Paths of Duty

Paths of Duty

American Missionary Wives
in Nineteenth-Century Hawaii

Patricia Grimshaw

University of Hawaii Press
Honolulu

94 93 92 91 90 89   5 4 3 2 1

Library of Congress Cataloging-in-Publication Data

Grimshaw, Patricia.
  Paths of duty : American missionary wives in nineteenth-century
Hawaii / Patricia Grimshaw.
    p. cm.
  Bibliography: p.
  Includes index.
  ISBN 0-8248-1237-9
  1. Missionaries' wives—Hawaii—History—19th century. 2. Hawaii—
Church history. I. Title.
BV3680.H3G75   1989   89–4956
266'.023730969'082—dc20   CIP

To the memory of my mother and father,
Florence Kennedy Sinclair
and Ernest Duncan Sinclair

CONTENTS

Contents

ACKNOWLEDGMENTS

Several people have taken an interest in the development of my research, and I should like to express my gratitude to them. Lela Goodell and Mary-Jane Knight of the Hawaiian Mission Children's Society Library, and Barbara Dunn of the Hawaiian Historical Society, remained helpful and enthusiastic about my enterprise during my research visits, and I appreciate their support enormously. Friends and colleagues offered useful insights at various stages of my work: Chips Sowerwine, Norma Grieve, Marilyn Lake, Donna Merwick, my husband Roger Grimshaw, and above all Greg Dening, who has with generosity shared the wealth of his ideas with me over the years. I am grateful to postgraduate and faculty members of the Melbourne Feminist History Seminar, who have provided a stimulating forum for pursuing the challenging insights of feminist history. I thank also Jane Koetsveld, who undertook the task of preparing the manuscript on disk with skill and patience, and Lynne Wrout, of the History Department office, for her continuing valued support. My children, David, Kathy, Sarah, and Andrew, cheerfully shared in this research project for many years. Finally I express my appreciation of the careful work of members of the editorial staff at the University of Hawaii Press.

Changing Worlds

It has been said that the lives of *happy women*
—like happy nations—are never written.
—H. A. Carter, *Kaahumanu,* 1899

Eighty women became involved in the work of the American Protestant mission to Hawaii in the first three decades of its existence, from 1819 to the mid-century. They were daughters, for the most part, of New England parents, some of whom had migrated eastward into New York State since the Revolution. They were daughters, too, of the enthusiastic nationalism of the early nineteenth century, daughters of the "second great awakening" and the "ferment of reform." From New England's shores they went forth confident of the moral superiority of American society, abounding in enthusiasm for transmitting its spiritual formulations and cultural systems to those ignorant of its virtues. These young women were not marginal figures in their own social worlds; on the contrary, they showed peculiar sensitivity to its tendencies and were representative of its central cultural beliefs. To understand the engagement of these women in the mission cause, and the nature of their life during the years they spent on an exotic and distant frontier, is to perceive the women's course within the context of American society in the first half of the nineteenth century. The women had been born and bred in America. During their years in the mission field, successive new arrivals, both to the mission and to secular pursuits, brought knowledge of the shifting life of their homeland. Avid reading of letters, newspapers, and books ensured, again, the continuing influence of American manners and mores.

The women of the Hawaiian mission grew to early maturity in a postrevolutionary northeastern America which was undergoing a significant economic and social transformation. Few lives remained untouched by shifts in the economy which ushered in the more urbanized and complex social world of an increasingly industrialized and capitalistic economy. The small-scale but influential shift from household to factory production was accompanied by increasing specialization in agriculture and dependency on wider markets. An increasing number of people became engaged in wage labor, the population became more mobile, and there was a concomitant growth of urban centers of population.[1]

The traditional labor patterns of women adapted to a situation where the traditional household economy felt the impact of new demands in the marketplace. Single women increasingly followed their customary work of spinning and weaving out of the home to assume it in revised fashion in the paid work force engaged in the new mills and factories. Others sought employment in the expanding common schools or private academies, an incentive to the furtherance of their own education as opportunities opened in the field of female education. Married women, by contrast, remained attached in a domestically oriented world in which they were increasingly relieved of their important productive labor. Wives' work for the physical maintenance of family members remained valuable, of course. Of enhanced importance was their child-care role, as men more often traveled to distant daily workplaces, leaving the supervision of children essentially to women.[2]

Simultaneously with the economic transformation of the early national period, a subtly related reformulation of definitions of femininity and masculinity took shape within a particular religious context from which it gained inspiration and legitimation. As workplace and home became divided, so too did specific gender identification emerge—the man associated with public life, the woman with the domestic arena, which was valorized in new, emphatic ways as the site of comfort, security, and admirable moral values. At the center of this sphere of human regeneration was the noble figure of the wife and mother, presented in idealistic form as giving moral and spiritual impetus to the family, not superseding the husband's proper authority, yet complementing his role, and influencing him always in an upright direction. Such a definition of femininity encompassed the duty of women to engage in charitable and religious activities, extending the moral values of domesticity to soften the ill effects of the harsh, competitive world of consumer capitalism.[3]

Within that public sphere were, of course, increasing numbers of single paid female workers: The contradiction was negotiated apparently rationally, as such employment, certainly with respect to teaching, and its educational prerequisites, were described in moral rather than in economic terms. "It is paganism to keep the female sex in ignorance," ran an article in the *Panoplist and Missionary Magazine* in 1819 which nicely captured the mood. Christianity had restored to women many of their rights and raised them from servitude; the light of the gospel inspired women's hearts as well as men's. "Then let the light of science illuminate their minds, nor let women be compelled to think that their sphere is that of the butterfly, to flutter in useless gaiety, and wandering thoughtless." As teachers, women could go where men could not be supported, even to remote places where God's angels, if no one else, could behold the pious female "in her little circle of affectionate pupils, laboriously and anxiously instructing the objects of her care to fear, and love, and serve their God."[4] Women's spiritual leadership could act as a regenerative force in the lives of future citizens whether in the home or in the classroom.

This redefinition of femininity was rooted in the Protestant forms of Congregational and Presbyterian Christianity that predominated in the region. The waves of religious revivals which waxed and waned through the villages and towns of the northeast at the turn of the century, led by such preachers as Asahel Nettleton, Lyman Beecher, and Charles Grandison Finney, modified Calvinistic beliefs to emphasize the individual's spiritual responsibility in the search for salvation; the thrust of duty for the convert was toward evangelical outreach of some kind. Women were central in the revivals, as participants and as prayer leaders among their own sex, even at times engaging more controversially in leadership in mixed gatherings.[5]

Women were central, too, in the social reform initiatives of the succeeding decades—distributing pious literature, redeeming drunkards from the slavery of alcohol, saving prostitutes from sexual degradation, promoting peace, teaching children of the poor in urban settings, campaigning for the abolition of slavery. For the most part the women's engagement was described in sex-specific terms with emphasis on their particular contribution to the redemption of the unfortunate, the ignorant, and the irreligious, especially those of their own sex. Women were urged to view themselves as moral crusaders and to associate in female organizations by virtue of a cultural definition which stressed their special nature, their special roles.[6]

Among the religious and philanthropic initiatives of the period was one which shifted its horizons beyond American shores to the many peoples of the world who stood outside of Western Christian culture and whose foreign ways were increasingly often described to an incredulous Christian public by travelers and explorers. Christian missionary outreach had previously directed its attention to the indigenous Indian societies, among whom proselytization persisted without notable success. Carrying the gospel to pioneers of the westward-moving frontier was another beneficent obligation; to send Christian envoys to the various non-Christian populations of the world, yet another. English Protestants had been early into the field of foreign missions, following the foundation of the London Missionary Society in 1795. American Congregationalists were not far behind: The American Board of Commissioners for Foreign Missions (ABCFM) was formed in 1810 and incorporated in 1812.[7]

From the first, women had been well to the fore in grassroots activities to support the mission cause—through fund raising, prayer groups, and the dissemination of information to encourage others' commitment—from the time of the formation in 1801 of the Boston Female Society for Propagating the Diffusion of Christian Knowledge. Evangelicals nurtured the deep-seated conviction that Christianity sustained a high status for women; the place of women in pagan societies was portrayed, by contrast, as desperately degraded. Such pitiful members of the female sex urgently needed the benefits of Christianity, drudges as they were for their lords and masters, slaves as they were to male sensuality. As Dr. Ashbel Green of Princeton told the town's Female Society for the Support of a Female School in India, Christian women must feel the most for those of their own sex in wretchedness and sorrow, must wish to raise them to "a state of rationality, intelligence, happiness, dignity, and the hope of heaven." He felt amazed that the known condition of these women had not operated with an "electrical force" on the whole enlightened part of the sex to arouse them to vigorous action. Catherine Beecher expressed similar sentiments even more romantically over two decades later in her influential work, *A Treatise on Domestic Economy:* "To American women, more than to any other on earth, is committed the exalted privilege of extending over the world those blessed influences, that are to renovate degraded man, and 'to clothe all climes with beauty'!" Women, then, had a special place in this mission endeavor.[8]

The first mission efforts of the ABCFM were associated with British missions, but none, by 1819, was operating independently of British control. The board's search for a field of independent endeavor came to center on the Sandwich Islands, the Polynesian islands of the North Pacific, discovered by the great explorer Captain James Cook in 1778. The British societies had dispatched missionaries to settle in the Society Islands (later named Tahiti) in 1797 and in New Zealand in 1814. New Englanders had become aware of the Sandwich Islands not only through sailors' and traders' tales, but through the arrival in port towns of Hawaiians who had worked their passage on American ships, the first as early as 1790. Some Hawaiian youths found themselves under the care of pastors, and in 1816 a Foreign Mission School was established in Cornwall, Connecticut, with a view to training potential missionary assistants. Sufficient funds were elicited from the Christian public to dispatch a pioneering company in the fall of 1819. The initial contingent was supported by successive reinforcements— seven in the 1820s and 1830s and three further groups in the 1840s, as well as several individuals who were engaged separately for the field. In all, one hundred and fifty-three people were engaged for the mission in the years up to 1850.[9]

A small tract issued for Sabbath School use in 1829, *Conversations on the Sandwich Islands Mission,* offers insight into the attitude of the American Christian public to the indigenous Hawaiian culture. A pious matron, Mrs. Barton, was pictured telling her children of the Hawaiian mission. When she produced a map showing the islands of Polynesia, young daughter Jane's curiosity was aroused and, drawing up her chair eagerly to her mother's, she asked with interest, "What sort of people [were they] who seemed to dwell in the midst of the ocean?" Her mother was prompt with a firm, unequivocal reply. "Heathen!" observed Mrs. Barton.[10] To Christians in general, including intending missionaries, Mrs. Barton's response represented succinctly the extent of interest in other indigenous cultures. Hawaiian society, however, was based on sets of understandings, webs of meaning, which were intricate, complex, and subtle, a code which would puzzle missionaries, essentially innocent as they were of notions of cultural relativism, in early years and in late alike. For mission women, gender relations in Hawaiian society constituted a focal point of interest, since the raising of women's status was marked out particularly as a matter for American female concern. Gender, in fact, was part of a system—of class relations, the organization of work, family, and leisure pursuits, all played out in the process of constructing and sustaining Hawaiian culture, a process which would remain essentially inaccessible to the American intruders.

Traditional Hawaiian society, before the arrival of Europeans to their shores, had been organized in a style reminiscent of feudal society. A chiefly elite, both male and female, maintained rigid control of the resources of land, goods, and labor, a ruling group divided into degrees of rank but all commanding the strong veneration of the populace. Elite power was underwritten by a religious system that enshrined the chiefs' sanctity, which was protected by a series of evasions and prohibitions, the infringement of which spelled danger, even death, to the common people. Chiefs owned the land, divided into jurisdictions of lesser chiefs who supervised the working of the land and the collection of tribute in produce and handcrafted goods. Nonchiefly Hawaiians farmed, fished, built houses and canoes, rendering perhaps two-thirds of all products to the chiefs. Not bound to an overlord like serfs, such Hawaiians could move at will to other districts but dwelled for the most part in close reciprocal relationships with a kinship group and community. The labor of nonchiefly Hawaiians was not usually onerous unless a project demanded swift completion; to procure the produce of land and sea customarily occupied no more than four or five hours of labor in a day and was interspersed with leisure for eating, sleeping, swimming, dance, and games. All lived basically on fish and poi, the pounded and fermented root named taro (kalo), with additional fruits and vegetables; the chiefs ate frequently and prized their enormous girths.[11]

The position of women was intertwined closely with their class position and their place in the life cycle. Chiefly women, along with men, though not as often chosen for political leadership, nevertheless enjoyed high status and could wield considerable power. Descent was traced through both the male and the female line; firstborn chiefly children of both sexes were specially honored. Nonchiefly women suffered the restrictions on their lives common to men of their class, derived from their low birth. All women, including chiefs, were sub-

ject to restrictions which sprang from the definition of the female element as dangerous or profane: Women were associated with the earth,
with darkness, with night, compared to the alignment of the male element with light, the sky, the day. Contradictions were clearly embedded in the circumstances of chiefly women, where the status of the
highest-born was in tension with definitions of their sex. Women were
debarred from eating with men, even from cooking the food; women
refrained from touching men's possessions, from entering men's
houses, from approaching the temples, from viewing images of gods;
women isolated themselves during menstruation, gave birth apart
from their homes, were avoided sexually by men before battles.[12]

Too great a concentration on the inferior status of women embedded in religious constructions distorts the broad canvas of Hawaiian
women's life experience. Women were advantaged by the gender division of labor. They undertook the making of bark cloth, *kapa*, from
the paper mulberry—used for the loincloth *(maro)* and skirt *(pau)*
worn by men and women, respectively, and for sleeping cloth. They
wove mats and took principal care of young children. Men farmed,
fished, constructed houses and canoes, carved bowls, spun fishing
nets, made gardening implements. Women, like men, had ample leisure time apart from productive labor. Marriage and child care were
not burdensome. Sexuality was positively enjoyed; sexual instruction
and games commenced at an early age, and a wide range of sexual
encounters was tolerated among young people. Parents gave some
direction to choice of marriage partners, but seldom went against children's wishes, and marriages were in any case terminated readily at the
will of either partner. Chiefs, both male and female, frequently had
multiple partners, and to keep blood lines pure they might marry siblings. Control of fertility was based on abortion and especially infanticide, apparently common when partners were of unequal rank or
resources seemed inadequate to the demands of further mouths to
feed. Infants were frequently adopted by kin, and grandparents
played a special role in their disposition. Adopted babies would be
fed by a substitute nurse or be taken after weaning, though contact
with the biological parents was sustained. Women of the commoner
class, therefore, though defined adversely in a metaphysical system,
enjoyed in sexuality, reproduction, child care, and productive roles a
situation not markedly more restricted than that of the men of their
class.

Into a society characterized by such gender relationships burst the Westerners who followed in the wake of Cook's visits of 1778 and 1779—explorers like La Perouse, Vancouver, Von Krusenstern, and Kotzebue among the earliest. As the fur trade of the northwest coast of America developed, traders called at the islands, swift to see the potential of sandalwood for the Chinese market, and from 1819 onward, whaling vessels sought recruitment in the port of Honolulu. Seamen jumped ship to become beachcombers. Other Westerners (*haoles*) set up commercial establishments to handle trade and provide goods for the better-off inhabitants. One means of barter was the sexual trafficking of Hawaiian women with seamen; women perhaps hoped to absorb mana from such apparently godlike creatures, and they certainly appreciated the cloth and the decorative ornaments which were their due. These new encounters were initially accommodated within customary forms; the unexpected and negative result was the venereal disease which began to take its toll of the population, causing sores, pain, and sterility.[13]

Frequent and continuing contact with members of such strikingly different and technically sophisticated societies, people who transgressed with impunity Hawaiian expectations about behavior, inevitably induced change in island culture as belief systems and behavior adapted to foreign ways. By far the most remarkable event, however, was the abrupt ending by royal decree of the *kapu* laws, the religious system which underwrote all social behavior, in 1819, after some forty years of intercultural encounters, by King Liholiho, son of the great chief Kamehameha, who had previously unified the islands under his political leadership. Much remained unchanged, including the power of the chiefs and their hold on land and labor. Nevertheless, the population now lacked a public focus for the manifestation of religious impulses. The missionaries arrived in 1820 to discover a community in which religious beliefs were in a vulnerable stage of transition, while they themselves sought, not material resources or sexual encounters, but the spiritual allegiance, the hearts and minds, of the inhabitants. A tiny band compared with the ranks of Westerners at large, over the next three decades the mission group gained an influence out of all proportion to their numbers. They had by the early 1850s made an indelible imprint on the fledgling state.

The experience of missionaries in early-nineteenth-century Hawaii has been described elsewhere by mission historians and figures prominently in the many general histories of the islands. The missionaries' importance in island history is undeniable. The conversion of the population to Protestant Christianity, the education system established, the provision of a Western language, the influence on chiefly leaders which resulted in a constitution, an elected assembly, and land redistribution by mid-century were striking events and critical for the future development of the island-state. Whether in the writings of early mission historians themselves or in those of later scholars, there is a fashion in which the enterprise appears predominantly a male endeavor and the participation of women is virtually invisible. The principal protagonists for mission goals, the central participants, are seen to be men; when the term "missionaries" is used, one senses that only the men are included.

The first historian of the mission, the pioneering missionary Hiram Bingham, coped with women's part in *A Residence of Twenty-one Years in the Sandwich Islands,* published in 1847, by the inclusion of flattering asides. "What a figure would a band of foreign bachelors have made in attempting this part of the work for the females of the Sandwich Islands, or for the children surrounded by heathen mothers," he reflected, when discussing mission attempts to correct "uncouth and disgusting manners." The long-standing secretary of the ABCFM, Rufus Anderson, referred to the women in similarly flattering terms in his 1870 *History of the Sandwich Islands Mission.* Mission wives had provided living models of domestic Christian life, well educated as they were not only intellectually but in domestic skills as well. "They were a pattern of what Christian wives and mothers ought to be." The major events of the mission experience were presented, however, as though men were the sole significant actors.[14]

More recent scholarly histories have not departed from this pattern of ignoring the crucial importance of women and indeed fail even to convey the flattery implicit in these early chronicles. Ralph S. Kuykendall, in his 1938 history, *The Hawaiian Kingdom, 1778–1854,* advises that for the work of missionaries to be properly appraised, "we must take into account not only the environment out of which they came, what manner of men they were, what they were trying to do, and the means they employed to their objects." Others have included women in a descriptive sense—principally, however, as comic relief in a tale that might otherwise be a depressing one. For the latter Gavan Daws, in his overall perceptive and sensitive history of Hawaii written in

1968, *Shoal of Time,* a renewed emphasis on the experiences of the indigenous peoples left white women still marginal to the period. There is no notion in these studies that mission history involved two careers, two life experiences, two centers of influence. Men were undoubtedly the dominant partners in the enterprise; the thrust of the narrative, however, threw all the attention on them.[15]

My study aims to recover the experience of women in the Hawaiian mission—firstly, because the women were present and their lives constitute a valuable human record; secondly, because such a record should produce a deeper understanding of the Hawaiian mission's activities taken as a whole; and thirdly, because that fresh insight might reorient aspects of the history of nineteenth-century Hawaii in which the mission played so significant a role. The task, however, has not been simple. Mission husbands gave wives a passing mention; few other literate people closely observed their days and lives. Reliance has had to be placed, therefore, on the records left by the mission women themselves, their journals and letters, which were certainly extensive and constitute a rich archive. The women themselves were constantly apologetic about their writings: They, too, sustained a sense of what was really important in the events of mission life, a sense that they were perhaps marginal figures, and yet as conscious subjects they inevitably had to place themselves at the center of their own accounts of life.[16]

In a letter to an American cousin, one mission wife confessed that she had taken for granted that the recipient of her letter would learn about the general state of the mission from the *Missionary Herald* and other sources, while she had filled her paper with subjects of a more private nature. Another thought her letters home were poor, in the sense of being uninformative about the crucial events, but she made herself in such intimate writing "the grand subject" and "disposed of other subjects as well as she could." To the wife of the American Board secretary, the same woman apologized for her familiar domestic letter. "I could not find it in my heart to do otherwise." To her absent husband, she in turn apologized for filling her letter with details of baby and nursery, material of a not very elevated character, but as a father, she hoped, he would be engaged in them.[17]

Women made constant complaints that their lives were too pressured for their writings to be characterized by any truly reflective quality. One wife wrote that she did not get time to indulge feeling "not pretty closely connected with the passing scene." Wrote another: "My letters nowadays are nothing but scribblings, for I have not time to digest any of my thoughts." There were other constraints. Some women's writings trailed off dramatically after the birth of their third or fourth child. Of the gaps in her journal between the fourth and eighth baby, Sarah Lyman wrote: "My large family and numerous cares prevent my continuing my journal letters but some of the time I have kept records of dates in small books, but nothing elaborate." Even the women themselves, therefore, feared the trivial nature of the tale they told, its anecdotal and descriptive character, and their inability even to keep that record complete. Out of such records mission women's lives had to be reconstructed, however, if recovered at all. And out of their records a consistent and compelling picture emerged —a picture of the mission experience perceived by the women themselves. The pursuit of Hawaiian women's experience over the ensuing three decades viewed in their own, rather than the missionaries', terms constitutes another highly significant, and different, study. Here the emphasis is on the Americans' story.[18]

The central questions underlying this study have emerged not only from Hawaiian history, although Hawaii is the geographical and social context of the narrative, but from American women's history as well— above all from recent writings on women in the early national and antebellum period. The mission wives in Hawaii presented an opportunity to explore the life experience of a group of female antebellum reformers, not in a dispersed fashion as they moved in and out of American associations, but in a continuous period in a peculiar reform endeavor, where workplace and home were closely identified and far removed from the possibility of ready withdrawal. The wives presented an opportunity to explore reformers' lives through a life cycle from the single state through early marriage to full maturity with their successive excursions into motherhood.

In *Paths of Duty* I wish to demonstrate that while almost all the mission women were married, their presence in foreign mission service was part of a separate female ambition for an important and independent career, the entry for which was marriage to a departing male missionary. The women were imbued with notions of reform derived from the same religious and social impulses as other reforming crusades of the period.

Once in Hawaii, the course of women's lives during the pioneering decades of the mission illustrates two points. First, the women, now that they were permitted participation in such public activity by virtue of an exaltation of femininity and female roles, soon discovered the sharp boundaries to legitimate behavior once they had homes to keep and children to rear. Their energy, zeal, and self-sacrifice could not prevent the demands of motherhood conflicting sharply with their public work, the more so since their ethnocentricity rendered them utterly intolerant of differences in Hawaiian culture, determined as they were to keep their children from being influenced by Hawaiians. Exotic though it was, their experience of the conflict between a new public role for women and the strengthening bonds of domesticity illustrated nicely a tension for educated, able women which continued through the modern period.

Second, the recovery of the part played by women in the mission, where they were the effective agents for transmitting to Hawaiian girls and women not just Christian beliefs but the notions of proper femininity and female behavior as defined within Protestant American culture, offers clearer insight into the place of the American mission in Hawaiian history. Rather than concentrating on the overtly public and political role of the mission by examining the male missionaries' relationships with Hawaiian leaders, this study, by uncovering in addition the private and often apparently mundane negotiations which took place between missionary wives and female Hawaiians, affords a deeper understanding of the process of acculturation on the islands, a process which eventually had implications for Hawaii's entry into the American sphere of influence.

The first chapter, "Christian Brides," describes the backgrounds of the women who went to the Hawaiian mission between the years 1819 and 1850, in terms of family life, economic status, education, adult work experience, and religious beliefs, as a preliminary for understanding their enthusiasm for missions and the highly unusual decision to marry virtual strangers in order to reach a foreign field.

Chapter 2, "Intrepid Pilgrims," examines in detail the experience of the first contingents of missionaries, from the time of their arrival in the islands in March 1820 to the conversion of the ruling chiefs in 1825; their discoveries about Hawaiian society, the nature of acculturation, and the problems of conversion emerge in a year-by-year descriptive account.

The following five chapters cover the period from 1826 to the early

1850s. The third chapter, "Dearest Friends," places the mission women in the social context of island society and looks at their relationships with Hawaiians, both chiefs and commoners, with other foreign residents and visitors, and with the members of the mission community, as well as their continued ties by letter with kin and friends back home. Chapter 4, "Pious Wives," examines the intimate marital relationships of the mission couples, reviewing the wives' experience of reproduction, sexuality, and power relationships in personal interaction.

Chapter 5, "Prudent Helpmeets," and Chapter 6, "Faithful Mothers," investigate the gender division of labor within mission marriages —the former in the general work of mission and home, the latter focusing specifically on the task of child socialization. Chapter 7, "Devoted Missionaries," evaluates the nature of mission wives' influence on Hawaiians despite the constraints of their complex work roles. The final chapter, "Family Fortunes," completes the story with a sketch of the women's lives in the decades following the mission's transformation into an indigenous church endeavor.

The women longed to know the path of duty and to follow it obediently; the way, however, was often confused, and the destination, when reached, different from the goal they had sought.

CHAPTER ONE

Christian Brides

> The cause of missions seems more glorious,
> more God-like, more worth living and *dying*
> for, than ever before. I long to be in the field,
> though I am learning some lessons on human
> depravity in a charity Infant School, which
> make my soul sink within me, and I am often
> led to inquire shall I have any courage to
> labour to dispel the still deeper shades of
> moral night which rest upon the hearts of the
> untaught, wretched heathen.
> —Fidelia Church to sister Maria, June 1833

Two young women, Lucy Goodale and Laura Fish, discovered that the path of duty for them led in the direction of enlistment in a foreign mission, that of the Sandwich Islands in the North Pacific Ocean.

One autumn day in 1819, twenty-three-year-old Lucy Goodale was taking her midday break from teaching her school in rural Massachusetts, just six miles from her home in Marlborough, when her call to foreign mission service came. Her cousin, William Goodale, soon to graduate from the Andover Theological Seminary near Boston, arrived at her boardinghouse with a momentous question. In six weeks time, a group of missionaries was to depart for the Sandwich Islands to found a mission supported by the ABCFM. Would Lucy, by marrying a complete stranger, Asa Thurston, who was one of this band, attach herself to this venture? Asa had been appointed to the mission but had no personal acquaintance with a woman who might be both willing and qualified to accompany him as his wife. William knew from his recent correspondence with cousin Lucy that she had a personal interest in mission service. Now he reminded her of the biblical Rebecca who had said "I will go." Lucy returned to her school in great agitation, longing for privacy; she could not eat nor sleep that night. Two sisters, hearing the news, arrived to offer sympathetic support. It was to her father, who had decided all the important questions of her life, that she turned for guidance. "Do you *advise* me to go for life to a foreign heathen land?" For once, he gave no directive. "Lucy," he said, "you must choose your own pathway in life. It is for yourself to walk in, apart from your father."[1]

It had been in a prosperous farming family of Marlborough, twenty-five miles west of Boston, under the rigid control of the father, that Lucy had been reared, one of ten children. Her father, deacon of the local church, had led his sons out to the fields each morning, while the daughters worked alongside their mother, preparing the food produced entirely on their land, spinning and weaving cloth for the family's clothing. A remarkable teacher at the local school which she attended for the three winter months each year had inspired Lucy to study alone in snatched moments throughout the year. The local minister, hearing Lucy and other senior girls examined in the higher rules of arithmetic, had dismissively responded with, "There is no use in girls going as far in arithmetic, other than setting themselves up as candidates for the wives of merchants." Lucy resented the clear message in her community that marriage was seen as a girl's destiny, while boys were trained for an independent livelihood. Older boys even received payment for farm labor, while their sisters, like children, worked without reward. Her schoolmaster had taught her that girls were endowed with minds capable of full intellectual development; Lucy for one would not regard education as a marriage ticket. With gratitude and relief, she won her father's permission to study at the Bradford Female Academy some forty miles distant, where she formed intense friendships with several like-minded young women. Returning to teach school, she had brought with her exciting thoughts of an active career as a mission teacher on some distant, exotic shore. Her cousin William had finally brought her to the fateful point of decision.[2]

Lucy consented to an interview with Asa, a graduate of Yale College and Andover Seminary, who had been reared in a large farming family at Fitchburg, Massachusetts, and had trained initially as a scythe maker. This tall, strong, athletic man presented himself at Lucy's home a week later. After the evening meal, some singing and worship, the other family members tactfully withdrew one by one, leaving the pair alone to discuss the future: "introduced at sunset as strangers, to separate at midnight as interested friends." The next morning, Lucy decided to throw in her lot with Asa, receiving this husband, she believed, as God's gift. They pledged themselves to each other "as close companions in the race of life, consecrating themselves and their all to a life work among the heathen."[3]

The marriage date was set for 12 October, some three weeks off. Asa then departed to attend his ordination and make final arrangements. Lucy dismissed her school and, with the aid of willing friends, cut out and sewed endless garments to outfit herself for her voyage and eventual destination. The wedding was celebrated in her parental home, sad farewells made, and the bridal pair departed for Boston in time for the sailing on the *Thaddeus* in just eleven days.[4]

Some eight years later, another twenty-three-year-old schoolteacher, Laura Fish of Oneida, western New York State, made an exciting entry in her diary: "This evening I received an application to go to the Sandwich Islands as a Missionary. I feel that I am placed in the most trying circumstances. If it is the Lord's will, I am ready to go." While her diary did not spell it out, the "application" had in fact been a proposal of marriage from a physician, Gerrit Judd, who expected shortly to sail with the second reinforcement for the pioneering band who had left in 1819 on the *Thaddeus*. This was the second time that God had apparently called Laura in this way. Two years before, she had consented to marry a prospective missionary, but circumstances inclined her to believe it was her duty to release herself, and she returned the ring and letters: a season of severe trial, she called it, when "darkness and doubt seemed to hang over my future destiny." Her original interest in missions had been aroused by reading an excerpt from the journal of Sybil Bingham, one of the first women in the mission, published in the *Missionary Herald* when Laura was boarding in the minister's family while teaching in another New York State town, Mexico. At nineteen, she had joined the church in Mexico when a revival swept the small community and she, along with so many others, had believed themselves subjects of "renewing grace." Thereafter her interest in mission work continued. She helped make up a box for one of the Indian missions, to which she donated a pair of thread stockings which were the equal of two whole weeks' labor. She began then to imagine herself in some distant, strange land, carrying personally the message of Christ's love to the heathen.[5]

Laura's life had been a troubled one. Her parents had migrated westward from Groton, Connecticut, to farm in Plainfield in Otsego County, New York State, where Laura was born into a family of seven children. After her mother's premature death, her father was crippled in an accident when he was helping to raise a bridge, and Laura, for most of her childhood, moved about among relatives' households and various village schools until she herself began teaching at the age of sixteen. Once bent upon mission service, however, she became determined to acquire a "thorough" education and entered the Clinton Female Seminary in Oneida, alternately teaching to earn money and studying:

> I was poor—entirely dependent on my own exertions for support— not a friend to furnish me with a dollar; I was obliged to dress very plain and practice the most rigid economy in order to purchase books, pay my board, half tuition. My friends were kind, and waited till I raised money by teaching. I struggled hard—I suffered many mortifications—shed many tears, but my aim was high—I was as proud and independent as I was poor.[6]

Now, finally, another summons to active foreign mission service had come. The prospective groom, Gerrit Judd, just one year her senior, was born similarly of New England parents who had settled on the New York frontier. Gerrit had served an apprenticeship to his doctor father since the age of fourteen, before formal training at the Fairfield Medical College. Like Laura, Gerrit had been converted to an evangelical, energetic Christian commitment in a Finneyite revival, this time in Utica, and Charles Finney, whose enthusiastic religion stressed free will and personal striving for grace, had since become his mentor. In need of a wife to qualify for mission service, he was led by discreet inquiries to the Clinton schoolteacher.[7]

Nine days after his proposal, Laura wrote in her diary: " 'The die is cast.' I have in the strength of the Lord, consented Rebecca-like—'I WILL GO,' yes, I will leave friends, native land, everything for Jesus." As she later reflected, it was not "love of gold, or thirst for fame, or a desire to see new and foreign countries," but the sheer desire to spread God's love which motivated her acceptance. She and Gerrit were married one month later. In the departing round in Boston, Theodore Dwight Weld and Mr. and Mrs. John Tappan joined American Board dignitaries to farewell them. (Her fellow voyager, Fanny Gulick, another Finney convert, laughingly wondered how Boston people dared to send Finneyites on missions.) In a departing letter to Charles Finney and his wife, Laura wrote: "God has heard my prayer and granted me my desire in permitting me to go to [the] heathen. He has prospered me far beyond my most ardent wishes in every preparation."[8]

The entry of missionaries to active engagement in foreign work during the nineteenth century has been described as a male endeavor. The women who accompanied the men have remained shadowy figures, appendages only, who appeared to have acquiesced loyally in an essentially male enterprise. The descriptions of engagement in mission work provided by Lucy Goodale Thurston and Laura Fish Judd indicate, however, that women had a separate path to mission engagement and that, moreover, their presence in the service was the outcome of an independently acquired ambition for an unusual career as Christian teachers on a distant, non-Christian frontier. The women, like the men, were prepared for mission service by education, by work experience, by the sense of a calling. They entered marriage with the intention of sustaining a significant part in the conversion of the world. There were two marriages, his and hers.

Between the years 1819, the inaugural year of the Sandwich Island missionary project, and 1850, some eighty women became enlisted as assistant missionaries under the auspices of the ABCFM, seventy of them married women. The majority had been born either in New England or in western New York State of New England parents who had migrated westward. What is compelling in their early life histories is the conjunction of their personal attributes and personalities with the economic, social, and religious transformations of the early national and antebellum periods. Such changes had shaped in women a particular sense of self, a special prescription for femininity and female roles, which resulted in sex-specific responses to the call for missionary endeavor.[9]

"God has been pleased to distinguish us above millions of our wretched race; and he demands of us in return for his favours, a willingness to yield up earthly comforts—to send the blessings we enjoy to the destitute," reflected Clarissa Lyman as she contemplated marriage to missionary William Richards in September 1822.[10] A study of the entry of women to the Sandwich Islands Mission shows the strength of the women's attachment to American nationalist sentiment, to an imperialistic, evangelical Christianity, and to a sense of specifically feminine competency. Women entered the mission to set themselves on the path of an independent endeavor to disseminate all three values.

Matrimonial Maneuvers

The women's entry to mission service may have been independently contemplated. It remained true, however, that their entry to the mission field was contingent on a previous male decision and endeavor. To understand the women's point of entry to the mission, therefore, one must have a prior understanding of the male search for a bride.

For the young men who claimed Lucy Goodale and Laura Fish as brides, and for their colleagues, the urgent search for a wife was a condition of their employment. It was no coincidence that the majority of men sent to the Sandwich Islands Mission were married. It was the firm policy of the ABCFM that married men made the best missionaries, unless the field appeared hazardous for women or a particular man was deputed for a job which entailed much traveling. The experience of celibate men in the Tahitian mission of the London Missionary Society had established clearly that, in the midst of a Polynesian community, celibate men were at risk from the sexual openness of the society. Although it was rare for men to form unhallowed alliances with local women, single men were likely to leave swiftly in search of a wife.[11] The ABCFM had taken the lesson to heart and for the most part refused to engage single men as ministers or teachers.

Rufus Anderson, the influential corresponding secretary of the American Board for more than three decades, spelled out the reasons for the policy in the introduction he wrote in 1836 to a memoir dedicated to Mary Ellis, a mission wife who had died. Anderson by no means failed to acknowledge the importance of women in the mission field, yet his depiction of the usefulness of a wife displayed somewhat chillingly the male agenda at the basis of the men's marriages. Male missionaries needed wives, asserted Anderson, because it was not good for men to be alone. The male missionary possessed the same nature as any other man, and his circumstances were not only scarcely fitted to better reconcile him to celibacy, but inclined rather to strengthen "that powerful law of nature." In short, "woman was made for man, and as a general thing man cannot be placed where he can long do without her assistance. You cannot educate him so that it shall be natural for him to live alone."[12]

As well as meeting the male missionary's sexual needs, the wife would serve as friend and counselor to her husband, would share his thoughts and feelings, would nurse him in sickness and cheer him in health. Indeed, it was almost impossible for a man in such an alien environment to secure domestic comfort, including a regular supply of food, without a wife's services. The presence of wives in the mission field, Anderson continued, had added advantages in terms of the conversion of the heathen. To begin with, women were potent symbols of peace and hence the strongest protection against violence that a missionary could possess. Their presence, moreover, afforded the indigenous population, whose domestic life was invariably disordered, the opportunity to observe the relationships of Christian families, a matter in which example was as important as precept. Lastly, the wife's potential for separate mission service could be acknowledged. The wife of a missionary could be expected to undertake schools for women and children, a highly useful role, especially if she had learned modern educational practices. Of course, the center of her appropriate sphere would remain the domestic circle, and Anderson stressed emphatically that every other concern must of necessity remain secondary to the care of her household.

The seventy-three men who engaged for mission service in the Sandwich Islands from 1819 to 1850 were the well-educated graduates of a variety of tertiary institutions, predominantly in New England. Congregational and Presbyterian by affiliation, their backgrounds were usually rural, and often farming had been the family livelihood. Like the women, they came principally from New England states (forty-six) and the New York frontier communities. Typically, they were drawn from "middling" ranks, not wealthy though certainly not poor, characterized by a determination to acquire advanced education beyond local school level and by geographical mobility. Their lives were marked by acquaintance with a variety of skills, hard work, self-denial, thrift, and personal initiative. Their college education and theological training had been gained at such institutions as Amherst and Williams, Andover and Auburn, in Massachusetts, Yale in Connecticut, Middlebury in Vermont, Bowdoin and Bangor in Maine. Some, in addition, had attended Princeton, the Lane Seminary in Ohio, and the Union Theological Seminary of New York. Their education had been preceded by engagement in various kinds of work, and not infrequently recent summers had seen them in the employment of charitable or religious concerns, traveling the northeast with tracts, Bibles, the missionary message, or the call to revival.[13]

When a young man of decent education applied for engagement as a missionary, his first hurdle was the acquisition of a number of written testimonials to his sterling character and Christian deportment. Referees were presented with a formidable list of queries into the candidate's character and standing as a church member; his judgment, discretion, and common sense; his literary and theological attainments; his "diligence in the improvement of time and opportunities for usefulness"; his leadership capacity, manners, appearance, and any "peculiarities of character, habits, or constitution indicating special fitness or unfitness for any particular field."[14] Delay in acceptance could seem agonizingly slow, as the men awaited the painstaking review of their suitability for the task ahead.

This obstacle negotiated successfully, the aspirant missionary, who had not infrequently spent recent years studying earnestly in monastic isolation for qualifications, found himself accepted by the American Board with one extraordinary proviso. Between the few short months which would intervene between his enlistment and the sailing of ships to the Pacific in the late autumn, a suitable bride must be found. During the entire period from 1819 to 1850, only two aspiring missionaries were already married, and only six were sent single (three as secular agents). Few had long-standing romantic attachments, and in such cases the young woman sometimes withdrew her involvement when it became clear that it was a missionary and not a conventional minister whose future lot she was expected to share. Some young men assumed the challenge to find a bride with alacrity, others with stunned amazement, a few with quiet despair. It had to be done, however, as the essential requirement, on top of all their study and good works, for entry to the field. It was a time of peculiar tension for the young men. News of their imminent departure for the mission field inevitably elicited praise and consequent fame amidst the evangelical Christian community in general and among their families and friends in particular. How ignominious to have the bubble of their pride and euphoria pricked by their failure to find a female companion.

The action being asked of the women was a dramatic one fraught with personal sacrifice and potential physical danger—quite apart from the uncertainty of entering immediately a sexually intimate and legally binding contract with a virtual stranger. The bride would be required to leave immediately her family, her home, her work, her neighborhood; to travel for a long time by a dangerous sea route under appalling conditions; to settle, with this comparative stranger most likely as sole company, among a people foreign culturally, and possibly frightening by repute, with an honorable undertaking not to return. In addition, the bride's parents had to be such as were likely to consent to losing their daughter to this rare enterprise, since the moral right of parents to intervene held good in theory if not usually often exercised in practice. For young women to pray for the global victory of Christ's cause at church, to thrill to the tales of missionaries' exploits in the *Missionary Herald*, to sew for fund raising in the mission cause, was one matter; to be a central actor in the drama was another.

Because of these difficulties, the American Board sustained a network throughout the northeast of contacts, usually ministers and college teachers, who supplied a confidential listing of women who might consent to marry missionaries under the necessary circumstances, women who were "missionary-minded" as well as being young, pious, educated, fit, and reasonably good-looking. Success could not be guaranteed, but it would be, at least, a possibility.

There was no doubt that the task which the young men confronted ran contrary to notions of proper courtship current in New England communities.[15] If marriages essentially arranged by parents were a thing of the past, marriages with the American Board as broker could only be highly unusual, however strongly underwritten by metaphysical justification. In one respect at least, however, these couplings were assisted by the current attitude to courtship, which left young women relatively free to take personal responsibility for accepting or rejecting an offer of marriage, although parents would occasionally exercise their right of veto. In terms of personal relations expected in courtship, the growing stress on mutual interests and friendship as a basis for marriage aided the supplicant, since shared beliefs and goals could at least be emphasized.[16] That granted, it could not be disguised that the men's quest was an extraordinary one.

Letters written during the courtships of two mission couples who had formed attachments prior to their decision to go to a mission indicate the developing bonds of friendship and sentiment undoubtedly more representative of expected behavior. While Mary Kittredge and Fidelia Church taught at schools in New Hampshire, western New York State, and Vermont and studied too at Pembroke Academy in Massachusetts and Middlebury Female Seminary, Vermont, they corresponded with distant theological students, Ephraim Clark and Titus Coan. Mary and Ephraim discussed at length the characteristics they most wanted in a partner for life. Mary admired "sweetness of disposition, cheerfulness, (to a degree) frankness, sincerity and constancy" while Ephraim sought a friend "who can smoothe the rugged way through life, pour consolation into your bosom." Fidelia could seek counsel from Titus about her "vile self," her "moral deformity," appeals which touched "every tender cord" of Titus' heart. Mary could recall evening walks with Ephraim when "every soft feeling of their souls" were awakened, and Titus could remember meetings after which he felt for a long time Fidelia's soft hand on his throbbing temples, her dear lips sweetly pressing his "with a long—long kiss."[17]

The leisurely courtships of the Clarks and Coans were a far cry from those of the majority of men who, between graduation and sailing, frantically sought the bride who would validate their selection for the Sandwich Island field. The distance from what was customary, and the variety of difficulties involved, can be judged by the stories of the courtships initiated by Lorrin Andrews, Bethuel Munn, and Dwight Baldwin. Their tales illustrate the extent to which the brides figured in male minds as a necessary adjunct to a male career; from the outset there was negligible sensitivity to the needs and plans of the particular women involved.

The two first, Lorrin Andrews, in 1827, and Bethuel Munn, in 1836, were some distance from New England working for religious causes when their acceptance for the mission came, and both looked askance at an arranged marriage sight unseen. Could he not go without golden or silken chains? asked Lorrin, from Marysville, Kentucky. He had no objection to marriage if it could be rationally and scripturally formed, but there was no probability of his making the attempt in that part of the world: The piety of the women was not of the "right stamp," and they were lacking the mental improvement which would be needed in a missionary wife. Greater success might be expected in the parts of the country where the females involved themselves extensively in mission interests, whereas in Kentucky missions were scarcely known and few would be willing to make great sacrifices. Bethuel Munn, working north of Ithaca, responded in his turn negatively to the discreet list of possible brides unveiled by the American Board. "I do not marry by proxy—It is personal private business." The subject was one of importance, since a companion would have great influence in aiding or retarding the efforts of a missionary. He wrote, "You will let me know what is wanting in a wife." The board took his objection in quite the wrong way. Perhaps at his age—thirty-three years—he needed "a very sparkling object" to tempt him into matrimony? Bethuel, in exasperation, reiterated his earlier point. If he could become acquainted with the ladies the board mentioned, it was a different matter, but he thought the subject of too much importance to hasten into a marriage with a stranger.[18]

An idea occurred to Lorrin Andrews in relation to the dilemma: If he could find a bride in Kentucky, it would have the important effect of awakening the attention of local people to missionary subjects. Certainly the female part of the church would feel more interest, and that way the most substantial part of the church. "With this view I shall make one effort. And I hope if I succeed not to disgrace the cause." Fifteen days later, on 16 August, Lorrin married Mary Ann Wilson in Washington, Kentucky, and a month later expressed the hope that God had given him a companion whose heart was in the work and, certainly, the novelty of missionaries' going to the heathen from that part of the world had caused wonderful talk.[19]

In his turn, "I can try here, and that I think I can get one, there is no doubt in my mind," concluded Bethuel Munn. He found Louisa Clark, a woman of only "common" education but with a good mind, a farmer's daughter who was acquainted with domestic economy although from "the better part of society." There were some doubts: She was shortsighted and wore glasses; her friends said she was prone to gloominess over religious doubts; her family had hereditary disease and she herself was easily fatigued in hot weather. But Louisa had one advantage which Bethuel did not mention—she had previously planned to go west as a teacher and thus was prepared for this more ambitious call. The pair married in November 1836 and planned to leave on the *Mary Frazier*.[20]

Even in New England, with every assistance from the American Board at hand, with mission interest apparent in many Christian communities, the men's search could be a harrowing affair. A doctor, Dwight Baldwin, in the late summer of 1830, had been swift to concur in the board's demand that he marry. He particularly hoped to find a wife who was so far a counterpart of himself "as to supply those qualifications in whh. [which] I think myself most deficient." Initially, all seemed well. At the end of August he found a well-qualified young woman in Auburn who was willing, but she expected and found adamant opposition from her parents, professed Christians though they were. The search continued. A month later he felt discouraged, for after wandering about New England making contacts, he had failed to find anyone suitable: "My way seems to have obstacles in it," he told the American Board. "One lady has *no left hand*— Would the Board object to that?" Obviously, they did. Around Albany, where he next pursued his course, he found "a different sentiment prevails there on the subject of hasty matches from what we find in other regions where I have been." He had been, he felt, in search of a companion as long as was personally creditable.[21]

Dwight was stunned to receive the American Board's response: Perhaps, if he seemed unable to secure a wife, he had best abandon thoughts of being a missionary at all. What would all his friends think if he gave up now, he agonized? Why had the board's estimation of him lowered so rapidly? In late October he was sent to interview a promising young woman in Chester, but though she seemed ideal, his ill luck held. Another missionary had just stepped in with a proposal before him. The ship's sailing date was delayed; he would try again. A woman, Emmeline Fowler, had sent a message that her cousin, Charlotte Fowler, might be just the bride he needed. One of her sisters was a mission wife among the Osages, and a younger sister was preparing for a mission to the Jews. One of ten children of farming parents of White Hollow, near Northford, Connecticut, her father a church deacon, Charlotte had for the past few years been so interested in domestic and foreign missions that she had refused other suitors. In the presence of cousin Emmeline, Dwight duly proposed, with lowered eyes and so delicately that it was only the next morning that Charlotte discovered that it was she herself, and not her cousin, who was the object of his attention. She, however, accepted promptly. On 30 November her testimonials went forward to the board from her pastor and the church committee. On 3 December, one short week from their first meeting, Dwight and Charlotte were wed, ready to sail on the *New England.*[22]

Female Ambitions

The male missionaries' courtships were decidedly unconventional and placed their own ambitions center stage: Brides were objects in a male project for transcendence. Even more extraordinary, however, was the women's acceptance of the men's proposals, and that too can only be understood when the women's projects for energetic endeavor are acknowledged. When the Reverend Heman Humphrey of Pittsfield, Massachusetts, was confidentially approached in 1819 about the suitability of Mercy Partridge as a bride for Samuel Whitney, he provided glowing credentials but doubted very much the likelihood of her acceptance. If she found the young man pleasing, and sufficient time was allowed, he could envisage a happy outcome, but if the sailing date was a mere six weeks hence, there was scarcely time enough to form a slight acquaintance: There were few young ladies prepared to settle such a significant question at such short notice. The reverend's voice was one of common sense and reason.[23]

But Mercy, in fact, surprised her pastor and her family by taking Samuel on sight. Unknown to them all, except the male cousin correspondent who had passed on the news to Samuel, she had cherished dreams of becoming a missionary for some time, reading their stories, projecting herself romantically onto a mission frontier. At times, she told her cousin, she had "almost fancy'd myself with the dear brethren, sharing their trials, and with them encountering the difficulties and hardships of a missionary life. I think I feel willing (were it the will of my Heavenly Father) to spend the remnant of my days in some little mission band, in a heathen land far from my native dwelling, and my dear earthly friends."[24] Mercy told her cousin Josiah that there could be no harm in a friendly visit from the friend he mentioned, even if it were never to be repeated: She had frequently meditated on such a situation. The young man gained her hand.[25]

Mercy was then left to explain her abrupt decision to absent siblings. To one sister she admitted she had been hasty in deciding "upon a subject of so much importance as forming a connection for life; and much more so, as it respects a Missionary." But her mind had been previously attracted to missions, and the call appeared loud and pressing. She begged her brothers not to brand her with "enthusiasm" nor to think she wanted to gain honor in this world; her decision was motivated solely by her desire to offer salvation to the "perishing heathen." As she faced the prospects of her imminent departure, she reminded herself of the trials faced by the twelve apostles.[26]

As had been the case of Laura Judd, of course, women who longed secretly for mission service did not always take the first offer which came their way. Sybil Moseley accepted the hand of Hiram Bingham at first meeting, after Dr. Worcester of the ABCFM placed the proposal before her that same autumn of 1819, when she was visiting east in a vacation from her select girls school of Canandaigua in western New York State. Sybil's dream had for a considerable time focused on foreign mission work; indeed, on her birthday on that very 14 September, she had privately written a petition to the Lord that if her life were spared, her next birthday would find her on heathen shores. Once before she had received a proposal from a departing missionary but had felt doubtful if it were right to accept as she felt no affection for him. A minister whose advice she sought had sensibly counseled that if the Lord wanted her to go to the heathen he "would make a way for her heart to go as well as her feet." On this second occasion, she did not hesitate to accept Hiram; they were married twelve days later.[27]

Others did hesitate, although they eventually gave their consent. Juliette Montague, a teacher from Sunderland, Massachusetts, who was also a skilled tailor and a graduate of the female seminary at Ipswich, delayed six weeks before giving an answer to her suitor, Amos Cooke. When critically ill with typhoid she had promised God that if her life were spared she would become a missionary. When the stranger Amos proposed in the autumn of 1836 she was contemplating a shift to the west as a teacher, but hesitated to accept the missionary marriage: She was not confident that she could commit herself to Amos as virtually her sole companion at a mission station. She sent to the board for copies of his testimonials and prayed with the church community, who counseled that she should consider the proposal as a call from God. (About to sail from Boston, she informed her mother that after glancing her eye over the other men in the mission contingent, she found her Mr. Cooke "a very kind friend, think I would not exchange with any of the ladies?")[28]

Seldom, indeed, did the prospective brides in announcing their intention of going to a foreign mission dwell particularly long on the man who was the catalyst for their action. When Clarissa Chapman accepted the proposal of Richard Armstrong in September 1831 after withstanding the strong opposition of her family, she wrote a long letter to her good friend Ludentia which was revealing of her attitude. Clarissa had struggled to gain an education at the Westfield Academy in Hinsdale, Massachusetts, where she assisted in the dairy on the farm where she boarded to pay her keep. Her upbringing on a farm in

Russell, Massachusetts, had prepared her for such work, since she had not only assisted her mother in household tasks like spinning wool, worsted, flax, and tow, but also her rheumatic father with farm work, the care of sheep and cows. After Westfield, she had alternately studied and taught, "to pay my way to knowledge," as she phrased it. She learned the new Pestalozzi system of infant management and was teaching in Bridgeport when "another call" came from "a remote, almost unknown part of the globe." This was her characterization of Richard's proposal.[29]

To Ludentia, Clarissa explained her decision to become a foreign missionary as an independently sought exercise. She told of her faith growing stronger—so firm indeed that she had decided to leave her native land forever "to labor, toil and die in heathen lands." She shared her grief at leaving family and friends, but also her conviction that she must endure all for Christ, "even if it be as painful as plucking out an eye, or severing a limb from my body." She expressed her excitement poetically: "In the deserts let me labor/On the mountains let me tell/How he died the blessed Saviour/To redeem a world from hell!" At the end of all this Clarissa mentioned, almost casually, "Tomorrow evening in church, I expect to become the wife of Rev. Richard Armstrong."[30]

Further evidence of the independent character of the women's commitments could be derived from the readiness with which several had offered to go to the mission as single women when the rare opportunity offered. On two occasions, the American Board, for reasons of its own, relaxed its customary ban on sending single women to the mission field and was flooded with applicants. There were clearly widespread doubts about the propriety of single women being sent to live amidst a large number of males of unknown sexual proclivities, an action which might likewise impugn the reputation for modesty of the woman herself. This attitude was reflected in Juliette Montague Cooke's spirited defense of two single women who were her fellow voyagers on the *Mary Frazier*. They were "girls of superior minds and devotedly pious[;] some might perhaps impeach the motives of two ladies who should go out as they do, but I do not theirs[;] I believe it is from a desire to do good." Rufus Anderson stated the problem in practical terms, eschewing sexuality. Single women would need a home of a married couple to reside in, where they could be assured of continuing acceptance and affection. Such situations were hard to come by unless there were already ties of friendship or kinship. The board had no qualms about commissioning Elizabeth Hitchcock, who had taught a school for Mohican Indians in Montville, Connecticut, to join her brother Harvey in 1834, Maria Whitney to join her parents in 1844, or Betsey Stockton, a freed slave, to accompany the Stewart family to the islands in 1822 in the somewhat ambiguous role of domestic servant-cum"humble friend"-cum-teacher. They also allowed in 1834 a safe fifty-four-year-old spinster, Lydia Brown, daughter of a physician, to travel, without ties, in order to teach spinning and weaving to Hawaiians. Generally, however, the American Board gave a cool response to single female applicants, and few knew it was even remotely possible to get to a mission unmarried.[31]

On the only two occasions when the American Board decided to send some single women, there was no shortage of applicants. The first occasion was in 1827, in response to years of pleas from their valuable secular agent, Levi Chamberlain, that a bride be sent: No one in the beloved homeland could, he said, remotely imagine the difficulties he faced as a single man. Levi's own list of potential brides proving unyielding, the board enlisted four single women as assistant teachers, all stunned to discover dreams so suddenly becoming reality but unaware of the ulterior motive.[32] The second occasion was in 1836 when missionaries requested single women for two specific posts, and when the missionaries Samuel and Nancy Ruggles, who were visiting the States, wanted a single woman teacher to live in their family on their return. Two spinsters were enlisted, the sisters Maria and Lucia Smith, graduates of the Clinton Female Seminary; Lucia had worked in the Tuscarora Indian mission. Numbers more offered their services, only to be paired off in marriage to single, needy, male missionaries. Mary Brainerd was one. She had previously attempted unsuccessfully to go single to the Constantinople mission; she agreed to the board's request that she marry one Mark Ives, once she had ascertained that she would go no more quickly with the Ruggleses. Another was Oral Hobart, who was a teacher at the Gouveneur High School, New York, a keen scholar of Latin, a skilled mathematician, combined, said her supporters, with "good practical commonsense, strength of character for decisions, perseverance, self-government." Oral was found "better company" with William Van Duzee for a husband.[33]

Two other women, Mary Barker and Elizabeth Edwards, would similarly have gladly gone single to the mission, because their incentive to service was a strong emotional attachment not to a male missionary but to a woman who married one. Mary's love was for Charlotte Fowler. "What is it that draws these tightening cords around the heart?" she asked herself of this friendship. Charlotte's departure for the Sandwich Islands with Dwight Baldwin brought misery: "My heart yearns to her." There was one star of hope only: "I think I shall see that beloved sister, yet again on earth. Then it must be—*We meet on that distant Heathen Shore* . . . soon I will follow!" Mary heard a talk in New York on a prospective venture of the Hawaiian mission to the Marquesas Islands. "I seem to hear a voice saying who will go to the Marquesas!—Who?—*Lord I will go.* Send me—is the heart's reply —Poor, *poor,* pagan." In September 1832, twenty-one months after Charlotte's departure, Mary made a fateful entry in her diary: "I take upon myself new and solemn vows—teach me Lord to fulfil them unto thee." She was, although she did not mention his name, about to marry one Benjamin Parker, commissioned by the ABCFM for the mission.[34]

Similarly, Elizabeth Edwards married Artemas Bishop in 1822 in order to join Lucy Goodale Thurston in the Hawaiian mission. Left fatherless and in penury at an early age, Elizabeth put forth a remarkable effort to gain an education through her own reading and her work to gain funds for her eventual enrollment at Bradford Academy under Miss Hasseltine, where she studied and taught alternately. (Artemas referred to Elizabeth as "a female possessing all the natural sensibilities of her sex" who had resolved nevertheless to rise above "unpatronized indigence by the dint of her own personal exertions.") At Bradford Elizabeth became involved in intense female friendships, most deeply with Lucy Goodale, who on one occasion wrote to Elizabeth of trying to compose her agitated sensations while contemplating the "deep waters" through which they would soon wade. Lucy's heralded departure for the mission field left Elizabeth solemn, lonesome, dwelling on the affecting scenes of the separation. Her diary recorded her agony at constant vile sin and careless unfaithfulness to duty, yet she summoned the resolution to repeat Lucy's path. At the end of August 1822 she wrote in her diary that a decision was pending on which hung her happiness and the salvation of multitudes of souls. Was it her calling to go to the heathen? God knew: "If there be an unholy motive within my heart O show it unto me and lead me in the right way." One week later she resigned her pupils to another teacher's care in order to prepare for marriage to Artemas and her departure from Boston in November. Again, her suitor's name was not recorded in her journal. In a jubilant letter to Lucy, Elizabeth wrote, "I long to embrace you, to talk with you of your dear friends."[35]

That Elizabeth and Lucy had jointly formed both a deep friendship and a missionary vision at Bradford was no coincidence. Such female seminaries were at the forefront of promoting women's exercise of moral and spiritual power in the world both near and far, promoting incidentally female bonding. No female educator in the period was more notable than Mary Lyon, whose influence touched numbers of women who reached the Sandwich Islands field. Julia Brooks and Abigail Tenney had attended the Ipswich Seminary when Mary taught alongside Mary Grant; both young women subsequently taught at the school. When Mary Lyon talked, said a friend to Abigail, of " 'The Mississippi Valley!', 'The American Indians!', 'Our duty to each other,' your heart would burn within you and you would feel that your life had been spent in vain." Other women, including Elizabeth Baldwin, Malvina Chapin, Maria Whitney, and Persis Thurston, encountered Mary Lyon at the Mount Holyoke Seminary which she founded in the mid-1830s. Persis Thurston thought Mary's whole aim appeared to be to train American girls to become "successful helpers in the work of leading wanderers to God." Everything was directed at the development of an active, self-denying, devoted character, privileged beyond words to learn from Mary, whose soul seemed "filled with heaven born benevolence"—so much so that in talking to the girls of their motives in carrying out the practical duties of life, it seemed as if "her eye pierced the veil which hides eternal scenes." Mary Lyon herself recommended Malvina Chapin to the board when she planned a marriage to the departing missionary, George Rowell, alluding to her "unexceptional deportment, good health, persevering industry, ardent piety, genuine benevolence." With female seminaries bent on producing women of such exemplary credentials, the mission cause was not unnaturally supplied with some volunteers to be missionary brides.[36]

When Samuel Castle had inquired, at the ouset of his first quest for a bride, about the requisite qualities, the American Board gave a prompt reply: "Fervent piety—An amiable temper and pleasant manners—Good common sense and a well cultivated mind, Good health, Cheerfulness, Industry, these are the important traits of character. A marked deficiency in any of them would be a total disqualification." (The board responded with alarm most frequently to any hint of religious unorthodoxy, which all but debarred William's own prospective bride, Oberlin graduate Mary Tenney, and to any history of "morbid" states of mind, or mental despondency, which brought Maria Smith under close scrutiny.)[37] In fact, the common characteristics of the mission women, married or single, lay not only in similarities of ideals of behavior but in shared backgrounds of upbringing, work, religious experience, and education.

Young Ursula Newell, a minister's daughter of Nelson, New Hampshire, whose sister was a missionary wife in the Ceylon mission, and who had attended the Bradford Seminary and Pembroke, was said to be a quick, efficient girl who could turn her hand to anything from milking a cow to harnessing a horse.[38] The rural background of almost all the women had endowed them with an adaptability in terms of skills, sometimes leading them in early maturity to earn a livelihood which not infrequently funded an advanced education. They came, like the men, from the "middling ranks," not accustomed to leisure or easy living (though far removed also from real poverty) and from families where some further education for girls was at least countenanced if it could not be generously supported in financial terms. When Juliette Cooke spoke in admiring terms of Charlotte Close Knapp, she indicated a combination of practical skills and intellectual prowess which was highly regarded. Charlotte understood "Latin and Greek—and all the kitchen branches into the bargain. Her being a plain farmer she has been accustomed to spin and weave and all kinds of house work."[39] Ellen Howell of Portland had attended the Gorham Female Seminary while anticipating mission service; Lois Hoyt attended lectures at the male Andover Seminary; Emily Ballard, "preceptress" of the Young Ladies Academy of Norridgewock, Maine, was an accomplished scholar. All three, however, understood the arts of housewifery.[40]

Few of the wives, however, had had the male privilege of extensive, full-time education for years, culminating in the granting of a formal qualification. Most had snatched their educational opportunities at intervals while supporting themselves by teaching or, more rarely, by farm labor or a skilled trade. While a minority had no formal instruction past district school level, such women had invariably enhanced their skills through self-education. They appeared to be seeking broader horizons than their mothers and grandmothers, independence of some kind, an ambition which took shape in an economic context of shifting opportunities for women, and in a religious environment which valorized certain styles of female public endeavor. The women had commonly experienced periods of uneasy religious contemplation in their early maturity, sometimes relished as a personal drama, but the call of the revivals of the period was for action, not undue introspection. Work with a moral reforming basis was the common goal.

Clarissa Lyman pointed clearly in this direction when visiting Newbury port in 1821, prior to her marriage to William Richards. At the boardinghouse where she was staying were a number of other young women, one of whom ran a school on the Isle of Shoals, twenty-one miles away, where there had been no minister for the past fifteen years. The woman had been forced to act the part of pastor, schoolteacher, and settler of disputes for these "miserable and degraded" people. Clarissa told her sister admiringly: "Thus you see what a delicate female can do when providence calls her to the duty for the amelioration of suffering humanity. She has done much towards advancing them in civilization and in the doctrines and duties of Christianity. Many of the females of this place have established schools in destitute places and have done much to reform and elevate the character of the inhabitants."[41] The legitimation for public female endeavor thus displayed had underwritten the women's decisions in work and education and was the incentive for involvement in an even grander plan: the conversion of the world. Their specifically missionary orientation had been nurtured in local congregations and institutions of advanced education, where the enthusiasm of a family, a community, or college peers was the catalyst for personal commitment.

That the brides' ambitions for a mission career had implications for the movement toward greater participation for women in public life could not be doubted; the striving for education, for meaningful work, for serious acceptance could only be read in that light. How the mission enlistment emerged from a significant reformulation of women's social status might be illustrated more particularly by the argument promoted by Fidelia Church in a spirited interchange with Titus Coan during the year 1831.

Fidelia described to Titus a revival she had attended at nearby Byron, in New York State, and mentioned that, at the request of two ministers, some of the women prayed aloud in the assembly of men and women. Titus took strong exception to this practice on several grounds: It disregarded the conscientious views of the majority of the church that women praying in mixed groups was unscriptural; it was in any case unnecessary when sufficient men were present to lead devotions; and, finally, "even nature itself" seemed to teach otherwise. It seemed "to be drawing the timid female from her proper sphere of action. It seems to detract from the natural delicacy and modesty, that disposition to retire from the eye of public gaze, which shed such a softened and ravishing charm over the female character."[42]

Undaunted, Fidelia pursued her support for the practice. In the neighborhood of Byron, Le Roy, Brockport, and Riga, men and women alike approved women's prayers as adding interest and good feeling to meetings. As for Saint Paul, could a woman not lead in prayer without usurping authority over men? Surely it was only "prejudice and education" which caused her even to waver? In any case, sometimes she had felt it her duty to pray aloud, and she had done so.[43] In Riga, the women who prayed were among "the most delicate, amiable, pious and prayerful women" in the town. There were some, of course, so delicate that they could not even pray before half a dozen female church members, or before their husbands and children, and yet they were voluble enough on any subject on any other occasion, including singing and piano playing in mixed company. Her observation led her to believe that true modesty accomplished much which false modesty, bashfulness, could not. She added, with some pain: "Why is it that the world so generally requires of our sex extreme sensibility and inflexible firmness, notwithstanding the existence of the one renders the exercise of the other so exceedingly difficult? You know if one of these qualities is suffered to supplant the other, we, are accused of weakness, or stoicism, as the case may be."[44]

Titus showed not the slightest hint of yielding his opposition. He replied that he was at a total loss to know what she meant by her question "Why the world requires of her sex etc."; he sent her two tracts opposing women's public praying, entitled *Women's Indifference* and *Female Suffrage and Obligations*,[45] prepared after a convention, adamantly opposed to women's participation, held in Oneida a few years earlier. Fidelia expressed constant distress that their views were so diametrically opposed, while he adopted a superior yet increasingly alienated stance. She let the matter drop, finally. (After all, she was in love and did not wish to lose him.) The mission wives, however, clearly had been engaged in a social environment in which new questions were being asked and new prescriptions for proper female deportment sought.

Setting Off with Expectations

The decisions to marry made, prospective brides faced the short and hectic period before the wedding day and departure. Final weeks were devoted to an excited round of preparation and farewells, a time of youthful excitement combined with heartache at partings and suppressed terror of the voyage. Friends and relations, unless the women were most unlucky, rallied to prepare their outfits, cutting and sewing the dresses, the petticoats, the nightgowns needed for the long trip and the first few years in the islands. Ten loose and twelve fitted dresses of calico and gingham were recommended, four thin and two flannel petticoats, twenty-four nightdresses, plus twenty-five changes of linen or cotton underwear, aprons, handkerchiefs, shawls, and stockings. For the most part, friends were sad, though supportive and duly impressed. Lucy Goodale's dearest sister felt the aftermath of Lucy's wedding to resemble a funeral, and the hired hand of pretty eighteen-year-old Betsey Lyons' family exclaimed, "That one oughter not to go. She's to purty. Them savages'll EAT her!" Others crowded around to fill the autograph books with tearful, loving messages of undying love, of meeting again in heaven, of admiration for heroism. Sybil Moseley, for one, sent her worldly goods of $800 as a gift to the American Board: "I trust it is not enthusiasm which makes me desirous of leaving my little patrimony in the bank of the Lord. I do feel that nowhere else could it do as much good—could it be as safe." Clarissa Lyman made a journey to meet a real live Hawaiian, living in Newburyport.[46]

Weddings were usually simple affairs, celebrated perhaps after service on the Sabbath or after the monthly "concert of prayer" for missions on Monday evenings, the bride in her best dress. The brides were on average just twenty-five years of age, twenty-three of them being twenty-three years or younger—slightly older than was normal for their contemporaries, but their preparation had also included a more prolonged education and varied work experience. Their grooms were on average just twenty-eight.[47] They left with earnest admonitions for zealous service ringing in their ears: "When the lassitude of a sultry climate oppresses you," the company of 1830 was told, "and tempts you to indolence, remember that you have no time to be idle; for you are executing an agency, which is of unspeakable importance, and admits no delay."[48] These brides were in a mood to take the message to heart.

When Abigail Tenney, about to marry missionary Lowell Smith, walked through the grove at Andover dedicated to Samuel Mills, instigator of the foreign mission cause, a friend was inspired to compose a poem dedicated "To the Missionary Mills":

> One of thy Spirit stands here now,
> *Thy mantle falls on her*
> Lo! on the spot where Mills did bow,
> She weeps for nations sunk in woe,
> In Sin's dark sepulchre.
> Go, Sister, to the wretched go,
> God will be thy guide and guard,
> Our parting tears will—they must flow,
> But God will grace and strength bestow,
> He will be thy *reward.*[49]

The poet friend purported to view Abigail as a missionary in her own right, carrying the banner of the mission pioneers. Abigail received such an estimation of her role without question. Yet, however much the brides set themselves center stage in their own life projects, they lived in fact in a male-dominated world which limited their potential in a fashion they dimly understood, despite such flickerings of recognition that Fidelia Church had displayed. They were setting off with expectations which were unrealizable. The women of the groups which departed for the islands in the first companies of missionaries were the ones who would begin to make that disappointing discovery.

CHAPTER TWO

Intrepid Pilgrims

> Indolence may be considered as a native characteristic. Little to excite them to action they spend many precious hours in sleep. Their women do no work of any consequence, they think it rather a disgrace. Their manner of living requires but little labor as the generality wear no clothing and live almost wholly upon raw fish and poa. . . . The curiosity and wonder of the native seems to be much excited to see women work. There are some times nearly a hundred persons standing round our fence and gazing at us while we are cooking. Before we had our yard tabood [*sic*] they were around us so thick we could hardly move for them. Whenever we walk out we are generally escorted by a large concourse of men, women and children.
>
> —Maria Loomis' Journal
> Honolulu, 21 June 1820

In the early afternoon of 23 October 1819, the first contingent of ABCFM-supported missionaries bound for the Sandwich Islands sailed slowly out of Boston harbor in the brig *Thaddeus*. Friends and relations on the wharf, who had gathered to farewell the departing group, sang with a tearful vehemence, "When shall we meet again?" Everyone waved handkerchiefs until no single face could any longer be distinguished. The sailing had been preceded by an exciting week of prayer meetings and farewell services, including communion for six hundred sympathizers in Park Street Church. Now the detached mission party, robbed of their ecclesiastical defenders, looked pathetically few and friendless.[1]

On board the *Thaddeus* were seven women. Lucy Goodale Thurston and Sybil Moseley Bingham were married to the two ordained men, Asa Thurston and Hiram Bingham. Mercy Partridge Whitney and Nancy Wells Ruggles had teachers, both named Samuel, as husbands. The sister of Samuel Ruggles, Lucia Holman, was married to the party's physician, Thomas; Maria Loomis' husband, Elisha, was a printer; and Jerusha Chamberlain's husband, Daniel, a farmer. The Chamberlain's five children, aged from one to twelve years, were in the party, along with four Hawaiian youths.

Dr. Samuel Worcester, secretary of the ABCFM, had publicly read the official instructions to the pioneer group. They were, he announced, about to direct their attention to a heathen population living "in the rudest state of uncultured man." The missionaries would offer them and succeeding generations the means to true happiness, honorable dignity, immortality through conversion to the Christian gospel. Their vision, however, must be a generous one. "You are to aim at nothing short of covering those islands with fruitful fields and pleasant dwellings, and schools and churches; of raising up the whole people to an elevated state of Christian civilization."[2]

The mission women, he continued, constituted an important part in the enterprise. The Creator had designed woman not merely as a temporal helpmate for man, but as rightfully placed in the task of recovering the human race. Had not such women as Phoebe, Priscilla, Mary, Tryphena, Tryphosa, Eudias, and Persis loyally supported the teaching and ministry of Christ? Similarly, upon the shoulders of the mission wives would much of the responsibility fall for the group's comfort, harmony, and success.

> In the domestic concerns, in the education of the heathen children, in the various cares, and labors, and trials of the mission, by their assiduous attentions, their affectionate offices, their prudent suggestions, their cheering influences, and their unceasing prayers, they will help cheer the brethren. And to them will belong to show to the rude and depraved islanders an effective example of the purity and dignity, and loveliness, the salutary and vivifying influence, the attractive and celestial excellence, which Christianity can impart to the female character.[3]

This was surely an uplifting message, if a daunting one, for these female pilgrims.

A seasoned shipowner had pessimistically watched the women embark. He ordered his ships' captains to give them free passage home if the request should come. The enterprise was foolish; every single one of them would be back within the year. The women themselves, however, were buoyed up with euphoric courage. No privation or trial, according to Lucy Thurston, would induce her to regret leaving home if she could bring civilization, the Bible, and literacy to "one of the tribes of men without knowledge of Christ." Sybil Bingham prayed she might become a light to benighted heathen. Nancy Ruggles' plan was even more romantic: "Who would not be willing to endure the scorching heat of a sultry region a few fleeting days if thereby they may be instrumental of plucking immortal souls from the scorching of eternal burnings?"4

The women had a five-month voyage ahead of them to get accustomed to their vision of the future. In itself the voyage provided a potent test of their fortitude. Most couples were crammed into tiny cabins which were jammed with ship's goods as well as their own trunks and their one narrow bunk. For the first weeks they were far too seasick to care. As appetites returned, fresh food had dwindled to nothing, and with weak hearts they faced salt meat, sea pie, water gruel, and hard crackers. From time to time terrifying storms blew up. Homesickness constantly hovered, ready to depress their spirits. The misery, increased for four brides by pregnancies, did provide the basis of shared suffering for the mission couples and, moreover, a swift bonding through the sympathetic help one received from the other. On better days, wives and husbands perched together on their bunks, or on some spot on deck, reading missionary tales and pious lives together. Husbands helped the women to improve their understanding of logic, philosophy, and Euclid, and all attempted to grasp the vocabulary of the Hawaiian language.5

The snow-capped mountain Mauna Kea on the big island of Hawaii first came into view at two o'clock in the morning on 30 March 1820. By nine, its valleys, ravines, waterfalls, plantations, and villages were clearly in view. Near Kohala the missionary party had their first sight of Hawaiians, who approached in canoes with articles for trade. Some women spoke to Lucy Thurston through a cabin window, exchanging a banana for a biscuit. *"Wahini maikai,"* "Good woman," they said. Sybil Bingham, appalled at the men's paucity of clothing, ran to her cabin to cry. "O, my sisters, you cannot tell how the sight of these poor degraded creatures, both literally and spiritually naked, would affect you! I say naked. They have nothing but a narrow strip, which they term a marrow, tied around them." The ship's officers returned from a visit on shore, however, with the remarkable news of the overthrow of the traditional religious system. "God in a manner unparalleled has prepared the way for His glorious Gospel," recorded Maria Loomis; and in Sybil's words, "The taboo system is no more—men and women eat together!—*the idol gods are burned*!!"[6]

When the *Thaddeus* anchored at Kailua, the present residence of the king, Hawaiians thronged into sight, women and men of all ages, floating on surfboards, sailing in canoes, sitting, running, or dancing along the shore. The missionaries would offer these obviously destitute, polluted, and ignorant people the advantages of "Christianity, literature, and the arts." When the offer was delivered by Hiram Bingham and Asa Thurston, King Liholiho looked doubtful and four of his wives began a queenly game of cards. Lucy Thurston and Lucia Holman were dispatched ashore in the next party, in the hope that a female presence would soften royal hearts. The white women most certainly created astonished interest. Upward of two hundred Hawaiians pressed around the embarrassed pair as they walked along the shore, shouting, trying to get hold of their clothes or hands, some running ahead to peer under their bonnets. Liholiho, however, despite his favorite wife's obvious interest, remained unmoved. The queen regent, Kaahumanu, was absent on a fishing expedition, he said. He would await her arrival before he would permit a landing.[7]

The mission party was not long making a discovery which was unexpected to them—namely the enormous power of the female chiefs together with the high-born males of the kingdom. Kaahumanu, it soon became clear, was a *kuhina-nui,* or regent, virtually coruler with Liholiho; at the least, he seldom took an important decision without her. They learned, too, that it had been Kaahumanu, along with other leading women, notably the king's mother, Keopuolani, who had urged Liholiho to break the *kapu* against the two sexes eating together, which had put an end to the traditional religious order. It was a political reality, though of a disconcerting nature to the mission men, that the elite women of Hawaii, particularly the former wives and daughters of the first Kamehameha, were a force to be reckoned with in the small kingdom.

With obvious reluctance and an unflattering lack of enthusiasm, Liholiho and Kaahumanu agreed that the mission party could live in the islands for one trial year. The chiefly elite might benefit from the

Nancy Wells Ruggles,
portrait painted in 1819
by S. F. B. Morse, N.Y.

Clarissa Chapman Armstrong, portrait
painted on the eve of her departure for
the Sandwich Islands, 1831.

Ursula Sophia Newell Emerson,
miniature painted in 1831.

Departure of the missionaries from New Haven, Connecticut, for the Sandwich Islands, 1822. Engraving.

View of Honolulu, 1821. Watercolor sketch.

newcomers, and a year's trial was clearly no great commitment. Yet there was also apprehension about the incursion of Westerners into their society. A Hawaiian youth who had been by ship to China reported that some people feared the missionaries had come to take the country. He pointed out to his apprehensive audience that the group had no guns, and if there were to be fighting, what would the missionaries do with their womenfolk?[8] Certainly at least one of the mission wives believed that it was the women's presence that had won the party residence rights. Lucia Holman reflected some weeks later: "I believe the females of the Mission have done more, much more towards the prosperity of it thus far, than the men—on account of the jealousy existing towards the white people. It has been thought by some, that they would not have got permission to land had it not been for the females."[9]

But the women did more than simply allay Hawaiian suspicion of male missionary motives over the course of the crucial first five years of the mission's life. The conjunction of powerful female chiefs and forceful American women was a critical one: The Hawaiian women were receptive in particular ways to the wives' influence. The interaction of the two groups of women was of incalculable importance in the complex intercultural negotiations and in the resulting balance of power by the end of 1825.

Acquiring a Foothold

The voyage was ended, landfall accomplished. The main object now must be to impress the Hawaiian rulers so forcefully with their worth that the mission would be granted permanent residency, a secure tenure for carrying forward their project. The first year and a half on mission ground, from April 1820 to late 1821, would be devoted to this goal, for women and men alike.

If there was one personal wish cherished by the mission wives, as they loyally threw in their lot with the men in establishing homes, it was that the small mission party should stay together. In particular, the pregnant women were fearful of separation from the sole doctor. This wish was denied them at the outset. The king claimed the physician's services at Kailua, together with those of the Thurstons. The remaining missionaries were permitted to proceed to Honolulu on

Oahu, the most populous settlement. Lucy Thurston felt she had been set down "in the land of pilgrims and strangers," not on fertile plains but on country as "dry and barren as the Arabian deserts." Kailua was built on black, volcanic rock, all fresh water had to be carried miles from mountain pools in calabashes, fires made with green brush on the ground. Moreover, the four, housed in a one-room Hawaiian cottage, felt desolate, cut off from Christian society, surrounded by "untutored pagans, whose strange dialect and clamorous songs vibrated on the air from morning to night, and from night to morning."[10]

"Do not be alarmed, dear sisters, GOD will be our physician," was Sybil Bingham's effort to cheer the other three pregnant women as the remaining members of the mission party departed from Kailua for the trip to Honolulu. There they were granted, by the chief Boki and his wife Liliha, the use of a large, thatched house; some other foreign residents there assisted the missionaries in accommodating themselves reasonably comfortably. Yet a further splitting off occurred within a short space of time, however, when the Whitneys and Ruggles were urged by the leading chief of the island Kauai—Kaumualii and his wife Kapule—to establish themselves under their protection at Waimea. There was no option but to take up the offer, though the wives were fearful. "Did not the path of duty appear plain, I think I could never consent to go," said Mercy Whitney plaintively. Kapule rubbed noses with Mercy and bestowed on Nancy the name of Kaumualii's mother.[11]

There in Waimea the wives settled to the task, like their Kailua and Honolulu sisters, of combatting the fleas by night and the mice—which ran on the walls and mats and fell in their dishes—by day. Windows were holes cut out of the thatch. The first task of the Honolulu women was to cart six months' washing to "a heathen brook" in the hills, where their arms burned and blistered under the heat of the sun, as they perched on rocks, struggling to soap their garments. Hundreds of Hawaiians crowded around to watch the women iron the clothes and to see them cooking over the open fire outdoors, their only kitchen. It was wearing on their nerves to have their every movement an object of such fascinated attention, but they bore it patiently. (Hawaiians described the white women as good-looking, with faces "round and far in," long necks, and wearing hats with a spout. They were all, apparently, employed as cooks, missionaries' cooks.) The chief woman at Kailua was positively alarmed at Lucy Thurston's and Lucia Holman's constant, frenetic, bustling busyness and handed over a boy from her own train to act as their servant.[12]

The mission wives in turn regarded Hawaiians in bewilderment across a vast cultural gap; Hawaiians' presentation of the body and all its physical functions, even expressions of joy and grief, were deeply distasteful to them. Wives heard with horror that Samuel Ruggles, on an exploratory trip in Kauai, was offered as sexual partners his hosts' wives or daughters in gestures of apparent warm hospitality. God, who saw all their actions, would be displeased, Samuel assured the men, but they replied, unmoved, that every other white man had seemed to think it was a good custom. The Hawaiian women themselves seemed far from averse to these goings-on and were clearly delighted when the arrival of ships opened the way to some trafficking of sexual favors for Western goods. Lucy Thurston's initial joy at the sight of an American ship at Kailua swiftly turned to horror when she witnessed men of the village willingly paddling off a whole company of women and girls to sleep on board ship, who then returned happily flaunting a "base reward" of foreign cloth. Lucy, alone among the wives, experienced fright at a sexual advance from a former priest, very drunk, who came into her cottage one day, removed his *malo,* and rolled suggestively on her bed. Hawaiian witnesses ran off, cowered by the priest's rank; Lucy administered a sturdy whack and made her escape. She experienced little anxiety thereafter.[13]

A fastidious Maria Loomis watched with revulsion as women picked and ate vermin from the dogs they held in their laps. The women had a "singular liking" for whitening the bristly foretop of their hair, carrying about a whitening substance and brush for the "beautifying" process. Sybil Bingham had to resist revulsion when embraced by a drunken, exuberant Liliha, bare-breasted and reeking of alcohol. Female chiefs, almost naked, to American eyes, often paid a visit on their way to or from their seabathing. Crowded social occasions became a trial. Mercy Whitney wrote: "Imagine how you would feel with thirty or perhaps forty naked Indians about you, some sitting in one place, some in another and others stretched out on the mats so thick that you must either step over or with difficulty get around them." She added pragmatically, "But placed as we are among a heathen people we are obliged in some measure to tolerate it, if we would gain the confidence and secure the favours of the chiefs."[14]

All wives were similarly appalled at the hula, or "horry horry," that "idol dance." Mercy Whitney, out of politeness, attended one such display. "Folly," "vanity," she called it and, as soon as politeness would permit, took her leave. All found totally distasteful and absurd Hawaiian mourning procedures. When one of Kapule's favorite friends died in May 1820, pandemonium broke loose: wailing, shrieks, and groans enough to shock the most phlegmatic. People covered themselves with filthy mats and *kapa*. Kapule, inconsolable, stamped her feet and cried vehemently. Nancy and Samuel Ruggles tried patiently to explain that "it was not good to behave thus, but they paid no attention to what we said." How could they behave so at deaths, demanded Sybil Bingham, and yet tell her that mothers sometimes murdered their own infants or threw them to sharks so that they should become gods? Lucy Thurston found "a lovely small girl whose eye had been put out, and who had narrowly escaped death, for eating a banana." Everything was baffling; there seemed no coherent ground plan which made sense of behavior.[15]

It was all too much for Lucia Holman; her evangelical zeal did not last three months in volcanic Kailua, where the chief attraction for Hawaiians, the surf, held no joy for the Americans. In letters Lucia lashed out at Hawaiians and their ways, deplorable beyond description, sunk to the lowest depths of sin and depravity. After two months in Kailua, Lucia wrote to her sister: "There is no sin, the commission of which, disgraces them—indeed, there is nothing that disgraces them but work." And by six months in the mission field, her mistake in ever coming there had become apparent: "Could any female know before she left her home, *all* the trials and afflictions through which she must inevitably pass, she would not *of herself* have strength or grace to enlist in so great an enterprize." Eventually, after the pair disregarded the small mission church's directives, they were expelled and left the islands; Lucia, according to Maria Loomis, was in excellent spirits and seemingly quite insensible to the injury she was doing to the cause. The survivors were temporarily gloomy, but remained to fight the good fight. The Thurstons battled on alone for some months at Kailua, and then joined the Honolulu group.[16]

The task the mission faced was unambiguous: to bring as much influence to bear as swiftly as possible on the king and leading chiefs to win their favor. It was not necessarily a strategy which accorded easily with their democratic and republican instincts. As the *Missionary*

Herald informed the American Christian public after reports from those in the field: "However strange it may appear, vast importance is attached to noble birth by all the islanders of the Pacific." The mission was forced to come to terms immediately with the sheer political reality of the immense, overriding power of the ruling elite. When Liholiho decreed that only the chiefly group, and wives and children of foreigners, could receive mission instruction, there was no alternative but to obey. Principles simply had to be swallowed. As Lucy Thurston put it, under such a despotic government it was imperative that those in authority be converted and educated, for thus was forged "a key that would unlock privileges to a nation." The American Board fully supported their political maneuvering. In June 1820, Samuel Worcester advised the men to secure the confidence of the king and principal men, to gain an influence directing their minds to "salutary principles," while the sisters should "cultivate acquaintance with the queen mother and other principle [*sic*] women and establish themselves in their favour."[17]

The most immediate, though scarcely most pleasant, means by which the wives could please the chiefs was through their sewing skills. For the chiefs, with their warehouses filled with silks and satins, the women were indeed a godsend. Orders for clothing, often quite elaborate, poured in. They dared not appear reluctant or tardy, however hard-pressed. Maria Loomis explained: "Chiefs, even the Governor, sent up his pantaloons to be made and though we scarce have time to breathe yet we think it a duty to leave all and sit down and do all work of this kind."[18] On one occasion, Boki and Naihekukui demanded full suits of superfine broadcloth. On another, Liholiho himself sent an urgent order to Sybil for five ruffled shirts. "To risk the displeasure of the king by declining we deem hazardous," she felt. Visiting Kamamalu, favorite wife of Liholiho, with a shirt for fitting, Sybil found her engrossed in cards. Kamamalu casually tried it on, then threw it back in her seamstress' direction for alterations. Sybil left, searching her heart anew "for a willingness to be servant of all, if by any means we might gain some."[19]

Mercy Whitney, sewing for Kapule and her train till her eyes ached, well understood the nature of the political process in which they were engaged. She managed thirty garments in the space of a few weeks. "In cutting and making clothes for them, etc., I have so gained the confidence of many, that they think that whatever I do is right, and are willing to confess themselves ignorant." And she had her reward. Kapule, "Queen Charlotte Tapoole," wrote to Mercy's mother, "I feel glad that your good women come here to help me. I want to learn to sew and read and do like them. I very glad they here. I take good care of them—they my children. I give them eat and drink. I love them much."[20]

In each station the wives turned with relief to opportunities for teaching, the principal work for which they had come to Hawaii. The male missionaries instructed whichever male chiefs showed an interest, while the wives directed their attentions to the chiefly women. Liliha was Sybil Bingham's first protégé. When, one morning, she found herself seated on a chair in the middle of a Hawaiian house, girls and women seated on mats on the floor gathered around her in apparently respectful attention, her joy knew no bounds. "It seemed like being where my thoughts had often, in past years, placed me—on heathen ground." Mercy Whitney had the pleasure of seeing her pupil, Kapule, with Kaumualii, standing waist-deep in the river, books in their hands, "delightfully repeating their lessons, b, l, a, bla, etc.," a sight to gladden evangelical hearts. In Honolulu it was Sybil who took the lead in establishing a school for wives and children of foreign residents, men like the Americans Oliver Holmes and Anthony Allen, traders, beachcombers, runaway sailors, some of whom swiftly subscribed funds for the purpose. Upward of forty soon attended. One woman, Pulunu, wrote on a slate one memorable day: "I cannot see God, but God can see me." It was hoped that such women would become mission assistants. In the meantime, the men often sent welcome presents; Anthony Allen made regular donations of goat's milk, kid meat, mutton, and potatoes.[21]

The mission wives rationalized their domestic labor, which fell squarely onto female shoulders, in order to allow themselves as much time as possible for teaching, entertaining, and conversing (through interpreters) with the chiefs. They moved swiftly to make their Hawaiian cottages comfortable with the addition of whatever furnishings came their way. Jerusha Chamberlain soon abandoned white clothing for her children in favor of dark-colored, sturdy garments. The wives organized the housework cooperatively. They set a long table three times a day for the whole group to eat together and took turns to oversee cooking and cleaning, although since Sybil was clearly the most gifted teacher, she was relieved more frequently.[22]

The first mission babies arrived in the latter part of 1820. Mercy Whitney's daughter was named Maria Tapoole (Kapule) "to please the Queen"; little Sarah Ruggles received the second name Kaumualii for Kapule's husband. Sybil, like the other new mothers, was determined that the newcomer should interrupt her teaching as little as possible. She had had a good pregnancy. She was in her school till the day before the confinement, and within three days of the baby's birth (at which Hiram was midwife) she was able to sit up in bed with her letters and journal. A nursemaid was employed to help care for baby Sophia. Sybil hoped the woman (although rather awkward) would relieve her hands somewhat from the "pleasant little burden" and thus give her more time for her "appropriate work."[23]

A good number of the half-Hawaiian children in her "heathen school," as Sybil called it, were invited to live with the mission families, a policy which had a dual motive: The children would be more readily converted and educated under a pious family's roof, while at the same time they would afford domestic assistance in the home according to their strength, gender, and years. Here would develop a pool of converts who would eventually assist the missionaries in their task of evangelization. American Christians had already shown themselves eager to donate money, and lend their names, to such protégés in the Ceylon mission. The Sandwich Island group had arrived armed with similar pledges, and the women kept a sharp lookout for likely conscripts. Mercy Whitney acquired a lad of eight or nine years whom she named Eli Smith after Samuel's cousin; within a month he knew his letters and had progressed to words of one syllable. Maria Loomis searched for a girl to be named Laura, who would be supported by a Utica woman. "I have not found one to my mind but hope to as soon as we get a little more settled," she wrote in May 1820. By November there were four children under Maria's special care and ten or eleven in the mission family as a whole, many of them offspring of European fathers.[24] Sybil Bingham's favorite was a lad aged about ten named William Beals. Of his recruitment she explained: "I picked him up by the fence, when I was searching for another child on whom I had set my eyes a few days before. He looked too *little* for what I wanted of a boy at that time. . . . But Mr. B. said, 'I know him; he is a sprightly boy, we will try him if he would like to come.' "[25] Soon she was extremely pleased with the lad, who made rapid advances "in American manners, language, and learning." She spared him much domestic work; in fact, he did none beyond fetching milk in the mornings and a few systematic chores for the good of his character. At Sybil's school he soon rivaled the other star pupil, Hannah Holmes.

At the examination in December 1820, held to promote interest in the school, William and Hannah received a Bible each as a reward for reciting correctly the Ten Commandments; they also knew by heart such texts as "Look unto me, and be ye saved, all the ends of the earth," "Thou shalt love the Lord thy God," "Love your enemies and do good to them that hate you." Sybil had prepared daily for them and all her scholars little lessons in Hawaiian and English to be transcribed on the slate and then onto paper. Hannah, along with other schoolgirls, was called away from her lessons to participate in the dancing when Liholiho and his train visited Honolulu. "It did one's heart good to see the joy she manifested in sitting down with us again, after two or three days absence in such drudgery," wrote Sybil, optimistically. In February 1821 William was brought forth as chief exhibit for the "orphans' school" when a Russian expedition called at the port; Commodore Vascilieff donated seven golden ducats and eighty-six Spanish dollars.[26]

The older Chamberlain children mixed freely with these Hawaiians, instructing them in English, and joining them in lessons and play. No one dreamed of restricting this interaction, just as they envisaged a day when mission offspring would grow up with Hawaiians for companions and eventually marry them. The facility of the Chamberlain children, meanwhile, in picking up the Hawaiian language was a boon to the adults, and the boys, Dexter, Nathan, and even six-year-old Daniel, were sent off to other mission stations as their services were required, without a qualm. Hawaiians loved the mission children. Indeed, the missionaries had to admit that Hawaiians, even if they had disordered lives, were generally hospitable people, and that certainly once the mission had the backing of a chief there was no reason to be fearful for lives or property.[27]

From February 1821 onward the missionaries sustained a constant barrage of requests to Liholiho, who was now more frequently in Honolulu, for permission to erect the frame house which had arrived in January from America and lay stored in Boki's yard. Acceptance would indicate the king's willingness to allow the missionaries more secure tenure than the one year initially allotted. Liholiho and Kamamalu were certainly impressed with the mission cottages when they paid a visit. The king threw himself on the Thurston's bed and rolled from side to side to test its softness.[28] Kamamalu, seeing the neat order of Sybil's room, called it "excellent" and picked up the sleeping baby from her cradle to show it to the king. The wives appealed to the king for the need of a house for their health, saying that they could not live, work, and sleep with only damp ground for a floor; they would become sick and die. Sybil Bingham and Maria Loomis took their babies on a visit to the chiefs, depending on the infants' amiable natures to win approval. Maria wrote of the visit: "Our babes in the meanwhile were exhibited and each lady must have them in her arms. We were also requested to take down our hair and display it before the multitude. This as well as the babes they all agreed was nue nue mite 'very good'."[29]

The king, unfortunately, was in a drunken sleep and did not awaken although they waited for two hours. Lucy Thurston was the one who claimed, finally, to have persuaded Liholiho, begging privately to him in what Hawaiian she could muster for American-style accommodation to preserve the mission wives' health. A few days later Liholiho agreed to the building and to the mission's continuance in the islands. By April work was started on the cellar. By August the house was complete, a two-story home fifty-four feet by twenty-two feet, with a mud and stone ten-foot-square cookhouse complete with brick oven. The women were thankful to move in, a family to each room, Lucy for the birth of her first baby in September, Maria for the birth of her second in December.[30]

Securing Tenure

The mission had acquired by the end of 1821 a secure foothold symbolized by a building of solid appearance in Honolulu. The women had been central to this achievement. The next three and a half years, however, until mid-1825, were to witness the development of a curious dichotomy between the fate of the mission, in terms of its public record, and the fate of the wives judged by their personal standards of achievement. The mission prospered, all had to agree. Yet at one and the same time, the work of the mission wives became increasingly problematic. As the impact of the group's Christian message gained force and credibility, the women, while working to the full extent of their strength, slowly and painfully began to lose their sense of being leaders, alongside the men, in the enterprise.

During this period the pioneer group of missionaries was aided immeasurably by an addition of valuable workers to their number. William and Mary Ellis, seasoned London Missionary Society workers from the Tahitian mission, unexpectedly threw in their lot with the Americans. In the spring of 1823 a reinforcement arrived from America on the ship *Thames*—six married couples together with Betsey Stockton and the secular agent Levi Chamberlain. Elizabeth Bishop and her husband joined forces with the Thurstons to reopen the abandoned Kailua station, while the Ruggles joined Martha and Joseph Goodrich at a new station, Hilo, on the northern shore of Hawaii; Louisa and James Ely settled a short distance off at Kaawaloa under the patronage of the female chief Kapiolani, at her request. Two other newly arrived couples, Harriet and Charles Stewart and Clarissa and William Richards, moved to the port of Lahaina on Maui at the behest of the king's mother, Keopuolani.[31]

There were now six separate mission beachheads. The mission continued its program previously laid out systematically on paper: teaching in a school; preaching and public worship on the Sabbath; learning the language; preparing and printing elementary books; visiting the chiefs, the sick, and others house-to-house "to instruct and impress their minds with religion"; cultivating small portions of land; training a family of heathen children and youth and providing for their daily wants; courteous treatment of foreigners; writing accounts of their labors, trials, and successes to their patrons.[32] The first reading material in Hawaiian came off the mission press in January 1822. Translation of the gospels and the facility to speak Hawaiian picked up swiftly with the Ellis' help. The missionaries saw the drama of Christian rituals as a means of attracting attention—in the first instance, a wedding.

The marriage of Kaahumanu to not one but two men, father and son at that, in October 1821, had not been an edifying sight. "It is a custom in the nation," reported Lucy Thurston, "that women, and girls even, become leading parties in proposing marriage." Kaahumanu and Kaumualii, leading chief of Kauai (who had perforce deserted Kapule), simply lay down side by side on a low platform, were covered by black *kapa,* and pronounced man and wife. On 11 August 1822 a Christian bride, Delia, carefully coached in wifely demeanor by Lucy Thurston, was wed in white dress and trimmed straw bonnet to Thomas Hopu, himself dressed in a gentlemanly black suit. The king and principal chiefs attended, appeared duly impressed, and shook the bridal couple's hands with cordiality.[33] A chance for an exemplary funeral came, alas, with a death in the mission ranks when Sybil Bingham's second baby, a sixteen-day-old son named Levi Parsons after the Alexandrian missionary, suddenly sickened and died on 15 January 1823. Kaahumanu, Kamamalu, and Kaumualii duly attended the solemn funeral and burial in the yard beside the church, where Asa Thurston expounded on the doctrine of the resurrection. Kaahumanu promptly requested a similar ritual for a young relative three days later, requesting a prayer that the child's soul go straight to heaven.[34] Kamamalu advised the missionaries what they already very well knew: They must convert the king if they wanted to convert the nation; Hawaiians would follow their leader. While assuring each other that they had come to serve subjects as well as rulers, the oppressed as well as the oppressors, the mission knew it was to the king they must look. Liholiho, however, was proving a difficult case, if for no other reason than because of his heavy drinking.[35]

The mission fared distinctly better with Liholiho's mother. Keopuolani became the first baptized convert, the first fruit of the mission, on her deathbed in September 1823. Keopuolani, after living near the Richards and Stewarts at Lahaina for six months, became ill. She had persisted in her interest in Christianity and had sent away the younger of her two husbands. She expressed the wish that the two younger children should be educated and Nahienaena trained to resemble the missionary wives. At Lahaina, Keopuolani built two houses, a prayer house and a schoolhouse. She firmly resisted protests of reluctant local chiefs, some of whom wanted to expel the missionaries altogether, while others said, "It may be well for us to learn the *palapala,* but prayer and *tabu* days will not enrich us." But on 16 September 1823 Keopuolani died, telling Liholiho to protect the missionaries. William Ellis arrived with Samuel Ruggles to be present at her deathbed and baptized her.[36]

This conversion was highly gratifying to the mission, but Keopuolani's political influence was now a thing of the past. Liholiho and Kaahumanu were the main forces to be reckoned with. At this juncture, November 1823, somewhat conveniently for the mission, Liholiho left the islands to pay a visit to King George IV of England. Meanwhile, Kaahumanu herself was becoming more sympathetic to the missionaries and their message. With Liholiho out of the way, her nascent interest blossomed. The first weakening in Kaahumanu's haughty indifference had come during a severe illness in December 1821 when Sybil Bingham had played the part of kindly visitor. Sybil wasted no opportunity to tell Kaahumanu the Christian belief concerning death, and found she listened with an interest she had never shown before. "All her affected airs of dignity were laid aside." Kaahumanu's general indifference to the mission, however, returned with her customary hearty health: her "air of superiority, and a heathen queen-like hauteur."[37]

One amazing day, however, Kaahumanu suddenly understood the link between speech and the printed word on the page and was instantly intrigued. Sybil and Hiram had called to show her a newly printed mission book. She put her cards aside, began studying the book, and asked for more books for her attendants. The very next day she arrived at church and sustained from then on a generous involvement in Christian instruction. Formerly, she told William Ellis, she and many leading chiefs had been suspicious of missionaries, thinking them "deceivers," but now they believed the missionaries to be their friends, genuinely seeking their good. Not that her Christian course followed orthodox lines; she would arrive at church with a train dressed in "showy" China crepe of red, orange, and blue, one of whom carried into church a branch on which perched three large green parrots. Their mistress would then, as often as not, stretch out along a seat and go to sleep during the service. But such matters were of minor importance when she called together the high chiefs and missionaries and announced that henceforth she intended to follow God's laws; she wished, also, that the people should attend to the *palapala* and *pule*, or learning and religion.[38] Her influence radiated out to other chiefs; some of them were antagonistic, but the majority engaged at least tangentially in some mission pursuits.

Kaahumanu's authority was overarching, but at least one other chief's conversion was of paramount importance at this time. Kapiolani, of the island of Hawaii, hovered on the fringe of the mission from the first, in what the missionaries termed "a very interesting state of mind," but declared herself "too wicked" to be baptized.[39] Now she dismissed all her husbands except Naihe and threw herself energetically behind the mission. She built a house, furnished it with tables, chairs, and china teacups, and put her hair up in a comb. Her magnificent gesture, however, to demonstrate rejection of old ways, was to undertake a daring mission to the mountain Kilauea to confront the high priestess of Pele, goddess of volcanoes. Kapiolani climbed Kilauea brandishing her mission book. When challenged by the priestess, Kapiolani read passages of Scripture to combat the unintelligible message which the priestess valiantly read from her piece of *kapa* from the god Pele. The female chief descended to the rim of the crater and cried out, "Jehovah is my God. He kindled these fires. I fear not Pele. . . . Great is the goodness of Jehovah in sending missionaries to turn us from these vanities to the living God and the way of righteousness."[40]

Diminishing Prospects

During this same period, however, when mission prospects were becoming so hopeful and when the mission wives were so obviously crucial in the process of persuading chiefs to the cause—Sybil for Kaahumanu, Mercy for Kapule, and Lucy for Kapiolani—the women themselves were losing their early buoyancy and optimism about their prospects for a useful life in the mission field. From the first it had been hard to sustain a heightened pitch of spiritual awareness without the services and religious community of home. "O that it were with me as in days past when I thought I enjoyed the light of God's countenance," Mercy Whitney lamented.[41] Life on the mission, even more significantly, was no longer working out as they had expected, and their ambition to sustain important roles as teachers was now confronted with awkward obstacles. Their subjective assessment of their lives sounded a decidedly gloomier note.

The wives' domestic labor, in the first place, instead of becoming easier with familiarity of local conditions, was becoming more onerous. In Honolulu, for example, even the task of organizing three cooked meals each day began to take on the aspect of a major challenge. Simply acquiring the food, by sale or barter, was an increasing headache. Whalers were anchoring at the port in growing numbers as the off-Japan whaling ground developed, pushing up the price of goods enormously. The American Board's allowance of trade goods was simply insufficient. The mission could not readily get enough of what they were prepared to eat. Sometimes they had beef, pork, or fish, potatoes, flour, and sugar, but they were destitute of them most of the time and frequently existed on sparse fare indeed. The mission table was more often these days extended to include room for ships' captains and officers, but the only upgrading in hospitality might be the use of a white tablecloth in place of the everyday red one. Counting in the Hawaiian children and domestic servants, there were often thirty-five people, or forty, or fifty, at each meal. Some of the fresh provisions for these meals were gained as barter for the wives' sewing skills. In May 1824 Clarissa Richards was still sewing hours every night for chiefs and had made eighteen silk or crepe gowns and two pairs of white twilled cotton pantaloons in a matter of weeks. Still, the gifts of food which came back in return were essential.[42]

The wives' energies were diminishing noticeably. There were further pregnancies, more new infants to be nursed. Charles Stewart could still witness in November 1823 Lucy Thurston, embarking for Kailua, intrepidly mount the ship's side by the manropes without waiting for a chair to hoist her on deck. Yet as some of their earlier zeal ceased to keep their spirits high, the increasing humidity and heat began to seem more oppressive. Mercy Whitney began to complain of headaches that drove her almost crazy. The women suffered bouts of unidentified fevers. Maria Loomis found the mission house at Honolulu a very inconvenient place to work in. The cookhouse was at some distance from the cellar, where meals were eaten. Since the cellar had no floor, crawling babies could not be brought below, obliging the mothers to climb constantly from the cellar to the bedroom upstairs. The sheer fatigue often affected their spirits, turning "molehills into frightful mountains." Conditions were sadly cramped in the house; altogether it called for "patience and prudence," wrote Sybil Bingham, to sustain good neighborliness. Daniel Chamberlain contracted rheumatism, so that Jerusha had a sick husband as well as a new baby on her hands.[43]

The situation brought to an end the women's experiment with cooperative housekeeping. They reverted to separate family groupings in November 1822. The mission general meeting in September 1823 deemed it proper, not only for every mission station to have its bell, spyglass, quadrant, timepiece, encyclopedia, gazetteer, chest of tools, and Scott's Bible, but for each family on that station to possess a separate dwelling with suitable provision for cooking and washing.[44] The wives divided up the crockery and cooking equipment and thereafter cooked for their own small families.

Abandoning the former division of labor had consequences for the women's teaching involvement. Maria Loomis confided in Nancy Ruggles her shame that her progress in learning Hawaiian was so slow. "So many cares and interruptions to engross my time, that I find but little time to devote to the language." Soon afterward she complained of no opportunity of calling her school together; sometimes she felt tempted to abandon her journal altogether, as she could not believe it was interesting; constant, tiring labor unfitted her mind for writing.[45] Sybil Bingham longed for more time to labor directly for Hawaiians. She wrote to her sisters: "You may wonder sometimes, what, in this corner of the earth, I can find to be doing, if it be not laboring for the heathen. . . . I have this consolation—I am allowed to aid one whose constant employment is in the way of direct efforts for their good."[46] Ten days later, she temporarily abandoned her school. Sybil was falling back on the role of the faithful wifely helpmate, though her heart yearned for greater engagement in what she termed "direct labor." The drain of domestic labor would not be lessened by reversion to the conjugal family unit, while their uninterrupted hours for teaching would be diminished.

The wives began to pay a high price for this acquisition of conjugal privacy. Their domestic and teaching involvement was also adversely affected by frustration in their task of raising Hawaiian children in the home as part of the family. Right from the start, the children, quick-witted, lively, and curious, had shown themselves also to be restless and impatient of restraints imposed on them. Not only did the wives lose sustained and increasingly skilled labor if the children decamped, but it was a severe blow to the teaching they offered in the home and the classrooms to which the children trooped off each day. The school at Honolulu had forty students by February 1822, with twenty-two children in the missionaries' families; there were in addition, on Kauai, twenty to thirty pupils with ten living in the family, but this apparent prosperity represented a shifting group indeed.[47]

Lucy Thurston had no sooner written in January 1822 to a friend of her delightful experience of presenting truths "to the dark minds of these untutored natives . . . to see the look of intelligence, of wonder, of gratitude and love" on their faces, than two of her five protégés absconded within the week. When another child, Charlotte Holmes, talked saucily to Maria Loomis and disobeyed orders, Maria tied her up by string to a chest till the family were called to tea. By this time Charlotte's mother had heard the news and angrily appeared to untie the child, whom she took away. Another girl removed in haste was a chief's daughter, whose father alleged that the Loomises had obliged her to work, which he considered disgraceful. The principal reason for the children's leaving, said Maria, was "aversion to labor, impatience of restraint and a roving disposition. It is generally thought disgraceful for females to work, especially for the younger part of them."[48] It was, alas, not just to return to their families that a number of pubescent girls departed; it was to the arms of Western men. Young Hua was "decoyed" from Maria Loomis' care by a white man. "Were it in my power to describe to you one tenth part of the iniquity and filth there is practised," Maria told a friend, "you would stare with horror and amazement. The village is almost overrun with runaway sailors."[49] And traders, and merchants, and adventurers of all kinds, for the most part men without women, with much to offer Hawaiian girls. The girls, as the mission wives saw it, were led into "disgraceful captivity." Charles Stewart described Sybil Bingham's heartbreak at the enticement by men of one after another pupil of her girls' school: "After being clothed and brought with much care and attention to habits of neatness and propriety in their persons, and made themselves to be deeply interested in various useful instruction —were borne off openly and forcibly by them, to become their mistresses, while the instructress herself could answer the appeals made to her for protection, only *by her tears*."[50]

The loss of the two star pupils, Hannah Holmes and William Beals, was the hardest blow of all. The sweet-natured, beautiful Hannah, the mission wives loved. She was, it eventuated, in and out of sexual liaisons with prominent Western men, first Captain William Davis, then John C. Jones, the American trade representative in Honolulu.[51] The mission wives kept hoping for victory in a tussle for her soul, but failed again and again. William Beals had become to Sybil Bingham like her own son, a bright, engaging, and affectionate boy. Some trouble had arisen in February 1822 through rival Westerners, and William spent two nights away from home. This first incident was negotiated successfully. William diligently pursued his studies and copied faithfully in his book, in regular, sloping hand: "I not go in the way of a bad boy. . . . For a bad boy can not go to God. . . . See not my sin O God and let me not go to the pit. . . . I may die to day, all men are to die."[52] And die he did, attacked by a raging fever after returning to the village to live. The day before his death, having been carried up to the mission home, he admitted having conducted himself improperly with Hannah Holmes: "He and she had done wrong—and that he should die—that he was wicked and should not go to heaven."[53] Sybil, recovering from her third confinement, was distraught and reproached herself as she made black armbands for the funeral and the boy's shroud. How could so promising a boy have fallen so tragically? That Hawaiian children and youth should be averse to chores or disobedient was one matter; that they should be sexually active at a young age was disgusting. All echoed Sybil's anguished cry: "O, it is a polluted land!"[54]

The London Missionary Society delegates, Daniel Tyerman and George Bennet, who visited the Hawaiian missionaries after a stay in Tahiti, had already advised the ABCFM that it was wasted effort for the wives to be feeding, clothing, and boarding indiscriminately chosen children in the hopes that they would serve the mission ten years hence. Day schools to which the whole population had access were certainly preferable and were working well in the South Sea islands.[55] A report written for the American Board at the mission General Meeting regretfully concluded that although Christian benefactors in America had generously pledged support for thirty-five Hawaiian children who were to bear their names, the mission was abandoning the policy.

The report in addition made a brief and carefully worded reference to an issue which had in reality become a matter of enormous importance to the mission wives: the wish to prevent the "exposure of our own offspring to the influence of the undesirable habits of native children to be trained up with them."[56] The two London Missionary Society delegates, plus William and Mary Ellis, had brought from their experience of the Tahitian mission other news and other forcefully expressed advice. Tahitian children and youth, they informed the Americans, were similarly sexually active at an early age. The practice of the English missionaries there, of allowing their own children to be raised by Tahitian nurses and to play indiscriminately with Tahitian children, had led to a shocking outcome: Some of the missionaries' children, girls as well as boys, had adopted the same sexual ways, cohabiting with Tahitians. One mission daughter had become no better than a prostitute.[57] A close scrutiny of the obliging and gregarious Chamberlain children revealed some alarming signs, as the Americans absorbed this extraordinarily disturbing news and reinterpreted these children's sociality. The family would simply have to return home. The missionaries wrote to the board about the Chamberlains, referring to "the infelicities in the carriage of some of their children and their apprehensions for their safety in this polluted land, where without the firmness of Christian principle they could not be usefully employed without coming into too close contact with the natives."[58] William Ellis backed Daniel Chamberlain up in a separate letter, referring to "the baneful effect the awful and shameless depravity of the place was likely to have on his family, particularly on the elder branches of it."[59] The Chamberlains left, looking downcast, in the spring of 1823.

In the meantime, other mission parents took stock of their own young children's moral welfare. Their babies were speaking Hawaiian, the "vernacular," more fluently than English. This no longer seemed quaint, or clever, but fraught with danger. Mercy Whitney set about teaching two-year-old Maria to read in order to stimulate the child's acquisition of English. By the age of two years and nine months Mercy had the child reading and spelling words of two syllables. Maria's book offered her much-needed amusement, for her day was a long and dull one indeed. Her baby brother now constituted her sole playmate. Much of the day she sat at the bedroom window watching the Hawaiian children at play nearby, without attempting to join them. Mercy strove to impress on her the "impropriety" of wasting time as these children did, and she was pleased to see how quickly Maria seemed to understand the rights and wrongs of the situation. "She has several times reproved them, particularly for playing on the sabbath," Mercy rejoiced.[60]

Meanwhile Lucy Thurston was imposing similar restrictions on young Persis and her little sister in Kailua. The family was housed in a single-roomed Hawaiian cottage, windowless and without light except from a door at either end, around which a throng of Hawaiians was constantly gathered. Her older daughter, swiftly acquiring language and receiving "permanent impressions," must be kept from communicating in Hawaiian; being an active child, she longed to run about outside, which was now denied her. Day after day Lucy could do little else but amuse the child, to shield her from the supposed danger. "It was this," wrote Lucy, "which, in feelings, caused the cottage to become the dungeon, and home the heathen world."[61] Ill health among the women abounded; some were forced to leave. These wives and pilgrims who had landed from the *Thaddeus* and the *Thames* with such excited expectations were soldiering on, but their situation was beginning to take a toll of their physical and nervous well-being.

Conversely mid-1825 found mission prospects at a more hopeful level than ever before. Kaahumanu found herself indisputably the strongest power in the Hawaiian kingdom, when news arrived in March that Liholiho and Kamamalu had died the previous July in London. Since the heir apparent, Liholiho's brother, Kauikeaouli, was still a boy, Kaahumanu's continuing regency was assured. As far as the mission was concerned, they had lost an erratic king, there was time enough to influence his young heir, and Kaahumanu in the meanwhile was the mainstay of mission support within the ruling elite. She now threw herself unambiguously behind the mission. In June, ten leading chiefs, Kaahumanu herself, Kalanimoku, Kapiolani, and Kapule announced themselves candidates for church membership and began a six-month probation which ended in December. Kaahumanu toured Kauai, Oahu, and Hawaii, exhorting her people to attend schools and worship; the demand for catechisms, hymnals, and spelling books escalated. At Lahaina, Kaahumanu foreshadowed laws against murder, infanticide, theft, boxing, and work or play on the Sabbath.[62]

In the midst of these exciting developments, one mission wife emerged briefly into a prominence of vaguely heroic stature, a state which had so far eluded them. Sybil Bingham and Mercy Whitney had approached that status when caught in the upheaval of a minor rebellion on Kauai in 1824, after the death of Kaumualii, but their exposure to the disturbance had been too marginal for more than passing admiration. In October 1825, however, Clarissa Richards had a moment of glory. The English ship *Daniel* anchored at Lahaina with a crew eager for the usual array of women. The ship's captain, Buckle, had attracted the ire of the mission some months before when he had paid ten doubloons to a female chief, Wahine Pio, for a young girl, Leoki, who was a promising scholar, and who, though unwilling, dared not disobey the chief's direction.[63] The crew, some armed, enraged at the *kapu* on women boarding ships and unrestrained by this captain, surrounded the Richards' house. Clarissa from the first had deplored prostitution in the port. Now she stood beside William and confronted the sailors, declaring she would die along with her husband if necessary, rather than beg for the *kapu* to be lifted. "I wish you all to understand that I am ready to share the fate of my husband, and will by no means consent to live upon the terms you offer."[64] The American Board was delighted with their heroine, and the *Missionary Herald* waxed lyrical about her bravery:

> It is difficult to say when or where, since the days of primitive Christianity, the heroism of Mrs. Richards has been surpassed. When she had great reason to expect that Mr. Richards would be murdered before her eyes . . . when there was no missionary brother or sister within a hundred miles . . . and when a single word of assent to the abrogation of a law in favor of public morality, would have removed all danger . . . she was firm and faithful.

What, the writer asked, would have happened if Clarissa, through feminine weakness, had yielded? "But she was sustained. The Lord was her protector, and the missionary cause was not tarnished."[65]

Ironically, the threat had come to this mission wife not from indigenous people, as mission women elsewhere confronted in situations with cannibalistic Maoris or cruel Burmese potentates, but instead from some Western sailors. It was for other mission wives to become the saints of missiology. The demands on the American wives' fortitude were to come from a less glorious, less dramatic, and yet no less difficult source. Their early dreams had focused on the heroism of foreign mission life, but the chiefs had in fact proved comparatively sympathetic to the mission's offerings. The women's ethnocentrism, their attachment to their own cultural ways of behaving, their utter inability to make sense of a society so different from their own, drove them to create obstacles which were of their own construction, yet which eluded their conscious control. The women's responses to the experience of the first years of mission life established the boundaries for themselves and for the women who followed them into this field over the next decades. With male missionaries the women stood, by the end of 1825, poised for a period of great influence on the Hawaiian population. If mission wives' life experiences over the next twenty-five years were to prove dispiriting and disappointing, this was because the women were to behave within the constraints established in these first years of mission life.

CHAPTER THREE

Dearest Friends

August 12, eve. Through night through day,
one form rises to view—the form of my dear
bosom friend. When may I again behold him
and mingle souls, and mingle praises and
supplications before the Throne of mercy! Is it
not nigh when I may unbosom my cares to a
faithful affectionate heart, when I may comfort and cheer and animate this dearest most
precious friend? Indulgent God, protect,
preserve, bless, return to my waiting heart my
dear husband, my soul's delight, support
and joy.

—Elizabeth Bishop's Journal
Honolulu, 1823

Mission couples had without doubt been oddly yoked together.
Remarkably, however, in the strained frontier conditions of the
Hawaiian islands, they entered relationships which became based on
the strongest of affectionate bonds. The women had entered marriage
with ambitions which revolved around a challenging role in public
missionary labor. Amidst lives on mission stations which they for the
most part experienced as alienating, frustrating, and lonely, an ironic
twist of fate ensured that it was in fact the emotional bonds which
developed within marriage that afforded women their emotional security, their greatest source of happiness, through the years of their
maturity. These close marital relationships were products of the particular social context of mission life in the islands. Mission life entailed a
scattering to mission stations where wives were firmly separated by
unfriendly terrain from most of their missionary fellows. Kith and kin
back home in America stayed in the women's minds and hearts, but
distance was a tyrannical barrier. Neither Hawaiians nor foreign residents offered acceptable companionship to those who could not tolerate cultural difference. For wives, husbands constituted their secure

source of support and friendship, on ordinary as on extraordinary days, a fact which they acknowledged with affectionate appreciation. The mission wives' experience over the twenty-five years of mission life following the early years of the first pilgrims was shaped by this relationship and its ramifications.

Lucy Thurston, writing from Kailua, once commenced a letter to the mission community at Honolulu with the words: "Lucy with Tatina, her husband, and all the children that are with us, to all that be in Honolulu called to be saints."[1] Like the saints of the early church, the Sandwich Island missionaries saw themselves as pioneering evangelists scattered about a pagan world which lay, as they often called it, "at the ends of the earth." They became isolated saints indeed. During the years up till 1825, only six mission stations had been established. As successive contingents of missionaries arrived from 1828 to 1848, the increase in numerical strength encouraged a far wider dispersal of forces. Waialua, Kaneohe, Ewa, and a school, Punahou, were begun on Oahu; on Hawaii, stations were established at Kohala, Waimea, and Waiohinu; mission schools were founded at Lahainaluna and Wailuku, as well as stations at Hana and (briefly) Haiku on Maui; stations were begun at Koloa and Waioli on Kauai; and a station was founded at Kaluaaha on Molokai. Two or three missionary couples at a time, as well as secular agents, a printer, and a physician, were located at Honolulu, by far the largest of the mission establishments. Most couples were located with no more than one or two others, often for periods of time alone, at stations established near the densest areas of Hawaiian settlement.[2]

Most women disliked the village of Honolulu on sight. It was dry, very dusty, with little vegetation. Indeed, mission herds grazing on the plain had denuded the surrounding area of what little grass had existed. Building had been higgledy-piggledy, building materials various. Mary Ives for one found that "its dirty streets, high mud walls, and brown grass huts, unsheltered by want of trees from the rays of the sun, do not strike the eye pleasantly."[3] Her negativism, however, was carried over by many women as they settled in their distant locations. Few could deny the remarkable sight of variegated mountains and valleys, numerous waterfalls and streams, beaches pounded by surging waves. It was magnificent, awe-inspiring, a testament to God's greatness. They were not birds of passage, however. For the mission women, this was their new home. It did not look like home.

As the wives went slowly about the process of establishing themselves in a situation where everything at first was difficult and unfamiliar, the scenery itself was an alien component.

Mary Ives moved to Hana, which at first sight seemed pleasant, quite like New England with its green fields, extensive forests, and little villages scattered here and there. "But these beauties are quite distant from our house," she complained. "There being no roads to mark the boundaries, objects appear to recede before one." Sarah Lyman responded similarly to Hilo: "Everything exhibits a striking contrast to the objects with which I was familiar at home. The houses are all built of thatch. The trees and the grass are not such as I have been accustomed to seeing." There were no fences, and no roads excepting footpaths "with rank grass on each side." Compared with the beautiful banks of the Connecticut River, one loyal New Englander found Lahaina a mere desert, "a land without order," like the valley of the shadow of death. The high mountain ranges behind the mission stations appeared to the women to imprison them, arousing "pent-up" feelings. For the wives at Hilo, the active volcanoes held out the terror of earthquakes, which sent them to bed each night in a fearful state of mind. But for most wives mountains implied loneliness rather than terror. Many a homesick wife sat staring out at the ocean, oblivious to its charm, thinking of it only as a barrier to "abodes of civilization and refinement."[4]

The mountainous character of the scenery, and their transference to islands cut off from each other by water which so often belied the name "Pacific," implied for the women an aspect of their situation which few had clearly envisaged. The extreme difficulties of traveling far—indeed, even further than a mile or two from their homes—would effectively shut them off from all society other than that found in their immediate environs. They were now situated in places both geographically and socially isolated, not just from their American homes, but from the mission circle which constituted their most natural friendship group. And they were so situated at the very time of their lives when they would be most dependent on others' help, as they began to bear and rear children.

"We are hemmed in on all hands," reported Fidelia Coan from Hilo. "No roads, no horses, no neighbors."[5] The geography combined with their response to it rendered the wives immobilized for years on end. Hawaiian women, it need hardly be said, found no difficulty in traveling far afield. They scaled high cliffs, forded swollen rivers, walked mile upon mile in a day, without fear or fatigue. American women, even those from farming backgrounds, were, by comparison, physically weaker and utterly unskilled in such demanding endeavors. Their menfolk were generally more robust, more suitably dressed, and accustomed to rougher living. Few of the American women could face any sort of expedition with equanimity.

Travel by land the women found virtually impossible without physical assistance from Hawaiian men, burdensome and dangerous even then. One of the first embarrassing discoveries on landing in Honolulu was the existence of a mission cart drawn, not by horses, but by Hawaiian men, which women found in turns comical and somewhat humiliating.[6] Wives were soon to discover that either they accepted such Hawaiian help, offered with the greatest good humor, or they stayed home. Travel on the islands offered fearful obstacles compared with the route from wharf to mission premises at Honolulu.

The nature of the terrain between the two mission stations of Hilo and Waimea, some thirty miles apart, indicated the problem of travel faced by mission wives. There were no fewer than sixty ravines, chasms from fifty to two hundred feet in depth, so steep that one had to clamber down the slopes using hands as well as feet. There were vast fields of rugged lava, and rivers, sometimes swollen by heavy rain, which had to be crossed by wading or on the back of a Hawaiian. Titus Coan, a restless spirit and enthusiastic evangelist, traveled about this district teaching and preaching. There was no way his wife, or other mission women, could envisage following suit.[7]

It became customary for women, with their children, to submit to being carried for a land trip in a *manele,* a type of Chinese palanquin, by Hawaiian bearers. The women would sit in a chair suspended at the middle of poles which would rest on the men's shoulders, the babies held in arms, the small children similarly borne in a cradle or a fruit box. A donkey or horse might be available from time to time, but the sheer slopes of the valleys made this, too, a treat only for the bold: If the beast took one false step, the rider could be plunged several hundred feet below. The mode of carriage, however, represented but one problematic aspect of travel. The women felt obliged to prepare beforehand all their provisions, such as cooked rice, a pie, or vegetables, cooking utensils for making tea, table furniture, bed and bedding, calabashes of water—the list was seemingly endless. On such a journey there could be seen, strung out for a mile or two along the road, dozens of attendants and bearers carrying *kapa,* calabashes, the missionaries' clothing packed in a gourd shell, all amidst the bearers of the mission family.[8]

The women thought they knew all there was to know about the miseries of sea voyages. They had discoveries to make at the Sandwich Islands. The Pacific Ocean seldom lived up to its name. Canoes, with Hawaiian rowers, were relied on for short coastal trips. High seas often made these trips hazardous, and the women, seated on a plank, clung to their struggling infants and prayed to escape, if not a wetting, at least being overturned into the sea. For interisland voyaging, there were schooners or brigs of thirty to sixty tons owned by the king or chiefs. The misery of such travel defied description. Mission families huddled together on decks surrounded by a lively throng of Hawaiians, with pigs, goats, chickens, and dogs; the Hawaiians' calabashes of food were spread about; smoking was prevalent. There, desperately seasick, the women crouched or lay day and night, driven to the stuffy cabins below out of the rain, wind, and sun only when huge waves swept across the boat. If she had ever imagined yachting by moonlight among the isles of the Pacific, declared Laura Judd, one trip dispelled the dream promptly. As their youthful courage and curiosity waned, and their families grew in size, the occasions for which women would face the rigors of travel slowly but surely diminished.

The daily social interaction of mission women would inevitably revolve around their neighbors. It was by no means the end, of course, of their ties with their families and friends in America. Despite the enormous distance, those ties remained highly significant to their emotional and imaginative lives. The journals begun on the voyages, or on first landing in the islands, were intended for their mothers, their fathers, brothers and sisters, to keep them in touch with the details of their activities and reactions, and they begged the same in return. Juliette Cooke began a journal for her mother on the very first day she stepped ashore. She would talk to her mother in this little book, settle on a particular time of day for the exercise, and try to imagine mother listening with her ever-ready interest in all of Juliette's affairs. She would write in a perfectly unguarded manner, only for mother's eyes, knowing she would not let anyone see any details which could embarrass the mission in any way. The American Board was delighted with graphic descriptions of "the world that lieth in wickedness," which gave superstition and misery a "local habitation," for this information spurred the benevolent to generosity. On the other hand, frank details about particular people in the Hawaiian community could cause the mission great embarrassment, as the wives painfully learned.[9]

In her communications home, Juliette, like all the women, engaged energetically in discussing all the concerns of the family, undaunted by the delay of long months before her letter would be received and a reply possible. Was brother Charles seriously considering marriage? He seemed far too young, though the Bible gave no command on the subject. He and sister Fanny should improve their mental powers and not neglect any opportunity to further study. Mercy Whitney similarly wanted particulars of all the family's movements and offered energetic comment and criticism. How were mother's eyes? Did they have hired help? How much cloth did they now manufacture each year? Was the new minister settled in? She was horrified that brother Edward had joined the sect called the Mormonites. The women focused again and again on the religious condition of their loved ones, and the reason was clear. The one consolation they had in their heart-yearning for all their kith and kin was the hope of meeting them again in heaven. The alternative—that they should be dispatched, unregenerate, to the fires of hell—was insupportable.[10]

Juliette Cooke expressed in poetic form for her mother the joy she felt when word came that a ship with mail from America had arrived:

> A sail from home! O how it makes the blood
> In its arterial courses leap for joy!
> And happy thought impatient of delay
> Starts on the wing and with the speed of light
> Flies o'er the boundless wilderness of waves
> To hold communion with the friends we love
> Then comes the golden freight of letters in
> Which with starving famished appetite
> We quick devour.[11]

Letters from home were the women's most precious gifts. They suspended work and sat up half the night to discover the news, pausing to weep at a death, to rejoice at a birth, to laugh at some comical scene, sharing all with their husbands. Women could receive rein-

forcement for their crucial decision to become a missionary, as when
Mary Alexander was told that for her labor of carrying light to Hawaiians, "blessed thrice blessed has been your lot; for these privations
have been endured in the service of your Lord and master."[12] In turn
they named babies, often, for their kin (though sometimes for mission heroes and heroines, and sometimes for themselves as well) and
could draw their relations into the circle of their new families by relating the prowess of their namesakes or describing how the little one
appeared in baby things sent from home. The sheer distance, of
course, created sadness. A wife might weep when she realized a
beloved sister would not even know of a birth for months, perhaps a
year, or when, having taught a "prattling" child to lisp the word
"grandpa," she discovered subsequently that her father had been
long dead.

The letters, however, did not come often and, as years went by,
grew fewer. Juliette pleaded with her family, "Do *dearest mother* and
friends write *more fully and frequently.*" Fidelia Coan thought her
letters were few because her brothers and sisters had never been eighteen thousand miles from home, whereas she could not think of them
and her parents without weeping. The fewer letters she received, the
fewer she wrote, in retaliation, feeling that to devote the time she
needed a fair prospect of "pay in the same coin," but this was a law of
diminishing returns. Maria Chamberlain was devastated when sister
Ann confessed that, after five years' separation, she now thought of
Maria less frequently. For Maria, neither distance, nor time between
letters, nor her new family, would alter *her* affections one jot.[13]

In fact, the women could not sustain the strength of loving ties as
they had experienced them in their youth. Brothers and sisters who
were children when they left grew to manhood and womanhood
unknown. Families shifted houses, and it was difficult to cling to the
memory of their daily round when the physical setting had altered.
("Do be more particular when you write," begged one wife, "to tell
me about the alterations and improvements which have been made.")
Village centers, they sometimes heard, had been rebuilt, no doubt
beyond their recognition. Perhaps they would feel like strangers in
their native towns, with so many dead, or gone, and another generation appearing on the scene. In the end many women were reduced,
for months on end, like Laura Judd, to clinging to some old material
token to conjure up vivid memories of home. Laura had an old carpet,

which she could never part with, a gift from loved friends, one of whom had since died; when she felt *moody,* she admitted, she would spread it, sit down, and think of other days.[14]

Strange Heathens and Heathen Strangers

Old carpets were a consolation in loneliness, but of little practical value. For day-to-day companionship wives had necessarily to turn to people nearer home. These were, most numerously, Hawaiians, for the sake of whose souls they had exiled themselves voluntarily. Far fewer in number, but not to be ignored, were other *haoles,* American and European residents, along with a passing parade of officers and sailors from the ships which recruited and traded at Hawaiian ports. With both groups, fragile bridges were sometimes constructed. Neither group could offer the quality of relationship which the mission women sought.

Mary Parker, alone with her husband Benjamin at Kaneohe on the northern shore of Oahu, once passed on to Fanny Gulick, a similarly isolated mission sister, some items of news which had filtered through from Honolulu. Perhaps it would do Fanny good "to give a new turn to thoughts which sometimes get solitary in solitude." She continued: "I feel sorry for those who live alone—'tis indeed a trial of bitter feelings yet I trust we all love our Savior sufficiently to serve him. . . . I think we who are situated alone degenerate insensibly to ourselves—in mind, body, and spirit—the tendency is downward and unavoidably, when surrounded day by day by a low grovelling people, and they our only society."[15] These dedicated but painfully narrow Christian missionary women lived year upon year with their spirits depressed at being thrust into the midst of Hawaiian society. One woman after another arrived, only to experience the same shocked and alienated response—like Mary Parker who, with chilling disappointment, described Hawaiians as "naked, rude, and disgusting to every feeling. Their little filthy huts tell their poverty of mind."[16] So thought Fidelia Coan, arrived among the "dark-hearted, stupid people" at Hilo, who seemed to her as surely on the road to destruction as when the islands were first discovered.[17] The scenery was beautiful, thought Clarissa Armstrong, newly marooned at Haiku: "But, O, the want of society! Week after week passes and we see none but naked, filthy, wicked heathen with souls as dark as the tabernacles which they inhabit. The darkness of the people seems to destroy the beauty of the scenery around us."[18]

Sarah Lyman's description of Hawaiians to her sister Melissa gave particulars for the basis of the American women's revulsion, specifics omitted from other accounts. The men's *malo*, she said, was passed twice around the body, just above the hips, and then between the legs "barely covering the private parts." Many of the Hawaiian women thought no more of bare breasts than Americans would of bare hands; their skirt covered them only from hips to knees. Even worse, women and men would sit down in the road "to do their duties, right before our eyes too. They seem to think no more about it than the dumb beasts." Finally, with whole families habitually sleeping together on one mat, sexual matters were "common talk" among children. "You must be careful whose hands this falls into," Sarah warned her.[19]

Some of the American women were warmhearted enough to respond to the initial goodwill and friendliness evinced by the Hawaiians themselves. Smiles, willing services, embraces, leis, visits, presents—all were showered on the newcomers by Hawaiian women. Maria Patton found the Hawaiians so pleased to have her in Lahaina that for the first few weeks not a day passed without a token of their affection. One of the female chiefs "took a fancy" to her and offered to be her friend; in consequence, presents of hogs, fowl, taro, and sweet potatoes arrived on her doorstep. On one occasion Maria wrote to her sisters with a wreath of beautiful scarlet flowers on her head and another of bright orange around her neck, kind gifts. "These we must wear or they would be very much displeased."[20] Few women were long in the islands, however, before giving voice to negative responses—no matter how mild, hospitable, or "harmless" Hawaiians may have seemed at first.

The manner in which newly arrived American wives responded to Hawaiians, virtually uniformly over three decades of first encounters, made little acknowledgment of the marked change in religious behavior which had taken place during those years. The mission prospered remarkably compared with the tortuous progress of the ABCFM ventures in the East. From her decision to espouse the cause of the Christian missions in 1825 to her death in 1832, Kaahumanu threw her considerable political influence in favor of the churches, schools, and legal changes congenial to the Americans. Mission-educated Hawai-

ians conducted schools for those beyond the reach of the mission stations. Attendance at church services was widespread, and under
Kaahumanu's leadership French Roman Catholic missionaries failed
to gain a firm presence in the islands. When Kaahumanu died in
1832, and the young king Kauikeaouli took the lead in policymaking,
there was at first some falling away of mission influence, which
proved, however, temporary. Other powerful chiefs, including the
new *kuhina nui,* Kinau, were strong adherents of the mission, and the
king himself eventually accepted advice from the same quarter,
appointing a succession of missionaries to his government. Church
membership increased sharply from the late 1830s after a religious
revival which commenced at Hilo and spread outward through the
islands. Chiefs who decided to throw in their lot with the missionaries
assumed leadership within local congregations and districts, taking
active interest in the schools, leading the sex-segregated prayer
groups. The high chief, Kakauluoki, explained to a newly arrived missionary in 1831 that once the priest used to pray on their behalf, but
now Hawaiians prayed for themselves; she herself, however, prayed
for all the people, for good chiefs and bad chiefs alike.[21]

From among the female chiefs, a very few mission wives found
women with whom they could sustain a relationship approaching genuine friendship, but even then it remained on the margins of reciprocal feeling. A woman like Kapiolani acquired enough of the character
and style of an American Christian to make mission wives feel comfortable. There was her two-story home, made of stone, with separate
rooms, furnished with Western goods from toilet tables to writing
desks and china tea services. She arranged her hair in side-puffs held
by tortoiseshell combs; her feet were clad in shoes and stockings; she
wore fitted dresses in sober colors, rather than red or yellow loose
dresses or *holoku.*[22]

But, in truth, even the Christian chiefs who most rapidly adopted
Western ways baffled the mission wives and left them uncertain of the
precise nature of their relationship. It was so difficult to read the
signs, to know who was the manipulator, whom the manipulated.
Juliette Cooke could speak of the chiefs as though the mission sustained the upper hand. She told a friend of a tea party she had
assisted in giving: "We do not often invite them but deem it necessary
once in a while that we may keep up the acquaintance and have their
co-operation in some plans we lay for the good of the people." Even

by 1828, however, Laura Judd noted that Kaahumanu "treated us like pet children." As Kaahumanu was an Amazon in size, "she could hold any of us on her lap, as she would a little child, which she often takes the liberty of doing." Kinau, Kaahumanu's successor, treated Laura in similar fashion. At a school examination, she called Laura across the room to give her an orange and "wished me to sit on her lap." A high chief called on Juliette Cooke and admired her straw bonnet; a mission sister warned her that the chief would most likely send for it the next day. Or, more threateningly, chiefs might ask, coolly and with the utmost assurance, for a child to be handed over to be raised as their own, as Kapulikoliko did of little Persis Thurston and Kinau did of newborn Elizabeth Judd.[23]

The situation was, clearly, a complex one. The missionaries ardently wished to view the chiefs as players in the mission drama. But the chiefs had an agenda that coincided in part with the missionaries' but had a vitality and plot of its own. They ruled the people who constituted the missionaries' congregations, they levied taxes, exacted labor, collected the goods that were their due, planned their political strategies, and fought according to cultural notions inaccessible to outsiders. Many chiefs shifted their metaphysical constructs toward a Christian vision, but this vision was incorporated into a worldview in many ways at odds with the Americans' own.

The mission wives' response to ordinary, nonchiefly Hawaiians was less ambiguous; indeed it was frankly condemnatory. Maria Dibble made explicit the logic of this response. She had known little before she came of the character, "if they may be said to have any," of a heathen people: They were ignorant and stupid, "nor can I say that our intercourse with them is in any way particularly pleasant but as we enjoy the happiness of seeing them improve by our efforts." Repulsive and wild they might appear, but, for Julia Spaulding, "we remembered that we went for their good, and not for our own gratification." If, in other words, Hawaiians had been acceptable as friends and companions, the mission wives would not have been there at all.[24] Hawaiians were automatically defined as "other," since they were subjects in the wives' own project for transcendence, their purpose for coming, their justification for staying.

From their statements, it would have been easy to believe that the mission wives viewed Hawaiians from a physical distance. Not so. Lucy Thurston, for one, likened her home to a public house. Hawaiians came into the mission homes as domestic servants. They visited for barter and for medicines; they came for spiritual advice and instruction, frequently spending entire evenings at the house. They slept overnight in the mission premises, offering protection, when the husband was away on a preaching trip or attending a meeting.

The American women appeared remarkably lonely souls to Hawaiians, and Hawaiian women tried to make up for their obvious lack of friends, calling to commiserate when the wives were left alone, but to no avail. When Kaahumanu visited Kuapehu, she found the cottage of the single woman, Mary Ward, inviting and proposed spending the night with her. Mary, hastily, "cheerfully gave her full possession" and slept in a corner at Clarissa Richards' house. When the Ives and Clarks suffered the misfortune of having their homes burned down, local Hawaiians offered them shelter for the night. Mary Ives' "heart rather revolted at the idea of taking my abode with fleas, lice, musquitoes, and half naked natives." Very, very occasionally, an exhausted and dispirited wife submitted to a *lomilomi,* a massage which one woman described as something between a squeeze and a pinch, which Hawaiians used for fatigue and minor pain. But women seldom wanted physical contact with Hawaiian women. They did not want them at births; they did not want their ministrations in illnesses; they did not respond to kisses and embraces. Mercy Whitney, in considerable embarrassment, once appeared in public in a "suit of native cloth" which her scholars had made her to match their own during the public examination of her school. Neither she nor any other woman hastened to repeat such a spectacle.[25]

One did not need the evidence of mission women to demonstrate the unusual personal warmth of Hawaiians, but in fact the wives gave ample evidence of it themselves. Sarah Lyman described her return, brokenhearted, to Hilo after burying her first-born baby at Lahaina. Their Hawaiian neighbors flocked to the landing-place to meet them, brought chairs, and they all sat down to weep together. She was carried to her door to be met by a church member who put her arms around Sarah's neck and burst into tears. To please her, the women made great efforts to turn out next day with clothes and hair acceptably dressed. Lucy Thurston was welcomed with great affection when she returned to Kailua after a long absence in America. "The natives were overjoyed at my return. Those who had lived in our family knelt around me, and wept aloud, bathing my hands with their tears." For several weeks a continual series of callers appeared, with kindhearted natives coming by schools and by districts to welcome her. Momentarily, an American woman might be touched by such personal warmth.[26] Overall, Hawaiians remained alien souls.

If the mission women rejected the Hawaiians as strange heathens, they similarly rejected the rest of the foreign community as heathen strangers. Hawaiians were a source of anxiety and tension rather than a pool of friendship because their way of living constituted the evil which Americans had sacrificed themselves to eradicate. The nonmissionary *haoles* outnumbered the missionaries many times over and grew in number at a far more rapid rate as each decade passed. It required much energy to prevent this group from subverting their entire enterprise of reform. The lines, therefore, became tightly drawn. Hawaiians might, in time, blossom into full-fledged Christians, unless they were seduced by *haoles* who were hardened in sin and whose regeneration seemed even more problematic.

It was at Honolulu that by far the greatest concentration of foreigners congregated, servicing the whaling, trading, and exploration vessels and their crews. In the 1840s the town was losing its earlier character of an overgrown village and taking on a more recognizably Western shape. Some foreign merchants had erected homes and warehouses of stone, others of adobe (sun-dried) bricks plastered with lime; the streets were bordered with shops; there was a windmill for water, and some trees struggling up on the plain. There were around six hundred foreign male residents in Honolulu by the mid-1840s, including representatives of the American and British governments. Some foreigners had *haole* wives, including wives of sea captains who settled from time to time in the islands, attracted like so many other outsiders by its particularly pleasant climate and easygoing ways of living. "It is becoming quite fashionable for Eng. and A. ladies to accompany their husbands to the Islds.," one mission wife reported in 1834. Such a concentration of Westerners and increasing wealth enabled entertainments and "social life" to prosper: balls, horse races, card parties, celebrations of national days and Christmas.[27] This was, of course, a very different social environment from that of the other mission stations, where a few scattered absconded seamen and adventurers lived by artisanal skills or agriculture.

The majority of foreign residents near the station of Waimea, reported the resident missionary, lived "like the veriest heathen."

They were not men schooled in the disciplined piety of New England Christianity. They lived with—or, more rarely, married—Hawaiian women and reared in their fashion the children of the union with little reference to the practices and teaching of the missionary churches. The most dissolute in mission eyes, men of the beachcomber variety, were responsible for the introduction of Western ungodly pleasures to a people already well endowed with their own variety. Said one missionary in no uncertain terms, foreign sailors, runaways, and other bad characters taught Hawaiians "gambling, profanity, intemperance, impurity of every kind, Sabbath-breaking, infidelity, etc."[28]

Something of the mission women's attitude to the sexual coupling of *haole* men and Hawaiian women can be judged from the response of Clarissa Armstrong to the marriage of one Nathan Mack in 1836. Nathan, a member of Clarissa's old church back home, had turned up unexpectedly on Maui and was taken into the Armstrong household at Wailuku. One evening Nathan announced calmly that instead of returning to America he had decided to stay and marry a Hawaiian. Clarissa was shocked almost beyond words:

> O what feelings of *sorrow, contempt* etc filled my breast. I have done nothing scarcely this P.M. but sorrow, and weep for the folly, of one I watched over as a brother. A member of our family, and we keeping him from temptations, and the[n] without asking even our advice, is going headlong into folly, and I fear what is worse!! What will his poor mother say, when she hears he is *married* to a *heathen,* who like the rest, regards not the truth, or the 7th commandment.[29]

As was the case in the first years of the mission, it was the conjunction of the Western male's sexual predacity and the Hawaiian's easiness about sexuality which most affronted missionaries' sense of propriety and drove a strong wedge between the mission and the rest of the foreign community. Laura Judd was "galled" to be forced to sit at table with John Coffin Jones, the American commercial agent, at a dinner party at Kinau's house—a man who openly kept three or four mistresses.[30] The missionaries refused to baptize illegitimate offspring of white men or to pray at the funerals of their mistresses, for which services the men often turned to the few Catholic priests.[31]

For the mission women, foreign visitors or residents occasionally provided welcome company. At a mission station like Hilo, well placed for expeditions to the volcanoes, the women were pleased to offer hospitality to scientists and other curious visitors who brought in their train opportunities to hear and discuss events of the outside world and intellectual interests to offset the work their stay entailed. Many of the ships' captains obviously pitied the isolated mission wives and offered hospitality on board ship, as well as gifts including books and newspapers. When the U.S. Exploring Expedition visited Honolulu, mission wives were part of a group of forty white women who were among the foreign residents present when the officers treated all to a picnic. There was a luxurious spread, something new to the wives. Laura Judd fancied that "some faces, little accustomed to smile, looked brighter and happier for a long time afterward."[32] Such contacts were ephemeral, however, could not be securely anticipated, and often passed so swiftly the benefit was transitory.

Few of the *haole* women were company for the mission wives. Laura Judd, for one, had at first been hopeful at the arrival of other white women in the islands: "Foreigners are crowding in, but we hope the poor natives will not be obliged to retreat before them like the poor aborigines of America. Vices of the most degrading kind abound but we do hope that *Ladies' Society* may have a happy influence in discountenancing and putting to shame some of them."[33] The majority of *haole* women failed to reach the stringent mission standards. Although the mission wives dutifully returned visits if foreign wives showed an interest in the church and paid them friendly attentions, true reciprocity of sentiment was absent and hence this social interaction became, frankly, yet another chore. By 1833 there were eleven foreign women in Honolulu besides captains' wives, who were temporary residents. All, said Maria Chamberlain, expected friendly attention from the missionaries, and to avoid giving offense one mission wife or another was obliged to entertain them, but it was an unwelcome interruption of missionary work. Maria attended the wedding of Captain Little to Miss Woods in September 1835, the ceremony followed by a grand party in the evening. Maria's eyes were almost dazzled, she told Fanny Gulick, by the fine vases, the handsome lamps, the variety of cakes, sweetmeats, fruit, and wine. She was quite willing, however, that her invitations to such parties should be few and far between; now, of course, she would have to return the civility. White women joined men to ride out on the Sabbath for pleasure, setting a dreadful example to Hawaiians. When Captain Hinckley's wife, who used to attend balls and card parties while also coming to the communion table, left her husband and went back to America, Clarissa Armstrong was not surprised: "She is rewarded even in this life, for her wickedness."[34]

Laura Judd once told an isolated mission sister that she would swap *"all her old shoes"* to be in their quiet retreat. She would share their sage tea and go without bread to escape the "distressing anxieties" of Oahu.[35] A fair share of that tension was produced by contact with their own compatriots.

"Sisters" and Husbands

When Elias Bond wrote from Kohala to ask Maria Chamberlain to come and stay, since "Mrs. Bond has had no female society for two years," there was no misunderstanding what he meant.[36] Neither the Hawaiian nor the *haole* communities could provide the mission wives with the reciprocity in affection the women had lost by severing their ties with home so drastically. There was only one group which promised such possibilities of real friendship, and that was the mission community itself.

In the alienating context of the island environment, other missionaries—and for women, particularly, their substitute "sisters" in the mission—were the one hope, apart from their husbands, of congenial social interaction. They longed for such contacts with the same vehemence as Louisa Ely, who wrote to her nearest mission sister that she longed to see her. "I often as I walk solitary and alone think how heart cheering the society of a dear female friend would be—I never can loose [*sic*] my relish for society—O how sweet an interview would be."[37] But, alas, her friend could not come. Mission sisters provided what solace they could for each other, but at the end of the day a variety of circumstances prevented consistent fulfillment of the needs of the women both personal and material.

There were circumstances in which mission women were able, for periods of time, to sustain close contact with other women, the most favorable of these being when women of congenial tastes were stationed together. While invariably sustaining separate households of sleeping and eating, wives under these conditions could coordinate other activities to some degree in order to offer some relief from duties which saved their energies. They took turns minding children and holding classes for older children or Hawaiian women. They took meals together when their husbands were absent. Acquisitions of food, such as meat, would be shared. They could help out if house renovations were under way; they could share domestic servants' services. Wives would help out at births and during times of family illness, watching at night in turn with a seriously sick child, taking the infants when mothers were ill. And the families could sustain "concerts" of prayer together, perhaps with a sermon in English.

The married women were particularly delighted when one of the single women appeared at their station. A persistent theme in letters home was a plaintive request for unmarried sisters to join them in the mission field. The request once made, the next news was often of the sister's marriage back home. Only one such effort proved successful. Rebecca and Harvey Hitchcock had twenty brothers and sisters altogether, fit and able. Just one, Elizabeth Hitchcock, joined them on Molokai, to their great rejoicing, especially as she arrived quite providentially to be present at Rebecca's confinement. Rebecca anticipated a great deal of happiness in having Elizabeth's society; her husband believed Elizabeth's prospects of usefulness were "flattering indeed." Several married siblings also arrived in the mission. "Oh can it be true that I shall see my sister, the former idol of my heart?" was Betsey Lyons' response to the news that her married sister, Emily, and her husband were on their way to the islands. By some macabre coincidence, in all three cases the death of the sibling first in the field followed quite quickly. These tragedies proved something of a test of faith and Christian resignation. After Betsey Lyons' death three weeks after Emily Bliss' arrival, Emily told how she "had once hoped to see an own sister at her dwelling, but the Lord's ways are not our ways, nor his thoughts our thoughts."[38]

If one's own sisters did not appear in the islands, some other single women did. When no fewer than four women—Maria Patton, Maria Ogden, Mary Ward, and Delia Stone—arrived on the *Parthian* in 1828, there was an almost demeaning scramble by the men and women of the mission to attain one as an associate. Maria Ogden responded to all the quarreling over her location with mild astonishment. "What a constant state of warfare to be a Christian," she observed.[39] That single women were highly valued was not surprising. Mission wives swiftly became hard-pressed with the variety of demands on their time as their families increased in size. The women were reluctant to ask for any help which might drain their married sisters' energies to the last ounce. Single women, however, were free of family burdens, and their assistance was therefore far more reliable.

The mission women needed to get along amicably with their female associates and clearly made a conscious effort to do so even where perhaps strong congeniality did not exist. (It was, after all, the male association which had usually brought the wives together.) Their hoped-for "union in sentiment and thought and feeling" did not always occur. At one informal discussion of the problem a number of mission women urged each other to avoid friction, to look to the Golden Rule, and to examine one's own faults rather than a sister's. They should suppress suspicion of one another and seek a fair explanation from a sister who harbored unkind feelings; they ought to study their sisters' peculiar temperaments and dispositions, exercising a forgiving spirit in all their dealings.[40] Lucia Smith expressed to Juliette Cooke the proper course she believed sisters should take: "If we differ in opinion, where that opinion affects our character and conduct: ought we not to labor to set each other right? You say, you do not see as it would do you any good, to convert me to your opinion. *Certainly it would,* if yours is nearer the truth than mine, and although I may be stubborn, where I think I am in the right, I think I am willing to recieve [*sic*] light from any source."[41]

Often, however, the friendship of women on stations was strong, and parting, when it came, a dreadful wrench. *"Man appoints—God disappoints"* was Clarissa Richards' reaction to Maria Ogden's transfer to the girls' school, breaking up the identification of their daily routine of duties which had proved so comforting. Nancy Ruggles and Mercy Whitney had similarly worked well together on Kauai. On one such occasion when Nancy had assisted Mercy through an illness, Mercy wrote: "Her kind attention to, and sympathy with, me and mine in this time of affliction has greatly endeared her to my heart. We have lived together so much of the time since we left A. that she seems almost like an own sister." Providence separated them when the Ruggleses were shifted to the island of Hawaii. At Wailuku on Maui, Theodotia Green and Clarissa Armstrong had a few years together before the Armstrongs' shift to Honolulu was mooted. Clarissa, on hearing the news, cried most of the afternoon. "O the thought of braking [*sic*] up all, with such a company of children, and my strength so easily exhausted, makes my heart faint!"[42]

Death removed some beloved sisters—either the death of the

women themselves or because they were widowed and hence departed from the islands. Wrote Caroline Bailey to Mary Ives of the death of Parnelly Andrews: "I would tell you how much I loved our dear departed sister, but I know you too loved her, and it is needless. I feel that wherever I turn there is a blank and I can only say, oh, my sister, my sister, art thou gone." A happier severance, but one which could almost as surely remove an associate, was caused by marriage. Single sisters tended to marry, and marry quickly, in the islands. Prompt proposals to the single women were forthcoming from the single and widowed male missionaries. Even the Hitchcocks, extremely disappointed, lost their valuable sister Elizabeth within a year to the arms of the widower Edmund Rogers of Honolulu.[43]

The alternative to an association with a mission woman was, of course, to visit one temporarily, but the women needed to feel that an expedition was essential before they could summon the courage to embark. Visiting for sheer pleasure was seldom a valid reason. When the Cookes had traveled over the mountain range from Honolulu to visit the Parkers at Kaneohe briefly, Juliette was glad to get back home and not eager to attempt it again. There was the trouble they caused their friends to consider, plus the guilty feeling that it was wasting time anyway, to add to the fatiguing effort of the journey. The one time women would make every effort to visit was when a mission woman would otherwise be left without female help during a confinement, and in that case they would brave a good deal if called on. Laura Judd, wife of the mission physician, became an intrepid traveler and once slid down a fearful slope on a sledge of leaves in order to reach a pregnant mission wife at Kaneohe. She clung desperately to the long grass at either side to check her speed, expecting any moment to fall to her death.[44]

The other occasion for which mission women faced the rigors of travel was to attend, at least occasionally, the General Meeting held for a month or more in Honolulu in the spring, when the business affairs of the whole mission were decided upon and the women had an opportunity of seeing one another for an extended period. Caroline Diell, for one, felt that "it seems to reawaken our sleeping energies (for union is strength particularly here), and make us feel more the importance of diligence, in the great work before us." When there was a suggestion that the meetings should be cut back as an economy measure, Fidelia Coan let the American Board know her thoughts through a letter to the treasurer's wife. It was so remote at Hilo, she said, that the tear "starts to my eye at the thought of spending my days with next to no personal intercourse with civilized society two families excepted." When she could not attend, as happened several years in a row, she felt herself to be living "an oyster sort of life—scarcely stirring out of my dooryard." It was a "dead level condition of existence," though perhaps, of course, meant as a "moral medicine" to her.[45]

The women urged one another to make the journey. "Seasickness, you know, when the passage is made, is soon forgotten," Sybil Bingham jollied along Nancy Ruggles.[46] The Honolulu women offered hospitality, if possible, or equipment to furnish a small Hawaiian house taken over for the occasion. Above all, the women reminded one another of the refreshing opportunity to pray together in something resembling old American ways. When Mary Parker returned from one General Meeting she suggested to Lucia Lyons that the sisters should try even harder next time to snatch time for prayer: "Yet I am satisfied that we should secure in some way more seasons of united prayer—we sisters—when we come together. It would facilitate our business maybe—but if not our temporal—it would the great business of life which is made up of our little daily actions after all."[47] As often as not, however, the women could not make it to the General Meeting. The husbands went as a matter of course. Illness, childbearing, terror at the voyage, a sense of responsibility to station business—any or all such reasons might keep them away. The "oysterlike existence" was the lot of many women at the outlying stations or, as Mary Parker wistfully expressed it to Fanny Gulick, "we who live away in the woods alone."[48]

Ironically, the most common way for mission wives to retain contact with one another was by letter writing—the same method, and a laborious one, that they were obliged to adopt for friends in America. The women dashed off brief notes to one another whenever an opportunity presented itself. They passed on the news, congratulated, advised, commiserated, urged each other to cheerfulness, to duty, to piety. But the overburdened women found letter writing a chore which chatting face to face never was. "I do not *like* to lose you entirely as a correspondent," wrote Clarissa Richards plaintively to Nancy Ruggles, "though perhaps I have been culpably negligent myself in that tender regard and unabated affection which I am confident I do really feel towards my beloved sister and her family."[49] There were many such apologetic letters. However willing and however kind, absent mission sisters could not offer the practical friendship which the women consistently needed.

Yet it was imperative that they have a personally close, secure friend. After merely a short time in their isolated situations in the islands, mission women would begin to experience an appalling sense, not simply of loneliness, but of anomie—a terror of losing the firm grasp of reality which sustained their personal beings. Some expressed their alienation in a joking fashion, as when Theodotia Green failed to date fully a letter to a mission sister: "I have really forgotten the day of the month." Juliette Cooke forgot her twenty-eighth birthday until two days later. Mary Parker had expressed this feeling seriously as a sense of everything being retrograde: "The strong current is downward here at Kaneohe—How easily we in a Heathen land assimilate with the darkness around us, and almost imperceptibly lose our sense of civilized life, if not our relish for it." When she once discovered a book tucked away in a box sent from home, Clarissa Armstrong was delighted, because, she said, they needed new publications to keep up with the times, "or we shall degenerate. There is a greater tendency to it [in] heathen lands than elsewhere—everything around us is in darkness, when at our station, and we become indifferent to ourselves—which is not right." To be effective proselytizers, and not succumb themselves to the cultural influences of their social environment, they needed on this alien frontier intimates who might join reciprocally in sustaining identity, constantly creating and recreating a grasp on a familiar, taken-for-granted sense of reality. It was husbands alone who could provide this support.[50]

The close bonding of married couples had commenced from the very start of their ship life, when suddenly a spouse had to take the place of all the family and friends they had ever known. Sickness itself brought couples together. Richard Armstrong on the *Averick* described how he and Clarissa lay ill side by side for days on end: "Whilst wd [would] hold the head of my C. with one hand and a tin vessel with another, I would be obliged to empty the contents of my own stomach at the same time into the same vessel." Many brides, some with pregnancy sickness, succumbed to fierce dysentery exacerbated by the foul bilge water, stale drinking water, and rancid food. Husbands provided all their personal care for weeks on end. Theodotia wrote gratefully of Jonathan's tender and affectionate care when she suffered "an untimely confinement after a nasty fall." Couples studied together, prayed together, jumped the rope on deck, labored over the washtub on rainy days. One or two wives sounded a skeptical note. Husband Benjamin, wrote Mary Parker to her sister, was "just what you saw him, better than I am but not perfect. I am not proud enough to think he is, nor vain enough to wish others to think so." Far more women echoed the wife who claimed always to have had an exalted idea of marriage, but found the joy far exceeding her most sanguine expectations.[51]

In the islands, marital dependence was intensified. No missionary, asserted Mercy Whitney, should even consider going to the field unmarried. Almost the only "enlightened" society that missionaries enjoyed was what they found in their bosom companion, and a person, to be useful, simply had to enjoy *some* society. Mercy described how, for years on end, alone at their station, she and Samuel had spent the long evenings together, he, often exhausted, lying on the settee while she read to him, or perhaps he reading while she was busy at her sewing or other work. "We were *happy* in each other's society, and while we could enjoy that, we sought no other." Here was described a drawing together in spirit which was striking, and typical.[52]

Over the years, some wives expressed their love in a stilted, romantic rhetoric, others in more mundane form, but the intensity of feeling could not be disguised. Juliette Cooke may have requested testimonials for Amos as a suitor, but she could write on their first parting in the islands, "Praised be the Lord for giving me such a kind husband"; and again, "May God return that dear one safe to my arms and make me a better wife than I have ever been before. How desolate the widow . . . " Mary Alexander, so arbitrarily chosen, could not bear William's absence. On one such occasion she shut herself in her room to weep when an expected letter did not appear. "I feel tonight my love, all impatience to see you"; and again, "I want you very much for a great many reasons, first because I love you and want your society. . . . Good night my dear, O you do not know how lonesome I feel without you and how I long to see you." If Clarissa Armstrong had failed to mention her prospective husband when she announced her immanent departure for the islands, she deeply felt Richard's absence: "When he is gone, *all* is gone—at least I think so." In her journal she expressed the fear held by many others: How painful, she felt, if she and Richard should be separated by death, as she often thought might soon be the case since "we are so much inclined to idolatry. This is a sin, that I hope grace will enable us to overcome." So strong was their love for each other it threatened, idolatrously, to supersede their love for God.[53]

The wives expressed such sentiments early and late in their marriages. Mary Clark, mother of eight, had been married nearly thirty years when she spoke to Ephraim of the "endeared" title of husband, "rendered so to me, by so much kindness and many acts of love. . . . Good night dear husband with an affec. kiss from your own Mary." When he was absent on a sea voyage, she pressed him to write letters to her every day, just as though he could post them, and bring them home for her to read. "Forgive and forget all my faults dearest, as my Saviour does." Another wife, Maria Chamberlain, mother of eight and married eighteen years, told of how, when having fruitlessly climbed the stairs to the garret time after time to search for her husband Levi's ship, she threw herself in a chair and wept inconsolably. She herself was not, like so many other wives, alone in terms of lacking adult company; indeed she lived in the bustle of a large household and Honolulu entertaining. "My cares are numerous and I am sometimes almost bewildered with the noise and confusion of so large a family. I am one *alone* in the midst of company. ah! I am alone! when will my beloved companion return?" She gratified herself while he was away by writing of him in her journal in the still of the night and retiring to bed thinking of him. "I dreamed, last night, of shaking hands with you," she wrote on one such evening vigil.[54]

One mission woman observed that the missionary husband and wife were all the world to each other, and a death was agonizing. "Well may it be said that when such friends part, 'tis the survivor dies." Mercy Whitney voiced such a feeling when consoling an Oregon mission wife on the loss of her baby. Think, she said, how much greater a trial it would have been if her husband was taken instead. "It appears to me that there is nothing except the hiding of God's face, which would be a greater trial to *me* than to be left a widow in a heathen land." Men wrote of the death of wives with genuine emotion. The death of Elizabeth, wrote Artemas Bishop, the "nearest and most beloved of earthly friends," was the greatest calamity which could befall him. Daniel Dole, grieving for Emily, hoped his colleague William Rice would never endure the anguish which caused his heart to swell almost to bursting, as the terrible realization came upon him, over and over, that he would never see her again in this life. "May you long be spared to your dearest earthly friend." Further: "Thus I have been bereaved," he told the American Board, "and though weeks and months have passed my heart still bleeds." Caroline Diell, newly widowed, spoke to a group of wives at Honolulu of her deep affliction as an affectionate wife called upon to bury the "husband of her youth," her first love, the father of her babes. Mercy Whitney experienced the loss of Samuel as more than all the other suffering in her life combined into one. [55]

Day by day, year by year, mission wives rejected as intimates, in the absence of kith and kin of like spirit, all who were different in cultural belief and behavior. Instead they invested the marital relationship with their fullest emotional resources. It offered women much joy. Yet the marital relationship itself was fraught with deep ambiguity in terms of their initial missionary ambitions. Even the intimate lives of wives and husbands, despite such affection, militated against independent activism; as "pious wives" they had this discovery to make.

CHAPTER FOUR

Pious Wives

In whatever situation in life a female may be
placed, ardent piety is the jewel which above
all others adorns and beautifies her character;
but more especially is this the case, in the wife
of a missionary. Indeed, without it, all other
gifts and graces would be comparatively
worthless. It is the mainspring which should
set in motion her every action, and guide and
regulate all her conduct.

—Mercy Whitney, Waimea, 1837

American mission couples in the islands, thrown into a special intimacy because of their cultural and social isolation, clearly shared a relationship strongly influenced by ideas of sharing and companionate marriage. But embedded in every aspect of marriage was an unequal balance of power which the genuine love that developed between so many mission couples mitigated but could not remove. American cultural expectations may have been given new emphasis on the Hawaiian frontier, but they underwent no notable transformation. Certainly, notions of companionate marriage afforded women a degree of informal power, yet there continued in force decided limitations to women's ability to negotiate on equal terms. Biological aspects of sexuality and reproduction were shaped culturally in men's favor. While sexual purity and fidelity were demanded of both sexes, and women's sexuality was acknowledged along with men's, there remained latent the belief that male sexuality was the stronger force, more urgently in need of an outlet. The greatest anomaly, however, lay in the unequal outcome of active heterosexuality. Cultural definitions of femininity severely disadvantaged women in the resultant childbearing and, together with barely restrained fertility, placed a heavy physical burden on mission wives. Companionate marriage could not neutralize these disabilities, nor could it place wives on an equal or parallel path alongside men in the search for a missionary career.

Mutual Society, Help, Comfort—and a Remedy Against Sin

One August night in 1831, Charlotte Baldwin felt obliged to write in her journal: "Have to regret that I have not maintained an entire evening of feeling—enclined [*sic*] to irritation but was in kindness reproved. Mr. B. and myself agreed to watch, reprove and exhort each other daily that we may have a knowledge with the Grace of God of our ways and be blameless."[1] The emotional attachment of these couples took shape and found expression within a particular cultural context. The "sexual politics" of these Americans' intimate personal relationships were defined in a complex fashion within the parameters of their Christian religious constructs. Their religious definitions were made all the more pressing because of the missionaries' urgent need to assist each other in sustaining religious faith and the external and subjective manifestations of true Christian piety. Any weakening in their spiritual experience meant inevitably a lessening of their conviction that the venture which had brought about their island residence was worthwhile.

Such reinforcement was singularly necessary because the Calvinism of many missionaries, especially those early in the field, offered little joy or satisfaction to conscientious souls. Mercy Whitney once declared that she had no hope of getting to heaven if she was forced to depend in the least degree on her own good works. "I feel," she told friends, "that I never did nor never can do one meritorious act in the sight of God, but that if ever I am saved it must be all of grace, *free, rich, sovereign, unmerited grace.*" Such views left many women on the brink of spiritual unease, sometimes of despair. A few incidents offer glimpses into their spiritual questionings. Sarah Lyman one Sabbath tried to pray for some Hawaiian lads, but there was so much "darkness" in her mind that she could do little more than plead for mercy for herself. Mary Andrews suffered a period of depression and was found one morning crying, unable to eat her breakfast. She said "in inexpressible anguish" that she had dishonored the cause of Christ and had lost all hope or evidence that she was a Christian. Sarah Smith begged Juliette Cooke to tell her no more of her lack of a spirit of prayer: "When I hear one and another say, I am cold, and dead, and do not enjoy God's presence, it makes me faithless."[2]

In a letter to Fidelia Coan, Titus made an apology: "My dear precious wife, I mourn before God, that I have done so little to help you upward and onward in your spiritual career. Your hint was well merited, and it is most thankfully received."[3] Husbands and wives assisted each other crucially in sustaining spiritual and moral belief and behavior, reinforcing their bonds of companionship. Both sexes continued to link spiritual strength with intellectual enlargement, a source once again of friendly, and necessary, interaction.

For a period of time, Juliette and Amos Cooke rose at four o'clock in the morning, this being the only hour during which they would be undisturbed, to read and study together, fearing that they might stagnate intellectually. The wives who had worked so hard in their youth to obtain an advanced education were not about to abandon entirely the effort despite the uncongenial intellectual climate of the islands. True piety involved expansion of the mind to incorporate the wonders of God's world. Fidelia Coan in particular bemoaned the tendency of married women, including many of the mission wives, to lose sight of that constant improvement, that completeness of character, attainable through expanding the intellect. "It is the power of educating oneself, the want of which causes so many to lay aside their books (especially females) and sink into insignificance as soon as they leave school." Fidelia, described by Titus as "an extensive eclectic reader," listed in one order from America works on botany, conchology, drawing, and the writings of Hannah More, whose *Strictures on Female Education,* stressing intellectual attainment for women, was popular reading among mission wives. Wives from time to time took up geology, chemistry, and theology. The reading of serious biography was widespread, works on such notable women as Harriet Newell, Mrs. Judson, Mrs. Huntingdon, Susanna Anthony, and Catherine Brown. Alongside their husbands, wives read American papers including the *Boston Recorder,* the *New York Observer,* the *New York Weekly Mercury,* the *New Englander,* the *Eclectic Review,* the *American Almanac,* the *American Journal of Science and Arts,* and the *American and Foreign Anti-Slavery Reporter.* Commenting on a review of Barnes' book on slavery in the *New Englander* in 1848, Fidelia Coan told Titus: "It is more satisfactory to my mind than any thing I have ever read before on the subject." As with their mutual devotions which fostered the mission couples' spiritual life, so this engagement in a search for knowledge drew husbands and wives together.[4]

The intimate relationship of couples was inevitably influenced by notions of "woman's place" sustained in the community. Mission wives from time to time articulated notions of wifely duty and made it a point of discussion in rare get-togethers. A group of wives in Honolulu read together a treatise, "Woman as She Should Be," which maintained that "woman's duty and sphere" was plainly marked out by Scripture, which elevated women's standing. Women, moreover, were naturally more pious than men because they were less exposed to vices, such as passion for gain; at home they were more exposed to sufferings and trials; and they were more accustomed to subjection. Women's lapses from piety were therefore more deplorable. Some women responded that the "deportment of the male sex, even the *best* of them, toward *females* is of such a nature as to *encourage idleness* and *vanity*, and a *neglect* of the *more useful and sound* pursuits." Such discussions recorded a range of prescriptive literature including John Abbott and William Alcott (on "wifely deportment"), works by Catherine Beecher (on domestic economy), Catherine Sedgwick (on manners and dress). Having read William Alcott's *The Young Wife*, the women agreed that they could all profit by his sentiments on submissiveness, kindness, thoughtfulness, confidence, and sympathy, "though we should not probably *agree* with him in all."[5]

In fact, as these deliberations indicated, the issue for mission wives of their proper deportment toward their husbands in terms of power and authority was a complex affair: "True womanhood" was by no means uniformly described. There was on the one hand a clear Christian prescription of wifely submission to a husband. There was, on the other hand, the injunction on wives as well as husbands to be effective actors in a situation demanding some personal resolution and will and, further, a Christian formulation which placed the personal conscience above adherence to the letter, as against the spirit of the models of femininity sustained in their group. One way or another, an acceptable compromise had to be sought. This tension was nicely illustrated in the case of Emily Bliss.

The husband of Emily Bliss, Isaac, was charged by the mission body in May 1841 with "violent and abusive treatment of his wife in a paroxysm of anger" and dismissed in disgrace. The crisis which precipitated this extraordinary charge had occurred when Emily, escorted by Isaac, arrived at a distant station to care for Lucia Lyons in her imminent confinement. Isaac, about to return home and reluctant to be long alone, suspected that Emily would enjoy this visit. To ensure her speedy return, he proposed taking their three-year-old daughter Mary back to his isolated station, a plan which Emily resisted adamantly. An enraged Isaac, after a nighttime quarrel, locked Emily, clad only in her nightgown, out of the bedroom and insisted that his shivering and weeping wife declare before Lucia and Lorenzo Lyons that he, Isaac, was in the right. This Emily, despite her distress, refused to do, since it was patently untrue—she would not act against her conscience. Isaac responded by handling Emily violently, until some Hawaiian men were called to subdue him.[6]

Among the unhappy catalog of charges produced against Isaac at the subsequent hearing was this: Whenever Emily expressed an opinion different from his, Isaac would repeat the Pauline injunction, "Wives submit yourselves to your own husbands as unto the Lord." Isaac attempted to put this dictum in a reasonable context. He almost always sought Emily's advice about his activities, he said, but sometimes he did not see things as she did. "In such cases I feel it is my duty to act for myself and it is possible I have quoted that injunction."[7]

The missionaries all liked the slight, pretty Emily very much. They wrote a strong defense of her to the American Board, stating that Emily was entirely free from blame and had led an irreproachable life. She had shown "a bright pattern of meekness, humility, discretion and patient devotedness to the duties of her sphere, and we most tenderly sympathise with her."[8] The mission, then, resolutely opposed Isaac's bullying of Emily, while Emily sustained the role of pious wife for refusing to prostitute her conscience. At the end of the day, however, Emily continued to play the dutiful wife by remaining loyal to Isaac and returning with him to America. Exemplary missionary though she was, she could not remain in the field as an independent agent.

In terms of ideal personality, the softness and kindness that spelled out femininity were ideally combined with firm convictions, developed through intelligence and education, which gave strength to wives' personal conduct. What was admired most in mission wives was caught in Juliette Cooke's evaluation of her friend Angeline Castle: "mild, meek and humble, yet firm where principles were concerned."[9] When Clarissa Armstrong observed Mary Alexander closely for the first time, she admitted that her new colleague was clever, amiable, and pious. Mary gave little indication, however, that she would prove a very great active missionary: "Miserable as I am, I shall have to lead in that. Her advantages for improving the mind have been rather limited—and a want of smartness will ever prevent making amends for it. She has not been brought up in wealth, but ease; therefore if work goes on, all is well, and if not, all is well with her. *I will work. I cannot help it. . . .*"[10] Many wives monitored their behavior in an attempt to fall between the weakness of passivity and the aggressiveness of determined activism. The "cult of true womanhood" was a complicated affair for women of their personal capacities and chosen vocations.

Lucy Thurston was one wife whose actions revealed the ways in which the demands on women to be effective agents influenced personality and behavior. When entering marriage, she had sought the Bible to learn its duties and acceded to notions of husbandly dominance. She had never felt it to be a servile position, when combined with the Christian duty of husbands to love their wives as Christ loved the church. This acceptance did not prevent her from displaying herself before the mission as a woman of forceful personality, as two incidents illustrate. In September 1830, Lucy was reprimanded by the mission for selling butter in Kailua: Missionaries ought not to be involved in trade. In reply she retorted angrily that her aim had been the purchase of schoolbooks for her two older daughters, who had readily agreed to raise funds by going without butter, which Lucy could sell for over a dollar per pound. Their New England mothers, she pointed out, "rose early, sat up late, and ate the bread of carefulness, that thereby they might grant advantages to their children, which would qualify them for the duties and services of life." She had followed in their footsteps, and defied the mission to press another interpretation.[11]

On the second occasion, Lucy was attending a meal with other missionaries in Honolulu on her way to visit America in 1851, where she intended leaving a daughter in college. She discovered that the mission community there utterly disapproved of her expedition: The girl was old enough to travel unaccompanied, and meanwhile Asa would be left alone at his station. Said one male missionary, "Mrs. Thurston is no wife for going off so, to leave her husband," and others chimed in their agreement. Lucy angrily replied that she went in response to Asa's own wishes. She thereupon described frankly, for all the missionaries to know, the main reason for her journey, which was to receive medical attention. Her "seasons of illness," menstrual periods, had always brought on severe headaches: "There I was in my fifty-sixth year, still taxed with the visitations of nature. In frequency, duration, and profuseness—excessive. Always debilitating. Many times alarming." Mary Castle responded apologetically that everyone thought that Lucy's constitution "had already undergone a change" and undertook to let others not present know about it. These subjects were by no means usual dinner-party topics, and Lucy herself said that if previously she referred to her difficulty as a "headache," it was because that seemed "most mentionable." Nevertheless, she blurted out the truth rather than submit to unfair criticism.[12]

Such incidents as these involving Lucy Thurston did not arise from naturally submissive personalities. While wives would undoubtedly see it as their duty to concede ground to their husbands when outright disagreement occurred, this often entailed disciplined effort to contain a strong will and not the absence of one. But they did take second place when it was unavoidable. The man's career and needs automatically took precedence, though male missionaries muttered from time to time about particular men who allowed their wives' wishes undue weight. ("Brother Dole wished to come to Kohala, or rather his wife did," was Elias Bond's terse comment on the jockeying for new placements in 1841.)[13] Although wives sustained a degree of informal power within marriage, in mission ideology patriarchal notions held sway.

To understand what place physical sexuality played in the marital lives of mission couples is a difficult task. Where notions of modesty demanded secrecy, few wrote explicitly about intimate sexual relations. Even the convention governing announcement of a pregnancy was circumspect. For every wife who wrote that she expected to be confined at a particular date, there were two who referred to such events in circumlocutory fashion. "As to the epidemic list, I suppose I may now add Mrs. Ruggles' name, and as a Bird of the air has brought me that news, will you not tell me when you write again, in what month you expect to be cured?" inquired Martha Goodrich of a mission friend. Caroline Bailey asked a friend if there was any *particular* reason why she might want to see a sister. "Do tell me you know you need [not] fear to tell me." And another, Sybil Bingham: "The dr. has had an invitation to visit Hilo last of June or first of July. Quite hush they have been." Others spoke of expecting "additional parental cares," expecting to be "laid aside," and of being "in the family way."[14]

   If one did not frankly exchange comment on the outcome of sexual intercourse, it is scarcely surprising that sexual intercourse itself was closed to public airing. The discussion of the marriage in the islands of two missionaries who had been sent out unmarried illustrates the delicate skirting of the fact that marriage entailed entry into a sexual relationship. When Levi Chamberlain, long hoping for a wife, met the four single women when they disembarked from the *Parthian* in 1828, his eye lit upon Maria Patton, and he was not slow to make clear his honorable intentions. Maria evinced suitable surprise. "My bosom is agitated, my thoughts perplexed at this unexpected interview," she wrote in her diary. Not much more than one short week later, Maria gave her consent. To her sister in America she confided the news. Levi's excellence as a missionary alone had won her heart, although she did admit that he was six feet tall with fair hair and blue eyes. Maria continued: "The finger of Providence has so plainly pointed out my way that I have not one remaining doubt respecting duty."[15] Levi himself prudently expressed the hope that this change in his circumstances would be conducive to his usefulness: "I shall indeed have more care, but I shall enjoy the sweets of a friendship, which will more than make amends for the solicitudes and anxieties, which will be occasioned by the increase of objects of attention."[16] The marriage took place after the usual Monday evening concert of prayer and was followed by cake and wine. The very next day, Levi attended an afternoon lecture, visited the sick, and the bridal pair took tea with one mission family and spent the evening with another. "May you both find your happiness and usefulness increased a hundred fold," was Nancy Ruggles' congratulatory wish, and Maria Ogden rejoiced that her friend had found "a kind and affectionate protector and friend." It was as though the sexual tie was irrelevant, though, indeed, Maria was pregnant within a month.[17]

   The convention held firm that public speech and behavior represented marriage as an affectionate and useful partnership rather than as a union based on sexual intimacy. This did not necessarily dictate, however, that sexuality was not a significant part of marriage and that it could not be viewed in a positive light by both wives and husbands. The male sexual drive was clearly seen as far more pressing and potentially disruptive of order. But women aimed to be modest, not coy, about sex, and there is no reason to presume that they found intimate sex distasteful.

Their attitude might be deduced from an interesting discussion that a number of wives engaged in during a women's meeting in Honolulu in 1840. The topic for discussion was at what stage they should inform their own children of "the connexion of the sexes" and of their "origins." One woman asked from what source everyone present had received this information themselves in their childhood or youth. Of fourteen women, only one could say that she had been informed by her own mother. Thinking of the various sources of their knowledge, the women felt that this maternal reticence had not encouraged moral purity in their minds, although they believed there was a "principle of delicacy," particularly in the female character, which would lead young girls to shrink from engaging in conversation about sex. They themselves certainly had done so. Their own children, they all vowed, would be informed in good time by their own mothers. Although there was in this discussion great concern for modesty and propriety, it did indicate an acceptance of sexuality in its proper time and place. (The women concluded the meeting "unusually impressed with the importance of being pure themselves in *thought, word,* and *deed.*")[18]

Wives were not, in addition, reluctant to have male doctors—indeed, any useful male missionary—present at their confinement. Not for them a modest death rather than an immodestly exposed birth. They often underwent considerable discomfort to reach a doctor when childbirth was immanent. If no doctor was available, any mission brother, even men who were close friends and associates, if they had experience in childbirth, were gratefully welcomed. When William Richards, father of eight, reached Mary Rice in time to assist at the birth of her first baby, "he seemed like an angel come to succour me in my need," she felt.[19] This was not the response of an overly prudish woman.

The marriages of the single women who came to the mission indicated that among them there existed no particular aversion to sexual intimacy. The few single women had reached the islands independently and had, undoubtedly, withstood some opposition in doing so. The light in which their action could be viewed might be deduced from the comment of an unfriendly Honolulu resident, Stephen Reynolds, at the arrival of the group on the *Parthian:* "Four single ladies and four native boys. All as Missionaries to this country. Single women!!! Decency art thou lost!!! Shame art thou fled the female breast!!"[20] A range of social pressures would of course have ranked the married over the single state. Nevertheless, the single women were warmly received by the mission families and welcomed into households; there appeared little in their situations that made marriage a retreat from difficulties inherent in the single state. Once in the islands, not only Maria Patton but five other spinsters chose to marry single men or widowers rather than serve the mission in the single state.

There was one wife in the mission, Emily Dole, who, quite privately, was not at all certain that her marriage had been a wise decision. A year in the islands, pregnant and already feeling overburdened, she wrote a frank and pessimistic letter to her two sisters back in America, warning them to destroy the letter when they had read it: "Sarah, I would say to you and Lucy: be not anxious to marry; there is a great deal of romance in the anticipation of it [which] *must* be a failure of course. D[aniel] is one of the kindest hearts in the world and he is one of the finest Christians but I often sigh for single blessedness as I never sighed for marriage. I believe I ought to have lived single." She could have supported herself quite well independently, and spared herself the "perplexities" that now pressed on her, she continued. But it was too late now: "I must submit like a tied hen to my silken bonds, but girls I say never marry because you are poor or put to it or because a man has money but you must feel that you approve his person and character throughout and then you will have enough to make you sorry unless you are fonder of these things than I am."[21] This could be read as a dislike for sexual intimacy, although the burdens she dreaded were clearly also those of parenthood and becoming coteacher with Daniel of the mission children at the new Punahou School.

This complaint, however, was rare. Most wives wrote to absent husbands in terms not inconsistent with a sense of loss of physical intimacy. In one case, the letters of Fidelia Coan to her husband, Titus, a hint of sexual deprivation was more apparent. Titus traveled frequently in his district, engaging in preaching tours often lasting two or three weeks at a time. He and Fidelia wrote to each other almost every day of his absence, sending their notes with Hawaiian messengers. The letters revealed a marital relationship based, as were so many, on the deepest emotional interdependence. "To speak moderately," Titus wrote on one occasion, "I know not how to live without you." He continued: "You seem a part of my identity. An essential element in my physical, mental and moral being." On their twelfth wedding anniversary, Titus wrote in a similarly loving vein: "You have been a faithful, 'prudent,' precious wife to me, and my love is deeper and purer than animal passion." Passion, however, there certainly was. "O that I could see you, kiss you, press you to my warm, warm beating heart!" he once wrote to her. On another occasion: "And can I say another sad and lonely good night? I am here like a monk in his cell. . . . O it is not good for man to be alone." He longed for her; it was hard to lay down his head without a sweet goodnight from his wife.[22]

Fidelia responded with warmth to her husband's avowals of love. "You are in my heart by day, and by night, and were the whole world around me it seems to me that without you, it would only add to my loneliness," she wrote. She often bade him goodnight, saying she would go to her lonely couch and "embrace her pillow." She ought to be ashamed to press him, she wrote on one occasion, but could he not return home on Thursday night instead of the next day? "I cannot help thinking how delightful it would be for you to arrive on a bright moonlight night when all is still, and no native company to distract our first interview. If you get home on Friday you know it will be all bustle till bed time, and half the pleasure of meeting will be destroyed." She would let him in secretly if he came to the bedroom window. When Titus read her letter his heart leaped "to reach her arms," he said. His heart burned toward her "with a love which amounts almost to idolatry." Their sexual relationship was undoubtedly strong and important to them.[23]

One year, a disgraced missionary turned up in the islands on his way back from South America. He had been dismissed "for taking improper liberties in kissing some one or more of the sisters." Lowell Smith for one took it to heart. "Let me and mine," he wrote, "take warning and never fall into this snare of the Devil." Female sexuality, though it may not have been publicly acknowledged, was clearly not denied. It was otherwise with male sexuality. Strong sexual feelings were viewed as an inevitable if inconvenient burden borne by the male sex, a condition that the mission could ignore only at its peril. The married men sent to the islands reiterated the well-established belief that single men were at risk amidst a Polynesian society. With the prospect of new recruits in the offing, "by all means I would advise them to come out married," Artemus Bishop urged the board. Twelve years later Harvey Hitchcock wrote in similar vein when he requested a man to teach at his station. "He will of course be a married man. The case of the woman is not so with the man. However good the arguments may be for sending unmarried ladies to this field, nothing can be said in favour of sending unmarried men."[24]

In fact, only two of the male missionaries ever fell from grace over sexual improprieties, and that at a late stage in the mission's existence: Samuel Dwight, a single man, and George Rowell, who was married. The disgust and horror voiced by their mission brethren indicated not only their strong attachment to the same rigid standard of sexual purity for men as for women, but a sense of their own vulnerability, their own temptation.

When Samuel Dwight's sexual propensities came before the mission in 1854, he had been stationed at lonely Kaluaaha for the six years since his arrival in the islands as a thirty-two-year-old bachelor. He had not made a favorable impression on the mission from the first. Titus Coan, for one, had disliked Samuel's "sing-song woman's voice" and voted "to send Dr. Dwight to Molokai, our Botany Bay." Early on the morning of 27 February, before breakfast, Samuel startled his colleague Claudius Andrews by sending urgently for him to come and perform a marriage ceremony for himself and a fifteen-year-old Hawaiian girl, Anna Mahoe, one of his pupils and a boarder in his household.[25]

The immediate circumstances surrounding this decision to marry appeared to his associates as simply appalling. Anna Mahoe, for whom Samuel had shown marked partiality, slept with another teenage girl in a room in Samuel's house, thinly partitioned off from Samuel's own. During the night, Samuel heard a noise in the girls' room and, brandishing a cane, had entered to discover a Hawaiian youth in bed with Anna. (The lad leapt smartly out the window leaving his *malo* behind.) Samuel decided on immediate marriage and treated the incident as an isolated event. Anna quite frankly acknowledged to others, however, that she had been "living in fornication" for several years with the youth. She would retire to bed, leaving her window open, and he would join her for the night. The other young girl in the room had her own male visitor.

Anna's past escapades were insignificant, however, compared to outrageous facts about Samuel which now came to light. Startled missionaries heard from a visiting Methodist preacher that Samuel had been in the habit of cuddling and fondling the breasts of children and young girls in his class at school and in his own home where he boarded two small girls, as well as the two teenagers. The Methodist had witnessed him often caressing and kissing the girls, while "feeling their bosoms," behavior which the Methodist preacher knew would have excited "very improper passions" in himself. But even in the public setting of the schoolhouse, deacons had seen Samuel, while supposedly adjusting the dress of the girls around their neck, "shoving his hands into their bosoms." No definite evidence of actual sexual intercourse was brought to light, but there was not another male missionary who believed that it was not a strong possibility.

At General Meeting, Samuel was charged with improper familiarity with native females, with keeping unmarried young females in his house, with marrying a native female under circumstances calculated to bring disgrace upon the cause of religion and the ministry. Samuel did put up a defense. Since the mission clearly believed that its work was retarded by the inadequacy of Hawaiian wives and mothers, he responded, he had decided on a course to uplift Hawaiian womanhood by concentrating particularly on the training of girls. In school he had ruled more by love than fear, and his familiarities had been misconstrued. To stop rumors, he had determined to marry, choosing the top girl in his class for a bride, hoping he could make her happy. He accused the missionaries of withdrawing their fellowship purely because he had married a Hawaiian.[26] His plea fell on deaf ears. The brethren severed his connection with the mission.

This was what could be expected when a male missionary did not have a pious wife. Even more disturbing was the fact that in the second case of sexual misdemeanor, George Rowell did have a pious wife yet even then he was not protected from sin. In 1864, a female church member at Waimea, on Kauai, accused George of committing adultery with Hawaiian women, a practice which he had indulged in for ten years or more. George flatly denied it, but finally grudgingly admitted to one incidence. Hawaiian church members universally supported the first informant, however, saying that they had kept silent out of fear that George would have killed himself rather than be brought to trial. George had gone on record, along with other missionaries, denouncing the Hawaiians in general for their sexual practices. Just three years earlier he had reported one Hawaiian pastor "under suspicion of the practice of seduction" and said that Hawaiian Christians persisted in "grossly coarse and impure habits." Now his hypocrisy was exposed. He was promptly dismissed by his angry brethren.[27]

Malvina Rowell did not shine in this adversity. She maintained that, since George had repented and confessed, he should be accepted back into the fold and supported him loyally. This was not, in the mission's eyes, the act of a pious wife: She should have loved the sinner, certainly, but distanced herself sharply from the sin. Martha supported George's efforts to sustain himself independently in the parish, causing Mercy Whitney to complain that Martha was aiding him "as though he was engaged in a good cause instead of disseminating heresy and error in our midst."[28]

The male missionaries' terror lest they, too, might ever "fall into the sin of the land" led to a difference of opinion between men and women in the mission over one issue: the timing of the remarriage of widowers. Men whose wives died either left the field altogether or swiftly put themselves in the way of obtaining a second wife. There was no doubt that although the bereaved men listed a number of urgent reasons for needing a new wife—not least the existence of young, motherless children—the most urgent incentive was the need to preserve their "characters" by acquiring a legitimate sexual partner. It was also clear that other men appreciated this need but the mission women did not. When a wife was left husbandless, the question was: How would she maintain herself and her children without a male provider? Nobody thought of suggesting that her virtue was at risk. Mission women were devastated when one of their sisters in the field died. A swift remarriage was seen as a denial of the personhood, the individuality, of the dead wife; it attacked their own sense of importance as unique personalities. When Mary Rogers died in May 1834, Edmund Rogers was so upset that for months he could not write about it without bursting into tears. Early in 1835, however, he applied to the American Board for permission to return to America to seek a wife, unless one of the women whose names he gave the board was prepared to come out to him. He felt the need of a friend and counselor very much; it was, he said, "a very trying situation." Rufus Anderson alluded to the request in a matter-of-fact tone: "Mr. Rogers has expressed a desire to visit this country, that he may repair the loss he has suffered." Clarissa Armstrong's reply was sarcastic: "Mr. Rogers, one of our printers, is going to America, *for a wife I suppose,* and will then return. You will percieve [*sic*] that *wives are important articles of household furniture* here. They cannot easily be sent in *boxes* so it costs some time and trouble, to obtain them." Providentially, Edmund obtained the prize of Harvey Hitchcock's single sister.[29]

Artemas Bishop might rejoice over his second marriage, to Delia Stone, in December 1828, just over nine months after Elizabeth Bishop's death. Delia was "worthy to bear the name and fill the place of one who has laid it aside." Laura Judd, by contrast, complained that though she had been prepared to face the marriage, she had certainly not been prepared to hear of such a *sudden* marriage. Mr. Dibble had gone "to obtain the lost wife"; Mr. Clark had "gone for a wife." So the mission women laconically noted this male behavior. Andelucia Conde was simply furious to hear that Edwin Locke was preparing to sail for America within a month of Martha Locke's death. Who could have advised him to go so soon? she demanded of Fanny Gulick. Her heart ached for the children and for the dead wife.[30]

Whereas the other mission wives saw these swift remarriages as almost traitorous to their dead sisters, in fact some of these men at least had certainly loved their first wives very dearly and continued to grieve for them many long years after they had remarried and founded new families. One such husband was Lorenzo Lyons, husband of Betsey, one of the youngest and prettiest of the mission women, who died in May 1837. To the American Board he expressed his loss in stylized form: Betsey had been "bone of my bone, flesh of my flesh, the partner of my joys and sorrows, the wife of my bosom, counsellor and companion of my youth." In his private writings he appeared distraught. He returned to his station miserable and feeling lost, gathered up Betsey's clothes to send away, as he could not bear to look at them. He threw himself into work day and night, not caring if he ever went to bed: "The bed was a desolate spot." A year later he noted a visit to Hilo to the volcanoes, "tho' a wife was the principal object." He proposed to the spinster, Lucia Smith, and was accepted. "Praised God for providing another companion; may she prove all that is desirable for usefulness and happiness."[31]

Four years and three new children later, he confided in his journal on the tenth anniversary of his arrival in the islands: "One who was with me ten years ago—where is she? Her lovely form is before me—but she has long gone to her rest." On the anniversary of Betsey's death a few years later, he wrote, "I loved her—yes, I loved her too much. Though ten years have passed away, yet my beloved Betsey is not forgotten. Forget her? No, never!" A new wife he had urgently needed in order to stay in the field. The mission women were reluctant to cede men this difference, but powerless to alter the practice or the belief on which it was based.[32]

Be Fruitful and Multiply

When she was still bleeding after the miscarriage in 1843 which almost cost her her life, Andelucia Conde, mother of three, wrote to a mission sister: "O what a suffering lot is woman's. Subject to such an accomplication of diseases, it seems marvellous that any should enjoy health or arrive at 3 score years and ten."[33] (She died, four births later, well below this target.) In terms of the intimate, personal relations of wives and husbands, there was one serious discrepancy between female and male life chances. The outcome of an active heterosexual relationship was a decidedly unequal one. Wives, as the bearers of children, faced a disadvantage resulting from biology which could not but set them well behind the starting line in any search for an active public role. It was undoubtedly true that the ways in which pregnancy, childbirth, and the postpartum period were managed considerably intensified their biological handicap, but this implied no measure of choice for the women concerned. There was one path they knew, one path of duty for them. This they struggled to walk.

For all but six infertile wives, the years spent in the islands from marriage until the end of their fertile span were dominated by the physical strain of childbearing. Of the seventy-six married mission women who lived for lengthy or briefer periods in the islands, seventy bore children, and most bore babies at regular intervals during their fertile years. Thirty-eight fertile women who lived in the islands until at least forty-four years of age bore a total of two hundred and fifty babies—on average, between six and seven children each. Only one of these women, Lucia Lyons, bore as few as three, and a further fifteen wives bore between four and six babies. But twenty-one of these women bore between seven and eleven babies; seven women had seven children, eight women bore eight, four had nine babies, two women had ten, and one, eleven. The length of time over which their children were born extended from, on average, a year after their marriage in their mid-twenties until their early forties.[34]

Fertile women generally greeted their firstborn children thirteen to fifteen months after marriage; a few babies were born as early as nine or ten months from the wedding day. When the first baby came later than average, evidence existed in some cases that a first pregnancy had ended in miscarriage. (This was true, for example, for Theodotia Green and Laura Judd, whose first babies were born sixteen and eighteen months respectively after marriage and who both suffered miscarriages during their voyage to the islands on the *Parthian.*) Subsequent babies then arrived at regular two to three-year intervals, with pregnancies tending to taper off at the later end of the fertile span. Twenty-seven of the thirty-eight women did not complete childbearing until forty years of age or older. Fanny Gulick, with her eighth pregnancy at forty-seven years, was the oldest to give birth.

When, in later years, Maria Chamberlain was asked by her married daughter Bella what she had done to prevent becoming pregnant (Bella was anxious that she was pregnant yet again), Maria replied: "You ask what I did? I frankly tell you, I never did anything to prevent having a family. I thought it was all of the Lord to give life, and I never did anything to destroy it." It is doubtful that Bella would have received a different reply from her mother-in-law, Sarah Lyman, or from any other mission wife in the unlikely case that she had asked others such a question. The childbearing patterns of the women gave no clear evidence that deliberate means of controlling fertility were being employed. Fertility was, of course, suppressed by lactation, and the wives customarily breastfed their babies at least for twelve months and sometimes as long as twenty months. When a baby died at a young age, and hence lactation ceased, the next baby usually appeared at a much shorter interval. Mary Clark, for example, lost her first baby at its birth, on 7 September 1828, and gave birth to her second baby on 20 September of the following year. Lactation was not a totally successful means of fertility control, and wives did sometimes become pregnant while breastfeeding. Martha Goodrich asked Maria Chamberlain in January 1833, "You say in Mrs. Lyman's letter that you have weaned your babe. Tell me when you write again why you weaned it so soon; is it as I suspect?" Her assumption was correct. Maria was pregnant again and had weaned the eight-month-old Maria Jane because a new baby was on the way. Martha Ann was born six months later.[35]

Little in the spacing of the babies born in the islands would indicate deliberate intervention in natural fertility. There were in some cases longer spaces between children toward the end of the fertile cycle, but this no doubt reflected decreasing fertility and an earlier age of menopause than was common a century later. There were four wives who ceased childbearing at an earlier than average age, before the age of thirty-five, which might have appeared the result of deliberate intervention. Sarah Hall and Rebecca Hitchcock were thirty years old, Mercy Whitney thirty-two years, and Lucia Lyons thirty-four years at their last births. In two of the four women's cases, those of Mercy Whitney and Rebecca Hitchcock, however, evidence existed that they were subject to serious gynecological problems resulting in miscarriages during the years following these last births. In one case of female infertility, in addition, gynecological problems existed—Elizabeth Whittlesey confided to her close friend Maria Kinney her continuing difficulties with miscarriages. A doctor warned her of the need to prevent a pregnancy; she must not do anything for a year, "so he told my husband if he wished to keep me. I think Eliph. does desire me to live and he will probably try to be more careful." Even some women, like Abigail Smith and Julia Spaulding, who were reportedly seriously ill for long periods of time, continued to bear children regularly, which suggested that abstention from intercourse for prolonged periods was not commonly practiced.[36]

In the earlier letter to her daughter, Maria Chamberlain showed knowledge of the current belief in periodic abstention from intercourse before, during, and after menstruation (which was seen as similar to the fertile estrus period of female animals). She advised the young woman that "if by mutual consent you both agree to wait 14 days or so, I do not think there is wrong in that, and if after that you should find yourself in such circumstances, I should say it is of the Lord, and if He gives you a large family, *he will provide,* and it is no matter what people say—it is none of their business." She did not necessarily indicate that she knew of this theory (ineffectual of course) during her own childbearing years.[37]

Maria's last comment indicated that the large mission families were

now considered somewhat prolific back in America, where, by abstention, lactation, and coitus interruptus, couples were reducing the rate
of childbearing. Some mild embarrassment had entered into mission
reporting decades earlier. When Abner Wilcox told his parents of the
birth of his second baby only sixteen months after his first, he tried to
turn it away with humor: "This, for your cold climate, would be
thought premature, but in a tropical climate like ours, it is nothing
unusual to have one or even two crops in one year." One missionary
on Hawaii joked, "The fact is we shall have to swarm! The hive is getting full. Won't they think so at Boston? The whole appropriation
from the Board will be absorbed in nursing babies." The American
Board tactfully attributed the large number of children in the mission
to the good climate.[38]

The birth of Clarissa Armstrong's third child in March 1835 illustrates something of the rigors of childbirth in the mission field.
Clarissa and Richard, already parents of a small girl and a baby boy of
fifteen months, were the only mission family at the new station of
Haiku on Maui. They were living in a poorly thatched Hawaiian house
which leaked in many places during a season of rain. Clarissa, daily
expecting another birth, caught a fever along with the rest of the family. In desperation at the thought of giving birth in this situation,
Clarissa sent an urgent message to William Richards at Lahaina, who
arrived on horseback to find Clarissa lying in pain on a mattress on the
floor, with her sick children at either side, while Richard, extremely
ill, had a half mattress on the bed. With Hawaiian help, the use of
horse and oxcart, the whole family was transported to Wailuku, where
another baby boy was born. The older baby, however, died a week
later in Richard's arms in the rocking chair beside Clarissa's bed. "The
anguish of my heart as I saw my child's sufferings and could do nothing to soothe or comfort it, cannot be described," she wrote. (They
called the new baby by the dead baby's name, William Nevins.)[39]

None of this was conducive to a good "getting up." Clarissa's pregnancy and birth were made more burdensome to her because of her
chronic fevers. This was no isolated occurrence. The years of pregnancy and lactation for the mission women were of far greater strain
because the women were often not in good health, undoubtedly in
part because they were physically weakened by insufficient exercise.
At home they all recalled walking long distances, which had kept
them feeling vigorous. The physical geography and social isolation of

mission life left them without this customary exercise, and many with no substitute. A few tried horseback riding, a few gardening. All were encumbered with corsets, petticoats, long skirts, poorly fitting shoes. Wives were extremely prone to a range of infectious diseases which were obviously more draining because of the extra physical demands imposed on their bodies by the cycle of childbearing. Clarissa Richards wrote in January 1836, "I am looking forward to the middle of March with more than ordinary solicitude—having been troubled with a *cough* for the last year which is increasingly troublesome just at present—I raise considerable daily from my lungs . . . am now hoping for relief after confinement." Troubles seldom came as single spies.[40]

Some of the illnesses which wives sustained were serious, even fatal, and little could have been done, given medical knowledge at the time, to have cured them. Even so, measures were taken, in full medical self-confidence, which could only have made the women more miserable if not hastened their end. Other illnesses most certainly were aggravated by the measures taken to counteract them, and such treatments as the mercury-based "blue pills," used constantly as an aperient, may well have caused serious symptoms themselves. The women's childbearing years were therefore complicated by the twin problems of ill health and medical ignorance. The men contracted fewer illnesses and hence were also acted upon less frequently.

As with Clarissa Richards, tuberculosis afflicted some mission women, causing the death of several and, in a chronic but not fatal form, undermining the health of others. Angelina Castle, Andelucia Conde, Mary Paris, and Louisa Munn died of the disease. A further few developed severe spinal problems which could have been caused by tuberculosis of the spine, also fatal. Maria Dibble, who had previously contracted rheumatic fever, had a stroke ("palsy") which paralyzed her right side. Again, little could have been done for her, although Dr. Judd's decision to bleed her, as he did the tubercular patients, was, not surprisingly, without benefit. Nothing, similarly, would have helped Sophia Lafon, who, suffering dreadfully with cancer of the breast just ready to ulcerate, went home "to die in the bosom of her mother."[41]

It could not be doubted that other illnesses were aggravated in severity, possibly fatally so, by following the medical books or, worse still, being physically within reach of the medical men. Fidelia Coan pointed out this paradox in 1837 quite innocently to her sister, a missionary in Bangkok. There had been few deaths in the mission, yet providentially there had usually been a medical man at hand when death occurred. Of the eleven children who had died, only one, the Goodriches', had no doctor in attendance. Of the four adults, three had died at Honolulu where a doctor resided, and the fourth, Elizabeth Bishop, had returned from Honolulu to her home when she had secured what medical advice she could. The previous year, both the Greens and Lymans had buried children while attending General Meeting, and that very year Betsey Lyons had died at the meeting despite the attendance of four physicians. "But do not think I undervalue medical skill. Nothing but a sense of duty would keep me easy, at such a distance from it." If no physician had attended and a death occurred, there was room "for painful reflections."[42]

Evidence would seldom support the idea that the presence of a doctor markedly helped in most cases of general illness, though the administration of morphine or opium was welcomed for severe pain. Women contracted a range of viral and bacterial infections, such as influenza, colds, cholera, typhoid, and erysipelas. Diarrhea and dysentery were also common ills that could be chronic, and alarming. Doctors tried a variety of cures, ranging from purgatives, bleeding, infusions of dandelion, courses of mercury, blisters, poultices, leeches, and the wearing of setons, cotton threads inserted under the skin as counter-irritants. Dysentery killed Parnelly Andrews, wife of the doctor Seth Andrews, within four days. (His ministrations of his own family proved particularly disadvantageous, since not only his wife but three of his four young children died in his care.) "Suddenly and most unexpectedly was Mrs. Andrews called to join her babes in heaven," the Kailua station report ran.[43] The practice of administering harsh purgatives to sufferers from dysentery can only have hastened their deaths.

Women kept going, through pregnancy, but life could be a struggle. A few had life-threatening conditions yet survived through successive pregnancies. Clarissa Armstrong clearly suffered from toxemia toward the end of each pregnancy. She would report that her limbs were so swollen she could scarcely stand erect or walk without pain; her hands were so enlarged that she could no longer sew, and wrote only with difficulty.[44] Abigail Smith experienced continuous vomiting with one pregnancy. She told her mother: "Well I was *sick* miserably so almost all last year. . . . At the time of my confinement I was mere skin and bones. I had not been able for nine months to make one tolerable meal . . . and was confined to my couch almost all the time."[45] Abigail had an extremely depressing experience of fertility, since she was subject to repeated miscarriages. Five infants she bore to full term died, and in between times she was frequently to be found prostrate on bed or couch, either attempting to ward off a miscarriage or recuperating from one with frequent spells of "flooding," profuse bleeding.

All the women feared miscarriages—interchangably termed by them "abortions," if they did not use the euphemisms "distressing turns" or "ill turns." Maria Chamberlain's advice was that newly pregnant women should be very careful of their activities, not to risk bringing on an abortion: "Then you are a broken down woman. It is truly alarming, even in the early stages, to have a flowing come down, and I would rather go through two regular confinements than have one abortion." Rebecca Hitchcock miscarried at General Meeting in 1841 and suffered such a "constant and inordinate flowing" that she stopped breathing, suffered "syncope" from weakness, but rallied unexpectedly after her fellow missionaries had prayed and farewelled her at the bedside. Mercy Whitney suffered a series of miscarriages during her thirties, one of which she described in detail to her mother and sisters. For twenty-four hours she experienced excruciating pain and such heavy blood loss that she was brought to "the borders of the grave," too weak to raise an arm from the bed or turn in bed without assistance. She miscarried twice again the following year, with further hemorrhaging. "I sometimes feel as tho' this poor frame would not endure many more such shocks," she wrote in misery.[46]

If the women dreaded miscarriages, they also anticipated their actual confinement with some fear and, for those who had narrowly escaped death on a previous occasion, even terror. Childbirth was not uncommonly called "the hour of trial and anguish." Many women suppressed news of a pregnancy from their mothers back home to spare them months of anxiety. Clarissa Armstrong was annoyed when Richard added news of her pregnancy to such a letter, when she herself had purposely concealed it. Well, Clarissa told her mother, if she survived she would write later with news of the birth; otherwise, her mother would hear of it from others.[47] Elizabeth Bishop was terrified about her second confinement after a disastrous first birth which others described as "a season of almost unparalleled sufferings" in which the baby died and she herself was left subject to "seasons of depression and deep anxiety." In the new year of 1825, a birth imminent, she wrote in her diary: "God only knows whether I shall witness its close. . . . O, God be nigh to strengthen, to uphold, and to deliver in this distressing hour. If it please thee, O grant me the desires of my fond heart in embracing a living babe. . . . If thou are about to take me away from this world, prepare me I humbly entreat for an admission to a state of purity and joy."[48]

When Clarissa Armstrong realized she was unlikely to have a doctor in attendance at yet another birth, she felt "this is a trial that females in America know not of—I hope they may never know from experience."[49] For once, their urgent wish to have a doctor present had validity: Doctors were trained to use not only drugs, to bring the afterbirth or stop hemorrhaging, but to use forceps, which often proved the difference between life and death for babies and sometimes for their mothers too. Dwight Baldwin believed that his own wife's life was probably saved by the use of forceps at her first birth, and most of her subsequent large infants were delivered similarly. (Baldwin described Charlotte's screaming for him to use the forceps for one and a half hours at the end of her fourth child's delivery, when the head became wedged.)[50] When babies arrived feet first, or labor pains ebbed, or the wife was faint with exhaustion, the physician and his forceps were invaluable. The pregnant women's calculations, however, had to be fine ones, for mission doctors did not appreciate being delayed several weeks at a station when an infant failed to make the scheduled appearance.

If no doctor was available, they could not reach one, and no mission woman was able to attend them, the alternative for many wives was delivery by their husbands. Such was the case in Mary Alexander's first confinement, when she had intended trying to reach a physician but the baby arrived early. She woke up her husband in the night with the startling news that "the hour of sorrow" had arrived. William's fear over his total ignorance of obstetrics was so great that, struggling in the dark to light the lamp, he fainted and fell senseless to the floor, was revived, and then hastily scanned their medical book.[51] The subsequent live birth was by luck rather than good management. The men dreaded the ordeal. When Elias Bond delivered Ellen's first baby, it was the worst night of his life. "Alone and no friendly hand skilled in such matters, my fears well nigh overwhelmed me, but the Lord enabled me to discharge the new and unexpected duties of midwife, and nurse, successfully."⁵² Much as the women loved their husbands, it was a situation to avoid, though there were the fortunate ones who gave birth between breakfast and lunch, or at night without disturbing the children sleeping in the same room.

Only two wives, however, actually died at the time of confinement. Emily Dole, who was appalled by the wan faces of the mission wives on her arrival in the islands in 1841, and vowed to preserve her own health carefully, died after the birth of her second son in April 1844. Her health undermined already by chronic dysentery, she was weak after the birth, with a severe headache, and expressed apprehension for her life. Since she was naturally of a "melancholy" disposition, no one took her seriously until she was suddenly "deprived of her reason," sank into a stupor, and died. The second fatality resulted from the first confinement of Mary Ward Rogers in May 1834. She had been in labor for two full days, with intense suffering that all but deprived her of reason, when a dead baby was removed by forceps. When the placenta did not appear, the doctor inserted his hand to remove it, only to discover yet another lifeless infant. "Her sufferings were extreme, and every heart present melted to tenderness," one of her attendants said. She had lost too much blood; she was utterly exhausted and dying. In her last words to her husband, she prayed that her sins might be pardoned, "which have made it necessary for me to suffer all I have suffered, pray that I may be prepared for more usefulness."⁵³

Martha Locke was able to boast that she was in the kitchen an hour before the birth of her third baby, and back there again one week later. Few women had to be warned, as Marcia Smith did her sister Lucia, not to follow such an example. Mostly they were physically so weakened that they were not remotely prepared to consider such energetic action. Lucy Wilcox was amazed to hear that Lucia Lyons could walk about within ten days of her confinement; she herself had not been well enough to sit up in that time. Sarah Lyman could scarcely walk across the room four weeks after the birth of her first child. The wives eased themselves gingerly toward one further effort each day, frightened above all of a prolapse of the uterus which, it was believed, resulted from overexertion too soon after birth. Both Julia Spaulding and Rebecca Hitchcock suffered from this condition; the latter was forced constantly to wear a pessary, though she hoped with each pregnancy that the condition might right itself.[54]

There were further ills. Childbed fever—or milk fever, as puerperal fever was named—occurred as the result of unsanitary birth conditions and reduced women on occasions to a very weakened state. Breast abscesses, also, occurred from time to time. With Malvina Rowell and Mary Alexander, abscesses broke out all over their bodies. Fidelia Coan was alone when she developed "broken breasts" after the birth of her second child. Shaking with fever, with aches in the back and head, she wrapped herself in flannel and took herself to bed with fomentations of hot vinegar on her breasts.[55] The women had usually at least a spell of time ahead of them, the postpartum period safely over, without the problems of menstruation to contend with. "Monthly headaches," sometimes attended by "local difficulties" such as vaginal infections, were then theirs for a time, before the next pregnancy pressed on them.

When Julia Damon was pregnant with her first child, Samuel found that his feelings became more tender: "I found my love to my wife increasing." When Fidelia Coan presented Titus with his first son, he promised her that "the reception of that precious boon, our little Titus Munson, has not divided but rather doubled our mutual affection." Their babies were "dear pledges of our mutual love." Mark Ives described his first two sons as given by God for the purpose of bringing his and Mary's hearts more strongly together. These babies were viewed as the inevitable and, indeed, fortunate outcome of entry into active heterosexuality.[56] Desired though they may have been, the lack of effective means of fertility control placed women at a considerable disadvantage in their quest for an active missionary career. Notions of wifely submissiveness, however modified, and a definition of women's sexuality as different from men's, implied an unequal place for women in intimate marital interaction. The reproductive experience of wives, however, intertwined as it was with persistent sickness and poor management of their health, contributed markedly to the inequality of outcome in marriage. Nature, and cultural definitions of nature, had dealt wives the poorer hand. The leverage in terms of sexual politics, which their Christian formulation offered women, was discounted by the nature of childbearing.

Men loved their wives and attached themselves to models of companionate marriage. Such notions could not counteract the effects of women's reproductive experience. "Prudent helpmeets" were to find, too, that companionate marriage did not alter the gender division of labor in the marriage, which established a firm structural basis for female inequality that further underwrote their biological disadvantage.

CHAPTER FIVE

Prudent Helpmeets

I see now how strong are the forces which
confine a woman to her orbit. God has wisely
and nicely adjusted these forces so that while
her own family is the center, a woman's orbit
still embraces objects enough to call forth the
feelings of expansive and genuine benevolence. But if the line is overstepped there is
discord and confusion within. At least it is so
in my case. If I am mainly occupied for a week
or two with my maps or pen or schools I find
that my wardrobe is ragged or my child's
clothes out of order or my house full of cob-
webs and cockroaches. So that with me the
centripetal force is in constant danger of over-
coming the centrifugal until my little circle
shall embrace nothing but my own domestic
establishment.

    —Fidelia Coan to sister Maria
     Hilo, 8 June 1838

When Mary Ann Chapin first arrived in Honolulu in 1832 and was
alone in a room of the Judd's house, lying sick on the couch, a Hawaiian woman entered. She fell immediately onto her knees, saying
"Aloha, aloha" repeatedly, clasped Mary Ann's hands, closed her
eyes, and knelt in an attitude of prayer for fully fifteen minutes. She
then pressed her hand, sympathized with Mary Ann's illness, and
retired from the room with further expressions of "aloha." This
extraordinarily deferential greeting to an American missionary was not
unique. When the Emersons first reached Waialua, a woman was
afraid because she thought they were gods. Even after a considerable
time, people some distance from the mission station would not talk to
Ursula or John without the help of an intermediary who knew them
well: "They only gaze at us with many exclamations of wonder."
Rebecca Hitchcock reported that in hers and Harvey's first years on

Molokai, people "seldom or never ventured into our house except on their hands and knees. We were called chiefs, which was not pleasant." When Mercy Whitney and Samuel returned to their Kauai station after a brief absence, people flocked from all over the island to welcome them, each bearing a present of a fowl, a pig, some *kapa*. "This mode of making presents to the *Chiefs* has been a custom of long standing; . . . I hope in *this* instance, it is out of sincere regard to us as *religious teachers,* and not from its being an old established custom among the Chiefs."[1]

The message from these various encounters was clear. First, the American missionaries, particularly at remote stations, were regarded with very considerable respect by Hawaiians. The idea that white people were gods was ephemeral, but the firm backing of local chiefs certainly transposed onto the missionaries a degree of chiefly, if not priestly, authority endorsed by the old order. Secondly, Hawaiians themselves made little distinction between American men and women in terms of veneration. The wives seemed equally different, remarkable, curious, and they commanded commensurate respect. The male missionaries, however, were not sensitive to the possibilities of this situation. There were proper ways for men and women to behave and no question, even in such a novel situation, of a gross reordering of cultural priorities between themselves and their wives.

Mission wives found themselves, on the Hawaiian frontier, participants in a gender division of labor reminiscent of the domestic economy of many small business or professional households in New England. The men possessed the major skills, and undertook the essential tasks, on which the family's material basis rested. Wives would be expected to sustain, however, a contribution to that enterprise—depending on their time in the life cycle, the numbers of their children, their health, and the availability of hired help. Their work was not inessential, or without significant economic implications, but it was undoubtedly more complex. While male missionaries certainly kept themselves busy, wives recognized their own lives as weighed down with "more cares, serious and perplexing, trying and neverending."[2]

In the islands, moreover, mission wives faced a far more challenging task in household work than did their American counterparts. Hawaii was not New England, and the missionaries constituted a vulnerable minority clinging to cultural forms in an alien environment, populated by souls whom it wished to win over to its own worldview. The wives' domestic labor would have to sustain a firm sense of identity for the mission enclaves and at the same time demonstrate an alternative way of behaving to the majority population. One aspect of labor which fell to the wives' lot, childrearing, would itself prove the most formidable obstacle to the wives' public missionary work and thus deserves special examination. The general domestic labor that wives performed, however, already constituted a brake on their ambitions, despite the availability of Hawaiian domestic assistance at negligible cost. When to this burden was added the convictions of the mission leaders concerning the proper place of females in teaching Hawaiians, the women's missionary careers could only seem marginal and un- heroic from the women's own subjective assessment.

Before any mission work could be contemplated, the onus was on the wife to establish the comfortable home on which the husband's mission endeavors would be founded and to provide, moreover, a suitable environment for the children he fathered. Of course, men should come married to the mission field, John Emerson declared from Waialua. Who else but a wife could cheer and comfort a man in a heathen land, and provide his meals, where no private board was possible? "I think some of my good friends at home who feel it is unnecessary and unwise for women to become missionaries to foreign lands, would change their minds if they should come here to live for a few weeks and see the thousand ways in which a good wife of a mis- sionary is *truly* a help-meet."[3] And this the wives strove to be.

Good Housewifery

Women and men together were complicit in the goal of sustaining American styles of living in the islands. Mercy Whitney once repeated Samuel's frequent comment, when he was at work on the house, that "if only we could live as *savages* do, we could dispense with this." But, she wrote, all these things were very properly a part of missionary work, a necessary preparation before the work of instruction could be fully entered upon. In a similar vein Juliette Cooke tried to wean her sister from the belief that missionaries lived like the savages among whom they dwelt. It was no object of missionaries to teach themselves barbarism, but to teach natives the benefits of civilization. They therefore lived in a decent respectable manner, in clean and orderly apartments, and wore appropriate clothing. Throw away all the mysticism and romance, she advised. Missionaries were not angels, but ate, drank, dressed, and slept more or less as Americans did at home.[4]

The burden the wives had assumed, then, was a heavy one. They faced the challenge to become exemplary housewives of an exemplary household, which involved a continual struggle to survive materially in unaccustomed circumstances, with the weight of this responsibility and pressure upon them. Before the wives could feel free to teach or engage in direct mission work, they had to be mistresses of homes, duly appointed and furnished in American style; to acquire "Christian" food for the family's diet; to fit themselves, their husbands, and children out in the proper clothing and footwear, varied for all occasions; to carry out, or see carried out, cooking, cleaning, washing, and ironing in proper styles. The two advantages of their situation—the steady supply of foodstuffs and manufactured articles sent by the American Board and the availability of cheap Hawaiian labor—failed to match the wives' requirements. Housewifery in the islands entailed an unending and unequal struggle for the dignified, acceptable subsistence they sought.

Until the early 1840s, the "common stock" system of material support continued in the mission: No salaries were paid, but goods supplied by the American Board were sent annually to a central depository under the control of the secular agent, Levi Chamberlain. Dry goods, salt meat, and fish arrived along with household goods, clothing, and tools. The inventory under "kitchen furniture" alone included bread pans, tin tumblers, coffee pots, Britannia metal teapots, lamp fillers, oilcans, dustpans, scoops, nurse lamps, milk skimmers, funnels, soup tureens, tea trays, nutmeg graters, tinderboxes, and molasses cups with covers.[5] Some goods were intended for mission use, some for use as barter with Hawaiians for other goods. They were collected when missionaries visited Honolulu for General Meeting, or dispatched by Levi Chamberlain as transport became available. The American Board itself cautioned the group frequently to practice the strictest economy as a matter of Christian duty; the missionaries in turn advised each other to refrain scrupulously from incurring the least item of expense not necessary for health and usefulness. They should think constantly of each other's needs and of their benefactors back home.

This communal economic arrangement was not likely to survive. An individualistic spirit entered missionaries' evaluations of their material support at a very early stage, mirroring the rapid growth of the marketplace economy of their native land. Some couples lived very sparely, performing tasks themselves rather than hire labor at the American Board's expense, and often doing without goods they might reasonably have acquired. Abstemious couples constantly had their heads over their shoulders on the sharp lookout for those who might be taking more than their share from the common stock. "Rigid notions of self-denial and economy," according to Laura Judd, "would incline some to refuse their allotted portion, but this only leaves a surplus for the careless, less conscientious member to appropriate and waste."[6]

More and more, the newly arriving missionaries pressed for individual salaries. Fair amounts were hotly debated. Some people were anxious that if salaries were introduced, they must represent ample, not partial, support or missionaries might be tempted to make up the rest by commerce of one sort or another. From 1842 salaries were paid—at the rate of $450 per year for married couples and $175 for a single woman, who was assumed to be living with a family to provide a roof over her head. In addition there was a graduated allowance ranging from $30 a year, for children under the age of ten years, to $70 for those over ten. Goods were sent from the States in the same fashion to the depository, to be purchased out of the new salary.[7]

If the first apparent advantage that mission wives had in setting up house in the islands was ostensibly liberal support from the parent body, the second was the availability of cheap Hawaiian labor. The first mission group had abandoned the practice of taking children and youths into the mission home in favor of employing adults, who were housed separately in Hawaiian cottages within the mission enclosure. It was not difficult to find volunteers for the position of servant to a missionary. The mission wives themselves airily rationalized this willingness as emanating from Hawaiians' unpressured lives. "Native help can be obtained in abundance merely for their board," reported Clarissa Armstrong. "They have nothing to do, and like to be employed by the missionaries." The Hawaiian servants were given in exchange for their labor their food, for the most part taro, poi, and fish, and basic American-style clothing. As much clothing, according to Mary Parker, was given as the missionary felt inclined—"not much, for if it is so they soon get above work and are more than useless." When the fiery abolitionist Thomas Lafon arrived in 1837 and denounced the system as a form of slavery, he swiftly instilled guilt in householders. Thus by the 1840s, wages were paid; but with board discounted, the labor still remained cheap.[8]

"Do you say we have three servants to wait upon two? Rather we have three persons under our especial training and care," Ursula Emerson interpreted her domestic situation for home digestion. It was, they agreed, a mercy to the Hawaiians themselves to be instructed and cared for, and a mercy to the nation to exchange Hawaiian labor for the services in schools of mission wives. This defensiveness reflected some embarrassment at their reliance on servants; no doubt they sensed they would be more admired by distant kin if they could claim to be managing all their chores themselves. Fidelia Coan supposed that she would be thought a better missionary by nine-tenths of American Christians if she could announce that she did all her own housework, and she had indeed done so in her first year. "But I became convinced of my error in season to save most of my health and vigor for these poor native children who are as sheep without a shepherd."[9]

Many another women confessed to changing her views on the employment of Hawaiian help radically after she arrived in the islands to discover that conditions made household work more onerous than even their farming backgrounds had prepared them for. Supplies of wood for fuel and water for drinking and washing were hard to come by at many stations. At Kailua, perhaps the most difficult case, water had to be brought two miles or more over rugged lava in large gourd shells suspended at two ends of a long stick resting on shoulders, and even brackish water was at a half-mile distance. Wood for cooking often had to be carried a similar distance since there were no roads and few beasts of burden. Taro patches were often at a distance from the mission station, so that regular tilling of the soil required extensive periods out of the house. And cows not only were wilder creatures than at home, but they often had to be fed on grass fetched from some distance.

Cooking, too, was an arduous affair. Many wives had no proper kitchens for long periods of time; cooking had to be carried on outside, or in a crudely constructed shelter, on a fireplace made among stones, without even crane or hook. Mission laundry had to be taken up to the hills where there was clear, running water; Hawaiians would sit in the cold water up to their waists, soap the clothes, and then pound them with smooth stones. House cleaning was peculiarly arduous, since even in houses made of mud, brick, stone, or timber, the dust and dirt penetrated through every nook and cranny, as there was always a shortage of timber to line the walls. The battle against rats, mice, lizards, ants, and cockroaches was a never-ending task. (Wives would wake at night to find the cockroaches drinking from their mouths or eating patches of skin off their hands.)

Amidst the particular difficulties of housework, wives had to face the effect of the warm, humid climate on their reserves of energy. A wife spoke of experiencing "a prostration of strength which I cannot describe, and which I never felt until I came to these Islands." All longed for a bracing, invigorating day, to experience the energy of girlhood when their frames were as though "set on springs." Sarah Lyman at first responded by lying in bed half an hour after the sun rose, feeling she needed more sleep than in a colder climate, but after reading *The Moral Reformer* she became convinced that this habit was laziness suitable only for invalids. Like others, she drove herself to greater effort, but few overcame the climate's effects. It was no surprise, then, that most households retained servants, often several married couples, to assist in the work. On one occasion, Rebecca Hitchcock detailed no fewer than four. One man cooked and milked the cow while his wife made the butter; another man washed, ironed, and fetched drinking water; a second woman set tables, made beds, swept the house, and helped with the sewing.[10]

Advantages, certainly, the mission wives had. Such was their urge to replicate American ways, however, that, even with a large number of goods supplied, even with ample Hawaiian household help, they could in a land of warm climate and abundant growth find housekeeping an exhausting burden. Mostly the struggle was to obtain the basic wherewithal of proper living; if and when that was achieved, they worried lest greed or ease were tempting them from the dutiful path.

Husbands solved the initial problem of finding materials for solid houses, stone or adobe brick or the scarce timber. Slowly and surely American-style homes appeared at mission stations, with front porches, cellars, and garrets, many double-storied because the cost of roofing was so high; some wives would have preferred a single-story house with a veranda all around. Most homes were simply furnished, perhaps with rag rugs on a painted floor, a cherry-wood table with folding leaves, a koa-wood settee, a mantlepiece with an American wooden clock, bookcases, a rocking chair plus a few cane chairs, four-poster beds, whitewashed walls and ceilings. (The Richards' stone house at Lahaina, complete with parlor and library, seemed overambitious; some queried the cost of its construction.) Whether couples felt guilty or not at the expense, there was relief involved in attaining such housing and laying out gardens, paths, and yards neatly designated for domestic animals, for domestic servants, for mission children. At Kaawaloa, Nancy Ruggles coaxed into flowering her favorite flowers, evening beauties, geraniums, pinks, mimosa, and roses.

Mission wives developed a range of strategies to sustain a better supply of goods and foodstuffs than the American Board allowed for. Much of the cloth in the depository was the coarsest possible, and if a piece of soft gingham or barred muslin was spied it was immediately stripped up for babies; a woman could not even obtain a soft ruffle for a nightcap. Sometimes ready-made garments appeared, but as Levi Chamberlain himself had to admit, they seemed peculiarly unfitted for any human form, and indeed they had been procured from unusable clothing left over in Boston slopshops. Shoes were of heavy leather, clumsy and hot; many a wife was lamed a week from awkwardly fitting shoes. Often food sent from the board was similarly deficient. Casks of flour invariably arrived caked hard or moldy and replete with large thriving worms which wives had to sift out before use.

By sustaining their range of contacts with others outside the family, mission wives controlled a network of reciprocity which attracted further goods. Their use of sewing and educational skills for chiefs formed part of the goodwill which eventually won for the mission, not simply permission to remain in the islands, but the right to use lands for grazing and agriculture and, not uncommonly, valuable gifts such as domestic animals. Missionaries were thereby enabled to produce some of their own food. From nonchiefly Hawaiians, presents of food were the most common recompense for services rendered, and wives took charge of the tedious bartering of depository trade items, such as cloth, fish hooks, needles, and scissors, for fowls, fish, *pia* (native arrowroot), taro, eggs, wood, medicines, mats, or labor. Scholars continued to bring food for their teachers. Some were the children of foreigners, like those of the sawyers near Hilo who shared some meat if they went to the mountains for beef occasionally. Sea captains in return for hospitality could offer useful gifts. Once Clarissa Richards received a few bottles of brandy and wine, lemon acid, raisins, molasses, bread, butter, oil, together with a bathing tub, two chairs, flat irons, and a shovel all from a particularly grateful captain. The return for pleasant meals ashore might be, as on one occasion to Fidelia Coan, the offer of the services of the ship's craftsmen. A blacksmith and cooper got to work for her and mended her stove, put hinges on a gate and new hoops on tubs, and made the baby a bathing tub.[11]

Within the mission and family, too, reciprocity was important. The kindly notes dashed off to mission sisters often went out with small gifts of preserves or fruit, and a note returned goods in kind. Lucy Thurston put up oranges for many stations. Mercy Whitney and others with herds sent butter and small cheeses; Martha Goodrich made guava preserves; many women exchanged babies' and children's clothing and clothing of their own which they had outgrown. Relatives abroad often sent presents to accompany their letters; the dried fruit from New England was especially welcome, since an apple pie was the height of culinary luxury. Rarely, clothes or money arrived as a share of a dead parent's belongings or from the division of the family farm.

The wives' own labor also contributed to sustaining the clothing and diet of mission families. In a land where "the arts of civilized life" were unknown, wrote Ursula Emerson, the wife had to be "tailoress, mantua-maker, milliner, and seamstress of the family." "I never felt so much the vanity of decorating these vile bodies as since I have been here," said another mission wife; and considering the amount of labor required, her opinion was understandable. The women sewed till their eyes ached—every waking minute that was not devoted to other chores, even when sitting up sick in bed or during rare sociable afternoons with other women. Children kept growing out of clothes; their husbands, as ministers and teachers, needed to appear respectably clad at all times. Men reserved black clothes for Sundays, though sometimes when the depository ran out of black cloth, wives had to watch their husbands mount the pulpit in blue, brown, or striped cloth. (In 1836 Sybil Bingham noted that Hiram had received over the past year only one made-up coat, which was too tight and already out at the elbows.) Three mission husbands in 1833 sent measurements and begged the American Board to provide their clothes ready-made to save their wives valuable time for mission work. Would the time wives spent making children's clothes not be better put to school teaching? Their quest proved fruitless.[12]

The women's own wardrobes, too, depended on their personal labor. They attempted to keep their wants simple. Missionary women, the wives agreed, should not give as much attention to dress as women of similar standing in America. They seldom sewed white muslin, silk, crepe, or bombazine for themselves; rather they kept mainly to calico, sometimes a coarse gingham or cheap figured muslin. Light colors were cooler and also made it easier to detect the fleas, though laundering was more difficult. Mostly they sewed light, loose dresses, with petticoats for underneath, keeping tight, fitted dresses near at hand for more public presentation. A few women in higher stations needed warm things occasionally. In the backwoods, Sarah Lyman on cold nights and mornings wore a flannel overgown and a pair of oversocks, her baby son wrapped in blankets. They made a ludicrous appearance, she acknowledged, but there was "no company" to witness it.[13]

Clarissa Armstrong would not have approved. Visitors there might not have been, but with Hawaiian spectators abounding, there existed the pressing need to set an example. "At best they are slovens."[14] This pressure to appear well dressed before Hawaiians and other foreigners, plunged wives into a constant state of anxiety, so complex were the possible differentiations in wardrobe for their days and so fickle the changing American fashions. Even ordinary Hawaiians soon developed a nice eye for determining when Westerners' dress was suitable to their station and tended to estimate people somewhat by exterior style. Particularly in Honolulu, where women were forced to the fringes of a growing foreign social scene, they struggled to suppress humiliation over their clothes. What was one to do when all one's dresses had short waists and tight sleeves, and suddenly even new mission wives appeared in a wardrobe of long waists, full skirts, and leg-of-mutton sleeves? Laura Judd, for one, passed around patterns and helped women modernize dresses they could not possibly discard. Unkind foreign ladies continued to make comments about the wives' old black bonnets and their attendance at the king's receptions in cheap calico gowns. The women sewed, and remade, and mended; still, an indistinct goal, that of satisfaction, eluded them.

Wives not only conducted the trading for fresh food but used skills in farming and housewifery to enhance the family's diet. Their general aim was, once again, to replicate the American pattern of meals and foods, making concessions to local conditions when necessary, without overindulgence. Said Sarah Lyman: "Our food should occupy few of our thoughts. I think it is very sinful to spend much time or strength in preparing it, or to allow ourselves to partake largely when set before us."[15] It was difficult to change tastes, however. Wherever it was remotely possible, wives kept cows and made butter. At Waimea, Mercy Whitney laughed at the pathetic size of the little cheeses she could produce with her clumsy equipment (a board with a stone on top for a press), but mission families elsewhere delighted in them.[16] Most families, however, went without such goods for months on end and had only goat's milk for drinking.

Wives assisted spasmodically in gardening in an effort to cultivate the string beans, pumpkins, potatoes, corn, cucumber, and cabbages, as well as a range of stone fruits and berries, which their appetites craved. The list of plants which were hopefully planted was almost equal to the list of failures. Indian corn would grow at Waialua, complained Ursula Emerson, but was not plump and sweet, radishes grew too big and strong in flavor, onions would grow no bigger than her thumb, they could not grow apples.[17] If wives tried to keep poultry, the dogs which abounded in villages killed them; eggs, too, therefore were scarce. In the end, wives had to place a good deal of reliance on what could be easily obtained locally—taro, sweet potato, breadfruit, squashes, bananas, sugarcane (for molasses), and pia, with such bread as they could acquire the flour for and the dried meat the board provided.

A common regimen would be a breakfast of fried taro or a bowl of pia or rice; dinner midday of salt meat or fish, boiled or fried, with taro or potatoes, and, rarely, a garden vegetable, followed by a dessert of pudding made from rice or pia; for tea, taro again, bananas, bread, and milk. Nothing was meted out in plentiful quantities, and women with poor appetites for such food clearly became malnourished. Special foods—a meal of roast turkey or chicken, for example, or fresh beef—were visitors' fare, not the usual family routine. Evangelical consciences frequently dictated fasting as good for the soul, a practice which added to frequent spells of deprivation in a land of plenty.

When Mary Clark's husband Ephraim was absent on a sea voyage, she felt lonely and depressed and acquired some wine. "You need not tell any one that I take wine," she warned him. "I felt almost discouraged before I took anything." She was rightfully ashamed: Missionaries were not supposed to take alcohol. The group who arrived during the 1820s and early 1830s did so, however, as a matter of course. Early annual orders went out for thirty gallons of rum, ten gallons of brandy, and thirty gallons of wine for what was at that stage a very small community. Some people might be surprised, Levi Chamberlain wrote, but alcohol was indispensable in a climate where no winter regularly braced the system. Particularly, thought Clarissa Richards, was this true for the women: "Wine and cordials of a medicinal nature are absolutely necessary for the females in this enervating climate."[18]

By the early 1830s there was sympathetic interest among the mission community in the temperance movement. The first formal resolution of the mission was against "ardent spirits," but soon even wine was proscribed, to be used only for medicinal purposes. Some went one step further. By 1834, Lucy Thurston could proudly claim that the eight mission families on the island of Hawaii had not only set aside the use of alcohol but abjured tea and coffee also. Thus began the retreat from all stimulants, as reformers were recommending back home. Lucy, for one, was grateful to be delivered from the slavery of these "stimulating draughts" and as a substitute to drink "from the crystal stream" or milk.[19]

Some remained defiant. Lydia Brown stated flatly that she took little meat, no milk, and was not going to give up tea too.[20] But most succumbed to this supposedly healthy and abstemious trend, looking wistfully to a kind sea captain for a little chocolate from time to time to add variety to their simple beverages.

Of the Hawaiian women and men who sought to assist the mission households in all the complex labor such living entailed, mission wives had scarcely a word of praise. One smart American girl, so one wife after another thought, would do as much work as all her Hawaiian servants put together. None of them had been taught to work when young, and the women in particular remained bone idle in maturity, refusing even to learn cooking. When Hawaiians finally, after much patient instruction, did learn housewifery, many wives complained that they would perform only one task at a time. What was worse, they held to a distinct demarcation of tasks. The cook would not even spread the table, nor knew how to, so that even washing and ironing had to be separate concerns. If a wife urged a servant to work more quickly, the calm response would come: "I will do it presently." You could never reprove Hawaiian servants, fumed Mary Parker, or they would leave and spread a report of your ill nature. "They are slow and dirty; all you can say is they are a necessary evil."[21]

Laura Judd was mortified to discover, when she was expecting guests to dinner, that the servant had set out spittoons at each place. Clarissa Armstrong was once exasperated to find that her cook had boiled, for a New England potpie, not only the chicken but its head, eyes, beak, feathers, feet, and intestines tied together with string. Her female servant used a needle like a crowbar; the women could be taught only plain sewing, and even then everything had to be prepared for them. Sarah Lyman gloomily looked over her linen when she was up and about again after a confinement: "It looks as tho it was washed by an unskilled hand and dried in the smoke. My man and woman are the most miserable washers." A sense of duty to their mission tasks, the wives agreed, was the only reason for keeping servants at all.[22]

With many servants, or few, the result of the wives' impossible demands on Hawaiian assistants meant that the mission housekeeper engaged in a range of routine chores herself, both those assigned to house servants and those allotted to husbands who were frequently absent. Wives usually performed complicated cooking like baking bread or pies, and they cooked for visitors. Some complained on occasion of exhaustion from scrubbing and scouring, often undertook spring cleaning or whitewashing walls while husbands were at General Meeting, and developed skills in carpentry and skinning and quartering sheep.

Mission wives picked up the slack of men's household work without much fuss. Men considered themselves grievously burdened if required to take over the women's load of work and organization. As a routine, men might assist wives with such heavy chores as putting up a bedstead, changing curtains, turning over mattresses. Such acts were a kindness, not a duty. When Daniel Dole proved himself able and willing to lend a hand with the heavier domestic work at Punahou School, the matron, Marcia Smith, was swift to defend him from possible criticism: Daniel was "no hen huzzy."[23]

Even when wives were ill, they hesitated to put too many demands on husbands. "A wife would rather suffer than call upon a husband constantly," said Clarissa Armstrong. If the wife was bedridden, husbands often had no choice. When women's illnesses appeared chronic, there seemed no point to staying on mission ground at all. As Alonzo Chapin explained to the American Board regarding his plan to leave the islands, since Mary Ann had been confined to bed, "much of the household drudgery" rested on him. At home, Mary Ann could have a sister's assistance, while he could pursue his medical career without interruption and feel as though he were living to some purpose. Whether Mary Ann, if in full domestic flight, would have felt as though she were living to some purpose appeared not to trouble his mind.[24]

Clarissa Richards wrote one day to Maria Chamberlain: "Dear sister how is it with you? Are you breaking away from the cares and entanglements of life and living more for heaven?" But Maria Chamberlain's examination of her conscience afforded no satisfactory response. She confessed that she wished she could live as though it would be a gain to die, but she was too much engrossed in the cares of this world. The drive to sustain a level of material culture that was in itself complex, and difficult to realize in an island setting, established mission wives in a thoroughly disadvantaged position in the mission field, through their designation by custom and male preference as "housekeepers."[25]

"Woman's Place" and Mission Life

When the male missionaries gathered for the yearly General Meeting in 1831, they calculated, as they were wont to do, a cash value on their work in the missionary cause: $8,320 for twenty years' labor. They continued with the observation that "one-third of our missionary influence is of a general character, exerted through the females of the mission in connection with our general system, aside from actual and effective labour."[26] From the commencement of the mission it was assumed that, however educated and capable wives might be, the men would undertake mission leadership and the major work which was perceived by them to be most important. Men took the initiative in treating with the ruling chiefs; men preached to congregations of men and women and undertook evangelizing tours; men translated the Bible and prepared exhortatory tracts and educational material; men trained advanced scholars for future leadership and directed the common school organization.

Within that overarching agenda, a place was carved out for wives.

Within classes, prayer meetings, and study and discussion groups, Hawaiian men and women would be separated, the responsibility for the women falling principally on the mission wives. As Hiram Bingham explained, the opportunity was thereby secured for the wives "to make their appeals, to read the Scriptures, and conveniently to give sisterly and maternal counsel to multitudes of their own sex." The system similarly gave scope for Hawaiian converts, female as well as male, to participate "in the public exercises of prayer and exhortation, and the details of religious experience."[27] This was, for wives, a subordinate role in terms of power in the mission, and it was an auxiliary role in terms of male priorities.

The preeminent position of men within the mission hierarchy was demonstrated symbolically and practically at the General Meetings when male missionaries conferred for several weeks together, making necessary plans for the coming year, apportioning finance, discussing station reports, appointing investigatory committees, allocating praise and blame to individual members. No women, not even the single women, were offered an active part in these proceedings. The women certainly attended, especially anxious not to miss the debates which affected their own situations most narrowly; they took their chairs, sewing, and babies along to the old schoolhouse. None dared speak, but they were quick to give voice to their opinions at tea breaks and at dinners. Given the close identification of many missionary couples, they sustained an informal influence which was not negligible.

Conflict abounded. Some quarrels arose from certain missionaries' attachment to a specific reform or issue of public policy, which they forced to preeminence in decision making, whereas others pleaded for unity around the essential goal of evangelization. Continual arrivals of fresh missionaries, and the reading of American newspapers and journals, kept the mission abreast of the wave of reforms and revivals at home, and the radicals took up strong positions. Slavery pushed a few into adversarial positions in the mission through opposition to the American Board's acceptance of donations from southern slave owners.[28] Anti-Catholicism surfaced over the entry of French missionaries; revivals on Hawaii brought dissent over Finneyite conversion techniques; there was debate over enforcement of temperance or anti-smoking rules; there were quarrels with the board over funding arrangements and the degree of control it could rightly exert over missionaries; finally, there were a variety of responses to such indigenous issues as the continuing autocratic power of the ruling Hawaiian elite. On all these issues women took up strong positions which they articulated forcefully outside the formal arena of mission deliberations. When Caroline Bailey heard of ministers harassed for their opposition to slavery she declared that words could not express her feelings about slavery in her native land: "Her ministers thrown into prison—for what! Let it not be told—if this does not arouse Christians to their duty is not the nation lost?"[29]

When at the 1839 General Meeting an outburst occurred over a new ABCFM ruling that missionaries should not leave their fields without first obtaining official permission, wives were swift to react. The American Board would prefer them all to die martyrs in the field, Mercy Whitney angrily replied. Unless missionaries stayed in the field for love of God and the souls of men, no law of the board was capable of keeping them there. She herself expected to live and die in the field, "but if the path of duty should plainly point me again to my native shores, this law of the Board forbidding my return would have very little if any weight, to keep me from going." Juliette Cooke was even more vehement: "Though missionaries we are *New Englanders* still, and the love of *liberty* is woven into every fibre of our hearts. It will take something more than an unjust law to quench this love of freedom."[30]

Mission wives found an alternative forum for airing their views: the Sandwich Islands' Maternal Association, which they formed at the General Meeting of 1834 on the model of the association of Utica, New York.[31] The women's's sessions were staggered at intervals in the male deliberations and revolved around a different focus—namely those issues which pressed most heavily on their own mission experience but which were ignored within the central body's discussions. In the Maternal Association they controlled their own agenda, chaired meetings, and spoke frankly in a formal situation about their mutual concerns. At each annual meeting, essay subjects were allocated to members for presentation the following year.

The primary object, explained Mercy Whitney, was "to throw light on the path of duty before us. It will also improve our minds, and qualify us for the better discharge of the duties of our station." The association enabled wives to promote to a generalized plane their mundane, individual experiences. It also reinforced their sense of importance as missionaries, temporarily at least, over the duration of

Devoted Wives, Mothers, Missionaries

Fidelia Church Coan and Titus Coan,
about 1850.

Asa Thurston and Lucy Goodale Thurston, about 1864.

Laura Fish Judd, date unknown.

Juliette Montague Cooke with her son
Amos Francis, about 1853.

School lanai and church at Kailua, Hawaii. Engraving.

Lyman House at Hilo, the home of David Belden Lyman
and Sarah Joiner Lyman, 1853.

General Meeting, in a community which marginalized them in terms of overt power and publicly acknowledged status.[32]

Mission life for women, however, did not consist mainly, or even more than occasionally, of attending General Meetings in Honolulu. The stark reality of their existence was the far more isolated life of the scattered mission stations, and it was here that the gender division of labor between missionary husband and wife established the limiting parameters of their days and years. Their first months, fresh to the field, were often characterized by an energetic and optimistic flurry of activity in the area allotted them as their duty. Charlotte Baldwin arrived with Dwight in Waimea on the island of Hawaii in 1832 to join Betsey and Lorenzo Lyons, and soon was involved in teaching two hundred and forty children five days a week, fifty women in adult classes, and a sewing school besides. Theodotia Green began "on a large scale" with a school for one hundred women organized on the monitorial plan. Sarah Lyman, whose husband began a boarding school at Hilo, wrote in her first year of teaching groups in map drawing, singing, and sewing as well as taking regular classes in reading and writing. The wives felt excited to have teaching under way. For the novice Juliette Cooke, laboring for the heathen was a "more exquisite pleasure than she ever knew." Such involvement in mission labor, however, and such euphoria, were an ephemeral experience for most fertile married women and associated with their very first months on mission ground. The wives' mission activity of a public nature was to be fitted around the edges of time left when the demands of their domestic situation had been satisfactorily met. Classes were movable feasts, schools began and closed at short notice, sewing and singing instruction were sometimes carried out on the mission house veranda. All wives tried to perform some "direct labor."[33]

It was harder for the women than for the men to acquire a grasp of the Hawaiian language, since they were out and about less among the people, but eventually they could assist husbands with translations. They assisted too in the men's medical and surgical operations among Hawaiians. "The blind, the halt, and the maimed are constantly calling for medical aid," one wife reported after she had helped tie the arteries after the removal of a tumor.[34] The wives prepared their own style of invalid food to take to the sick, imparting their own lore on nursing. At the most minimal level of direct mission work, wives met regularly with female church members to pray and discuss moral issues. Those involved with husbands in boarding-school work, women like Juliette Cooke and Sarah Lyman, possibly sustained the most active labor, since they could opt in and out of an ongoing activity as circumstances demanded. (Two brave but relatively brief attempts to carry on a female boarding school of their own were made by Ellen Bond and Fidelia Coan.) It was for the most part mundane, unexciting labor.

Mission wives did demonstrate their capabilities unequivocally during their husbands' absences. In Sybil Bingham's case, this sometimes meant protecting Hiram's privacy when he immersed himself in work in his study for weeks on end in order that translations could be completed. "I have got such a habit of concern lest he should be needlessly interrupted that I know very little, from week to week, of indulgence with my pen, my book, or even the rest of my chair," she wrote to a mission sister. Journeys, such as those for attendance at General Meeting, could mean an absence of six weeks at a time. Various reasons led wives to stay home quite frequently, and among them was a sense of obligation to monitor parish work. Sarah Lyman admitted in 1841 that she was perplexed as to duty, but she and Fidelia Coan had decided to remain at Hilo "to check the progress of sin, and encourage the saints to go forward." In Fidelia Coan's case, for one, her husband was absent so often on his evangelical tours that she became accustomed to acting independently in many regards. She had felt justified in staying behind from the 1839 General Meeting because there had been less "dropping off" than usual. "I have done more (or tried to do)," she told Titus, "than when you are here, and I have had my reward." She put two names on the blacklist for smoking, heard three cases against church members for adultery, and counseled a female church member against marrying a "China man." On other occasions she gave out hymnbooks (a little anxious in case Titus would not think she had made a judicious disposal of them), checked numbers at meeting and church, supervised repairs to buildings and grounds, and gave out medicine. During one of Titus' absences, Fidelia took the initiative of sending a note to the captain of a whaler demanding bonds that he would not be whaling on the Sabbath—the condition for enlisting two Hilo church members in his crew.[35]

When left husbandless, wives could at times have an unusual influence in their parishes. Nancy Ruggles found, for example, that when Samuel was on a trip for his health in 1829, her temporary jurisdiction attracted surprising interest. A considerable number of people came to the station from neighboring villages, pressing her to discuss religious matters or, as she phrased it, "to talk about the word of God and to inquire the way to heaven." Attendance at her Friday meetings for women rose dramatically to eight hundred souls. The revival persisted for a short time after Samuel's return, and he could write of their being worn down "just in the way we would wish to wear down."[36]

The effects of Clarissa Richards' independent exercise of spiritual leadership at Lahaina in 1832 was the undermining of the "reigning evil" of Lahaina—namely, smoking. Assisted by Maria Ogden, she first encouraged energetically total abstinence from smoking among her domestic servants and the female moral reform society. Once converted, the Hawaiian women themselves pressured their husbands until they too streamed into the mission house with their pipes (beautifully ornamented pieces) for Clarissa's bonfire. Others sent word that they would hand over their pipes when the last of their tobacco was used up. A total of twenty-five hundred signed the pledge—all brought about, in the absence of male missionaries and chiefs, by the "moral suasion" of the two women.[37]

Mercy Whitney stayed at her station after Samuel's death in 1846, compelled by a sense of duty to continue their long work there. She undertook the entire labor of the station except for the preaching, which was carried out by a graduate of the mission seminary at Lahainaluna. On his deathbed, Samuel had commended Mercy to Hawaiians as his successor. "Here is my dying charge to you," ran Mercy's report. "Take good care of her (pointing to me as I sat by his side); she will be my successor: obey her as you have obeyed me." Mercy found that the people regarded her "as a kind of deaconess." Occasionally some would say that her elucidation of Scripture was the most enlightening they had ever heard, and they felt highly favored to have her instruction. Even after George and Malvina Rowell joined her, church members continued to regard her as their teacher.[38]

"Mr. Lyons is greatly blessed in his labors since the death of his wife," reported Ursula Emerson in *Mother's Magazine*. "Ninety have been added to the church since general meeting." Wives could contribute to the cause of the mission by dying a saintly death on the job. Angeline Castle, for example, wasting away with tuberculosis, was seen, thankfully, as "calm as the summer's evening" and "waiting

patiently and joyfully the coming of the Lord." Asked the preacher:
"Who will not embrace and cherish that religion, which can thus take
away the sting of death, dispel the gloom that hangs over the grave,
and 'light up our way to glory and immortality'?" There were many
such deaths of mission women, valuable for sustaining others' religious beliefs.[39]

The case of Elizabeth Bishop was ironical. She died in a state of
despair, calling herself a hypocrite, warning others not to neglect their
duty as she had, her mind "dark and often comfortless." She began to
spit up blood and pus, regretting how little she had accomplished in
four years as a missionary, and telling Hawaiian women who visited
that "I shall soon die, and my unfaithfulness to you makes me afraid
to meet God in judgement." The Hawaiians appeared amazed: "If
after doing so much for us, *she* is afraid to meet God, how will it be
for *us*?" They flocked to her funeral. Her death in fact proved to be
the catalyst for the foundation of a church at Kailua, where local
Hawaiians showed a new excitement about religion, as they expressed
regret that they had neglected Elizabeth's instruction. The *Missionary
Herald* could now refer to Elizabeth as the "youthful heroine" who
had found an early grave that others might be saved.[40]

Overall, for the living, there were few high points to the female
missionary's career in the islands in the ordinary course of affairs.
Mercy Whitney made something out of the story of the *L'Artemise*
affair of 1839, when a French frigate of war under Captain Laplace
threatened to bombard Honolulu unless guarantees were given concerning freedom of religion for Catholics. Mercy wrote that the
Hawaiians' "Protestant teachers also were proscribed and doomed to
suffer, with the poor natives, all the ravages of war and bloodshed. It
was indeed a season of trial, but trials we are taught ever to expect."
("The 'Beast' has come with his wrath," said Fidelia Coan.) Mercy
Whitney had read the disclosures of M. Monk, "Six Months in a Con-
vent," as well as "The Lady Superior's Answer," and knew all about
papist iniquities. Mercy conceded, perhaps half-wistfully, that on this
occasion God did not suffer even a hair of their heads to be hurt.[41]

In one particular situation where three mission wives were called to
rise, with their husbands, to the demands of a genuine challenge to
courage and fortitude, they failed miserably. Three couples were dispatched to the Washington Islands, the Marquesas, where they
arrived in August 1833; few Westerners had lived there and a short-

lived English mission had failed. Marquesans were considered to be wild, possibly dangerous, even cannibalistic. In November 1832 Clarissa Armstrong had written home: "What, my friends, will you say? Clarissa expects to go amidst ignorant degraded filthy beings, & more than all they are cannibals. . . . We are to go to the Marquesas Islands. . . . My life may be destroyed by cannibals, but no matter if I am prepared to die." The Armstrongs, Parkers, and Alexanders sailed from Honolulu on 20 July 1833 to the tearful farewell and praise of the mission body. Mercy Whitney wept, expecting never to see them again on earth. Said Hiram Bingham, "The faith and courage with which the ladies, two of them with their tender babes in their arms, set off in this new enterprise were highly commendable, and their unshrinking heroism too admirable to be soon forgotten." The Christian public in America awaited anxiously to hear that the "Light of life" had risen on the dark valleys of Nukuhiva.[42]

The light brought by the American missionaries flickered fitfully and was swiftly extinguished. The group was horrified when presented with real live Marquesans in the flesh instead of the imagination. "Their looks strike terror," Mary Parker wrote in her intimate notebook.

> Disembarked today to live among cannibals—They seem to me more like demons than men—I think they are fallen spirits, inhabiting a prison house of flesh, to tame them.
> My heart never sank so low, as today. The tears course freely, down. Our dwelling is surrounded by hundreds of these savages, their eyes glaring out on us, through every crevice—their words, their gestures, shame the very brutes.—Gracious God—Can these be men and women! It seems impossible![43]

And so thought the rest. It boded ill for their project.

On shore, the couples set up house, the women clinging to each other by day as the men made nervous forays into the neighborhood. The wives attempted to set up a small class, but the Marquesan women said reading made them ill and stopped coming. Mary Alexander, like her colleagues, looked in puzzled dismay at the "taboo" system which greatly oppressed the women, she insisted. "They are forbidden to enter many of the houses of the men, and have few of the privileges the men enjoy; they are also abused and cruelly beaten by their husbands. Yet they plead for having five or six husbands. They ask who will prepare their food if they have only one husband.''[44]

Infants were born to both the Armstrongs and Alexanders, adding to the store of fear since the Marquesans offered constantly to rear one or the other child. The wives' second great terror was of rape. As Clarissa Armstrong explained to Richard's sisters, "The lust of the men seemed to rage towards us, to such a degree, that I sometimes feared they would not be restrained by our husbands, but lay violent hands upon us." The men's resolution failed equally. All felt desolate, ineffectual, and constantly fearful for their lives. In April of the next year, indecently precipitously, the group decided to return to Hawaii. Clarissa pondered on the bad effect their defection would have on the mission cause in America, "but my judgement must of course yield to my husband's." They returned to a reception so cold, she said, that "it seemed like a Greenland climate." (All these couples were dispatched in retribution to new island stations, solitary and distant from their fellow missionaries.)[45]

The lot of wives in the Hawaiian mission was not a heroic one, nor was it an environment where female intelligence and capacities could be used to the full. Few challenged outright the boundaries of a proper female public role in the first three decades of the mission. A controversy over women's right to pray aloud before men hovered, however, in the mission. A male visitor might ask a mission wife, in the absence of her husband, whether she might not consider it her privilege, rather than his, to lead in family devotions. Marcia Smith, a forthright woman, was clearly restive about the prohibition. ("Thus you see that the czar is not the only man who rules in this world. Some women are the greatest men of their kingdoms," Titus Coan commented rudely with reference to Marcia.) She once confided in annoyance to Lucia, her sister, that at a prayer meeting she had heard fourteen men contribute three prayers among them while women kept silent. Mary Castle, fresh from Oberlin in 1843, was moved by a yearning for the Christian perfectionism discussed by the followers of William Lloyd Garrison. She was known to spend agonizing periods at personal prayer, struggling for enlightenment, sometimes in the company of a kindred spirit, Mary Parker. Mary Castle once stepped beyond proper bounds by praying aloud at a public gathering of both sexes—to the disapproval of many of her colleagues. A mission wife could go into the pulpit to interpret in Hawaiian the sermon of a newly arrived male; a wife could temporarily take over an ordinary classroom from a male teacher, despite male scholars as old as thirty. They were not, however, to usurp the dominance of men in the mission church.[46]

One wife, the same Clarissa Armstrong who failed the Marquesas test, did once try to extend the boundaries of "woman's place." In December 1847, by now forty-two years of age and a mother of ten children, Clarissa was the central figure in a religious revival in Honolulu. Richard Armstrong, pastor of the central Kawaiahao Church, went to the island of Hawaii for some weeks on church business. Hawaiians, not only women, but men also, began soliciting religious instruction from Clarissa, who had pressing domestic cares with three young daughters not yet at school, including a nursing baby. She applied to the other men at the station, the printer, the binder, the secular agents, but all were too busy or too ill to assist her.[47]

At that point, Clarissa Armstrong decided to put aside her sewing and other domestic chores for the time being, and, her small ones with her, she confronted the work in earnest. Women flocked to the morning meetings, overflowing the schoolhouse; they shifted into the church. Men came into the service. Clarissa asked them to leave—this was a women's meeting—but they persisted and Clarissa acquiesced. Might not the Holy Spirit have sent them? The king, the queen, and all the high chiefs joined the throng. At first Clarissa led the singing, but she asked the king and leading male Christians to pray and address the congregation. One woman, however, her heart full, prayed aloud, and then another. After Richard returned, delighted with this new enthusiasm of the parish, Clarissa continued a meeting of men and women on Fridays, believing she had a strong hold on people of all classes. Richard arranged, in addition, for Clarissa to instruct the men at the prison.[48]

Clarissa was astonished at the strength she found to press on with this work. Years before she had resigned herself to a marginal position in mission labor as the weight of domestic duties had descended upon her. When she expressed her sadness at not being able to do more for the "heathen," Richard had tried to comfort her by saying that she might perhaps be raising children who would become missionaries while she mourned: "If it is my duty to raise a family, it is my duty to do it cheerfully."[49] Yet she became dizzy in the head, confined at home, felt the need of more exercise in the open air, suffered from headaches and ill health. Now that she was engaged in mission work these troublesome headaches diminished and her health improved. For the first time in years she felt she was accomplishing a great deal and was not "living in vain."[50]

It occurred to Clarissa that the Honolulu mission community, except Mary Castle, kept aloof. In fact, she was not long in learning that they were highly disapproving of her activities. Women should not preach; women should not pray before men or instruct men. Condemnatory letters from Honolulu went swiftly to the other stations, and Clarissa soon faced the same mortifying response from others. She was accused of the misdemeanors of the Garrisonian wing of the antislavery movement. She was reproached as another "Abby Kelly," the feminist abolitionist. She was accused of being a proponent of "woman's rights." "She had better wear pants," quipped one missionary. She had neglected her family and her children. She was clearly, thought Clarissa, seen as insane, or heretical, and in need of being halted in her course. She herself was utterly confident that God had blessed her efforts, and blessed her own soul. "I knew," she wrote, "the Theology was 'let your women keep silence,' yet God has led me on and greatly blessed me in breaking that silence. My husband, like others, learned the same Theology, yet never reproached me for what I had done, but encouraged me."[51] Hostile male missionaries finally prejudiced Hawaiian Christians against her leadership, however, and she realized that she had no alternative but to drop her work. She had lost her valiant fight for a place in the forefront of mission activity.

The pressure on wives to sustain a conservative attitude toward their role in the mission can be demonstrated by the response of Fidelia Coan to an account of women's prominence in the abolitionist movement, culled from the *New York Observer* in 1839. Fidelia wrote to Titus when he was absent at General Meeting in 1839. Did the ladies take part in the debates, she humorously asked, or sit on committees? If not, the mission was quite behind the times, and anything but liberal-minded abolitionists, judged by some reformers. "Can you believe it that females are acting in public—making speeches, acting on committees, etc., with the other sex at anti-slavery conventions and anniversaries?"

Some of these women, she continued, were calling for emancipation, for the yoke to be taken from their necks before the negroes were freed. "Surely they must feel their bondage to be a terrible one, if they are willing to let the African wear his chain until this much desired female emancipation takes place." Then Fidelia, who as a young, reflective woman had once asked how men could require of women that they be simultaneously yielding yet strong in defense of principle, who as a married woman was at that very time attempting to teach a school, showed how conservative she had grown in her intellectual convictions:

> I am afraid they would find some of their sex as unwilling to accept this liberty as some Africans are to be liberated and transported by the Colonization Society. I think some of us would feel quite as much expatriated to be taken from our homes, our nurseries, to make a speech in Philadelphia Hall. . . . I am grieved that the cause of abolition should have so many excrescences which must be offensive to many good men and good women of all parties.[52]

The work which Fidelia and many of her female colleagues were engaged in constituted in some ways a novel situation. Her shift in attitude shows how such work could be incorporated within a context which avoided conflict with the prevailing gender order, unlike Clarissa Armstrong who had moved beyond acceptable limits.

CHAPTER SIX

Faithful Mothers

I have a continual fear lest I ruin my own
children from neglect and exposure to native
influence. It lies upon me like a dead weight.
. . . This is a missionary's trial. It is comparatively nothing to leave one's house—the loved
spot of our childhood, . . . to be located in a
distant lone Isle of the ocean with the heathen
for our associates and neighbors. This one can
bear with an unruffled spirit, for we know that
the trials of earth will soon be done away. But
our children have souls that will live forever!
and when the sorrows of earth are over they
will enter on an eternal existence.
—Juliette Cooke to her brother Charles,
1842

Lucy Thurston once offered a graphic and agonized description of
the experience of motherhood in the Hawaiian islands: "Crucifixion is
the *torture of days*. These maternal anxieties which prey upon the
heart, and produce so many sleepless nights, is [are] the *anguish of
years*."[1] The deeply felt concern of mission wives with their maternal
role reflected the enhanced emphasis on childrearing and childhood
as a special state which became widespread in antebellum American.
There, in the northeast, Maternal Associations proliferated in villages
and towns, in which middle-class mothers met for earnest discussion,
the tenor of which could be judged from their popular journal, *Mother's Magazine*. Mission mothers, too, covered the whole gamut of
godly childrearing problems in their own Maternal Association, a
great blessing, they agreed, on Hawaii's lonely shores. Swift to order
the magazine, they examined articles such as "Errors in the Education
of Children," "Begin Discipline Early," "How Shall a Mother Secure
the Confidence of Her Children?"—ever mindful of their deficiencies
in training immortal souls, aware that when their children moved far

from them in adult life, the character of the mother would be read in her sons and daughters.[2]

The physical drain of childbearing and associated ill-health had diminished the mission wives' capacity for energetic engagement in mission work. The gender division of labor, which allocated primary responsibility for domestic work to women, provided a second disadvantage which heavily curtailed the wives' attempts to sustain a public presence in mission work. There was, however, this key element in that division of labor which proved the death knell to any ambitious teaching role: It was on the wives that chief responsibility for child care rested, and on the Hawaiian frontier this charge proved a peculiarly heavy burden. Many wives harbored the sickening fear, derived from their Puritan heritage, of their children's naturally degenerate state. When to this was added their children's attraction toward the indigenous Hawaiian society, and their eager attempts to acquire Hawaiian culture, the ingredients existed for tension. As prudent housewives, the mission wives directed their labor toward reproducing American material living conditions. As faithful mothers, they faced an even more arduous task—reproducing young Americans.

Maternal Perplexities

The rearing of mission children occurred in a context of sharp philosophical debate combined with intense emotion. Within the mission group itself, the anxious preoccupation of all parents centered on the educational responsibility of mothers toward their children, on the one hand, and Hawaiians on the other. Between the missionaries in the islands and the American Board yet another ongoing discussion, heated at times, revolved around the duty of missionaries to adapt their childrearing to local circumstances versus sending them for protection from that environment for an education in their parents' homeland.

Mrs. Whittlesey, editor of *Mother's Magazine,* whose policy was to sustain a generous mission outreach, expressed her concern that, when even American mothers who were favored with "heaven-born, inestimable" privileges still sighed over their own ignorance and indolence and wayward children, what must be the "darkness which broods over the pathway of their sisters in heathen lands?" Laura Judd attempted to describe to *Mother's Magazine* readers the feelings of those in the Sandwich Islands. They were not forced to bury as many infants as mission women in the East, for which they were thankful. Nevertheless, they carried the burden of caring for the bodies and minds of their young. Mothers in the islands had no day schools, Sunday Schools, or religious services in a language the children understood; the children were exposed to Hawaiian "corruptions"; and the claims on mothers of mission work were pressing: "Among the numerous miscellaneous duties the path of duty is often obscure. Our poor hearts are sometimes sad and our pillows and the cheeks of our little ones are often witnesses to the tears we shed over the neglects of the past day, and the resolution that, with the light of another sun, we will be more faithful in the discharge of our maternal duty."[3]

And what of fathers? The Maternal Association members of Honolulu met on one occasion to read an American treatise, "Address to Mothers," which stressed that the duties of the mother began in the morning and did not end with the day but pressed on her until she reached the grave; she must expect no return for her labors and could not be sustained by any theory which could not be reduced to immediate and constant practice. This was too much for some of the women present, who objected to "the recent practice of authors throwing *all* the care and responsibility of training children on the mother."[4] Their experience nevertheless accorded with the writers' observations. Lucy Wilcox reported home that "Mothers here have to perform the labour of Mother and teachers and I had almost said Fathers, for the Fathers have so many other duties that their own children are many times neglected by them."[5]

Men would speak seriously of the duties of parenthood, reminding themselves as did Richard Armstrong on the birth of his eighth child that the little one would exist as long as God existed, "and what he is to be millions of years hence will depend very much upon the influences exerted upon him in early life."[6] Yet in practice, the day-to-day burden fell on mothers, and this the wives had slowly, and sometimes painfully, to accustom themselves to. When Lucia Smith, still a single woman, traveled on an interisland schooner, she witnessed a clear indication that for all practical purposes, "parents" often meant "mothers." She thought the male missionaries very selfish in staying forty hours on deck, unencumbered, in the fresh air, while wives lay miserably seasick in the cabin below with their little ones to attend to.

"I found myself revolving the question in my own mind many times, why all this thrown on the mother? Is it right? I fear if I had been in the place of some of them I should have said Aole no. Enough of this."[7] But mothers perforce accepted the burden, willing or not. The essential depravity of their offspring remained an article of faith. When Mercy Whitney heard people expressing the opinion that children were perfectly innocent and free from sin, she concluded at once "that they are strangers to vital godliness, and have never seen and felt the workings of a depraved nature, or had any true sense of the evil of sin." The growing child's essential sinfulness was every day made more and more apparent. One proof, if proof were needed, was the child's propensity to love the company of Hawaiians, human beings in a "low and wretched state" akin to the natural depravity of children.[8]

Mothers of quite young babies were shocked to discover how swiftly infants could assimilate Hawaiian ways. "This is a sad place to bring up children: so many heathenish customs, lewd words, and unbecoming gestures are used by the natives, that it is exceedingly difficult to keep our little ones from being corrupted by them," was Maria Chamberlain's fear when baby Warren was fifteen months old. Babies as young as seven, eight, or nine months were judged to have picked up "bad habits, gestures, turns of the mouth, soon forgotten at that age, but what did the future hold?" Prattlers spoke first in Hawaiian, believed to be "peculiarly adapted to the imperfect organs of children."[9]

Henry Parker by two-and-a-half was speaking Hawaiian very fluently. By the time Caroline Armstrong was three-and-a-half years, she imitated *all* Hawaiians did, understanding and repeating in English everything they said. Her mother reported: "In imatating [*sic*], she scratches her head, squats on the mat, spits, and clears her nose, and many other things just like the natives—and it is exceedingly difficult to prevent it." Young Curtis Lyons alarmed his mission aunt by assuming a boldness unlike "that retired unassuming appearance so lovely in the character of a child." She overheard him frequently playing with a good deal of glee, talking Hawaiian loudly to himself so that the natives heard and called out that he was smart.[10]

The realization that young children could acquire so readily a culture quite different from their parents' was a shock to successive missionaries, as it had been to the pioneers. They fell back on a homely comparison to explain the situation. Missionaries at one General Meeting, examining the sad fact that their offspring developed a relish for "heathenish habits and vices," asked: "Who does not know that the children of the same neighborhood and circle have the same general habits, manners, taste, and language, even though there may be a difference in the characters of their parents?" Divine grace, said Mercy Whitney somewhat doubtfully, could keep the children from "giving loose to the sinful propensities of a depraved and wicked heart," but nothing short would be successful. In the meantime, strategies would have to be devised of a more human type.[11]

That this was an urgent need was made even more apparent from the continuing, distressing news of the fate of the English mission children which continued to arrive from Tahiti, whence had come the first warnings. Some men of the American mission visited the Society Islands on an exploratory trip to the Marquesas. William Richards summed up their findings in general terms: "Chastity is almost as rare among the children of the missionaries as it is among the natives!!! How much good will those children do to the cause of missions?!!!"[12]

Lucy Thurston provided some details. About two months before the Americans had arrived, an unmarried mission daughter became a mother; her child was part Tahitian. Another mission mother, hearing a noise one night, lit a candle, entered the bedroom of her three daughters, there to find three Hawaiian men; she fainted. Two mission sons had recently been expelled from the mission school, the South Sea Academy, for seducing Tahitian girls. The school principal had advised the Americans frankly: *"Unless you wish your sons to become vagabonds and your daughters harlots, remove them from the Islands!"*[13]

The result for their American colleagues was a terrible struggle between wives' sense of duty to the mission and their maternal responsibilities. For women who had come to the islands to be missionaries, the tension between being energetic mentors toward Hawaiians and being faithful mothers was ironic. What would it profit the women as missionaries if they sacrificed their American homes to cloister themselves with small children in a wing of their Hawaiian homes? But what would it profit the women as mothers if they redeemed a portion of the Hawaiian population for a new life in Christ, only to witness their own beloved children rapidly turning into pagans? The life of a mission mother, from the time her first baby arrived, was to center on this challenge—to fit in missionary labor not only around the edges of time left after she had performed or organized general household chores, but in a way that necessitated the least possible personal interaction of child and Hawaiian.

The most extreme position was taken by Lucy Thurston. Were missionaries to labor to bring a revolted race back to God, and in doing so, in practice, give their own children over to Satan? No, the mission mother instead would establish a moral atmosphere for her children. All communication between children and Hawaiians must be prohibited. Children would, therefore, have separate rooms and yards, and the Hawaiian must be told honestly the reason for this. "It would break our hearts to see our children rise up and be like the children of Hawaii, and they will be no better if exposed to the same influences." When the children were in the dining room and kitchen with Hawaiian servants present, only the most tersely stated instructions would be exchanged in the native tongue. When the children were in their own rooms or the "taboo" yard, surrounded by a high wall topped by a projecting paling, or when they were asleep, then Lucy could instruct Hawaiians. To her own children, she admitted, she was forced to be servant, playmate, and preceptress. This regimen she continued until her oldest child reached nineteen years.[14]

Three other pioneer women, Mercy Whitney, Sybil Bingham, and Nancy Ruggles, countenanced a solution which to Lucy Thurston was an anathema: to muddle along for a number of years, minimizing but not totally stopping contact of their first children and Hawaiians, with the intention of sending the children back to America at the age of seven or eight, before too great damage to their Americanization could be inflicted. Sybil Bingham told an American friend in December 1828 of her little Sophia's exile at the age of eight: "Our first born, our little Sophia, we have pressed to our bosoms, given her, probably, the last parental kiss, and voluntarily sent her far away. You will say, how could you! Truly, how could we? We had long made it a subject of serious and prayerful thought—We had settled it in our minds as expedient." Six-year-old Maria Whitney had already been dispatched two years earlier. "None but a parent knows the anguish of a parent's heart," wrote Mercy, as she described the severe struggle she had undergone until her duty became plain: to give the child up.[15]

While some missionaries followed the lead of the Whitneys and Binghams, others apart from the Thurstons began to have serious doubts about the humanity of the procedure. To begin with, it proved unbelievably hard to find host families to take the children in. Little Maria Whitney was shunted from one home to the next. Mercy's relations disapproved of her sending the child; they believed that if the move were truly imperative, the parents should have returned with their daughter. Some of the mission wives, Fidelia Coan for one, had seen such mission children, cared for but unloved, before they themselves departed for the islands. Children educated by strangers, she thought, could never have the benefit of that "social sunshine" which brought out the gentler, interesting features of their natures. "Home, though it may be an imperfect one, is the heaven-appointed nursery," she believed. Laura Judd watched with pity the two little Chamberlain boys, aged six and eight, take leave of their parents and witnessed a heart-rending scene as another small girl shrieked while the boat parted her from the shore, "Oh, father, dear father, do take me back!" She wrote to Fanny Gulick, "My dear sister shall you and I have to come to it? or will the Lord direct some other way?"[16]

From the first baby's arrival the strategy of each mission mother's days and weeks was to sustain some public presence in the mission while turning with the utmost vigilance to the supervision of their children's days. Juliette Cooke held Lucy Thurston in high esteem as a successful mother whose children demonstrated the faithfulness of her care, but she confessed that Lucy had taken a different stand from most of the mission women, in her belief that training her children was her first work. "I cannot say whether she was right or wrong, but I can say that we cannot all do so. I cannot for one, and there is a majority that cannot."[17]

Typically, young mothers worked while they had one infant, taking the baby with them to classes or leaving them, hopefully asleep, with a nurse. Controversy raged over the latter practice. Some, like Laura Judd, urged new mothers to conserve their strength and not to go about their work constantly with a little one in their arms when a Hawaiian could be trained to care for the baby. Others, like Marcia Smith, claimed that Hawaiian nurses spoiled babies if they liked them, and neglected babies if they did not, unable in any case to meet the child's needs for "physical, mental, or moral culture." Even with one child, women nevertheless felt tired as they raced between breastfeeding an infant and teaching a classroom. The worst conflict arose with the arrival of a second baby when the first was now talking and active all day but certainly needing a mother's, not a Hawaiian's, attention. "My strength is not sufficient for my undertaking. But what can I do? There is no one to aid me," mourned Sarah Lyman. Lucy Wilcox, a second infant in her arms, said flatly, "My school is the nursery *now* and will be I think for some time to come." Some reduced their direct labor to a minimum; some gave up for years on end. It was the rare wife who counseled her sisters that children should be taught that others had claims on her time: A mother's entire attention should not be devoted to "watching and quieting its own little self."[18]

Fidelia Coan was one who began motherhood determined to persevere in her teaching. She felt that too many mission wives, having left home with exaggerated plans for usefulness, were so discouraged to find their dreams thwarted that they sank down and gave up the struggle too easily. With one small infant often beside her in a crib, she began teaching a small girls' boarding school and wrote in optimistic vein to another teaching mother, Lucia Lyons, that they should together aim to demonstrate to the mission that "married ladies and mothers can labour systematically and efficiently in schools without injury to their own families." With a second, third, and fourth baby in swift succession, her adaptive strategies were pushed to the limits. She ran from one room, to yard, to school, back home, a babe on her arm, trying to separate children and Hawaiians, guiltily aware that any mother who did not prevent her children from acquiring Hawaiian was virtually designated a heathen missionary. After ten years of the most resolute effort, she abandoned her school, finally defeated. "*Home* is the mother's place and here must her best energies be expended," she conceded despondently.[19]

It in fact required an Amazon's strength to meet the demands of domestic cares, including childrearing, and ample mission labor. The energy and drive required were illustrated in the daily round of Delia Stone Bishop, stepmother to two children. She rose every morning at 4:00 A.M. The children would hear her call to Artemas, "Mr. B., I think it's past four. Look at your watch." Her husband would strike a light on his tinderbox, only to discover that it was perhaps only three thirty. The whole family breakfasted at five, and school for the children followed till 9:00 A.M. At that point, Delia moved across to the adjacent schoolhouse, where she taught Hawaiians for six hours, running back and forth to the mission house to check that the children were performing their set tasks. This was an arduous program such as few women cared to sustain.[20]

On the one occasion where the traditional gender division of labor was broached and the children were clearly acquiring Hawaiian ways, the couple was sent home rapidly, charged with inefficiency. The culprits were Martha and Joseph Goodrich, stationed at Hilo on Hawaii in the early 1830s. Letters of accusation against the pair flew between their colleagues and between mission spokesmen and the American Board. Martha Goodrich, in a plaintive letter, described the way in which the couple organized their day. First Joseph would teach school in the morning, and then at 1:00 P.M. Martha would go into the school while he took his turn caring for the children, so that she might have the opportunity of trying to do something for the "natives." The chief complaint against Joseph was that he spent far too much time in secular pursuits: He went fishing and bullock hunting, made sugar, and not only built a six-room New England–style house but undertook a range of carpentry for others, including Hawaiians. Joseph in turn explained that he undertook the latter pursuits when he was caring for the children. Unfortunately Martha, though apparently an anxious mother, was inefficient. "Many are my responsibilities; that of a Mother is perhaps the greatest," she mourned as they were being hustled away for being "cumberers" of the mission ground. Not only did Nancy, her four-year-old daughter, often wet her bed at night, but she spoke Hawaiian far more fluently than English and did not like her books. It appeared that the rest of the family would soon follow suit. The whole situation was intolerable for the other efficient members of the mission.[21]

The American Board officials and mission leaders participated in a running debate for thirty-odd years over the group's childrearing practices. From the first, the board counseled the missionaries against sending young children back to America. The board had no wish to accept either the financial or personal responsibility of caring for mission children. But there were other considerations. Children should be educated under their parents' watchful and loving eye, and that was more important to their development than the social environment. If mission children were all sent away, moreover, the pagan world would lose the example of Christian family life, except for the regimen of the nursery. In a fatherly fashion, Jeremiah Evarts counseled the mission: "You will be likely to think, from the fact that all your experience as parents has been obtained at the islands, that the difficulties you find in governing and educating your children are chiefly owing to the peculiarity of your circumstances; whereas parents find trying difficulties every where."²²

Never could the mission parents make any board official understand the policy of segregating mission children, a practice which, from the safe distance of America, appeared to make "exotics" of the children. "It shuts them up in hot-houses, instead of exposing them to the open breezes of heaven," Rufus Anderson of the ABCFM wrote on one occasion. They must liberate their children from this species of quarantine. "Put them in full sympathy with yourselves, if possible, in your labors as missionaries. Make them teachers in the Sabbath schools, and your helpers in every way. Make them interested in the Islands and the Islanders."²³ It was advice which the missionaries were ill-prepared to take. The parent body and the island group remained at loggerheads over the issue.

For mission parents, their children would be described as their treasures, their only priceless possessions. Yet it was not surprising that Mary Tinker looked at her newborn baby daughter in 1834 and felt "a gleam of sadness steal over me when I think of her lot, in common with us all, should she live to become *a mother.*"²⁴ The practice of mothering, performed on this distant plain, brought more tension than satisfaction. Amidst the pressure of the enhanced stress on motherhood, with fear for the misalliance of unregenerate American children and unregenerate Hawaiians, with the continuing battle of wills between mission abroad and mentors at home, missionary mothers took up the challenge to rear godly American children with understandable anxiety.

Training the Child in the Right Path

For mission parents, the birth of their first child was a momentous event, their entry into full maturity, the beginning of their strength. For the first two years of life, the particular responsibility of mothers revolved around the infant's physical care, combined with the compulsion to commence moral training as early as possible. Both duties were carried out under the overarching fear that the baby would die, breaking their hearts because of the love they felt, while raising the painful question of the child's salvation.

Mothers generally enjoyed breastfeeding their infants. "Juliette deems it one of her greatest blessings that she can nurse her own babies," Amos Cooke reported.[25] To keep the baby well fed (indeed fat) appeared the best defense against ailments and the most likely avenue for nurturing a quiet baby. New babies slept on their mother's arm in bed at night so they could suckle frequently without unduly disturbing her rest, and even after they were transferred to a crib close by the parents' bed, babies were fed at night often until their first birthdays. Occasionally, recourse had to be made to a wet nurse, or to artificial feeding, when a new mother died or proved deficient in milk. Both alternatives were heartily disliked. It was considered an arduous task to hand-feed a baby from a spoon or bottle, made more so by the difficulty of keeping milk fresh or even of procuring a steady supply. Goat's milk took on an unpleasant taste within a few hours. With the attitude the wives sustained toward Hawaiian women, resort to a wet nurse was considered only when the baby otherwise failed to thrive. "Judge of my feelings on committing my lovely little William into the arms of this Indian woman," wrote Clarissa Richards, "to be pressed to her bosom, and carried about on her back, as mothers here usually carry their little ones."[26] Wives tried to insist that wet nurses live in a cottage within sound of the mission house, so that they could be summoned only when the baby required nursing, but few Hawaiian women were willing to be tied for a long time to a mission baby, and often successive wet nurses had to be anxiously searched out.

By the time a baby reached five or six months of age until molars appeared, much fretfulness was attributed to teething, a period dreaded by mothers since they assumed infants were now predisposed to common ailments. The teething period overlapped with weaning, usually at around twelve months, and the introduction of mixed feeding, which certainly made the child more vulnerable. The "first great agony of bereavement," Laura Judd called the weaning period, and, like many mothers, Clarissa Armstrong noted the reluctance with which babies exchanged their "best food" for goat's milk. (Not infrequently the baby developed diarrhea, or thrush, and mothers were forced to find breast milk once more.) It was common, when infants appeared peevish, to lance their gums in order to enable teething to take place more easily; indeed, it became a cure-all (along with purgatives) for a range of symptoms.[27]

Yet mothers had to be wary, and remember, as did Mary Rice of her little Maria, that a baby gave at the same time "increasing evidence of the depravity of her nature." Was it not a fearful thought, Mary wrote, that Maria was by nature "an enemy of God"? By the time baby Munson Coan was ten weeks old, Fidelia was convinced that his crying was a display of passion and unsubdued will. "I cannot bear the thought that our child should live an enemy to God, one, two, or three years, were I sure his heart would be sanctified then," she confided in distress to her sister. If anxious mothers thought that willfulness might be at the bottom of peevish behavior, prompt action was taken. Little Henry Lyman's first words were "kiss" and "stick," a sure indication of the combination of affection and chastisement that was put in train. The rod was employed quite early; one loving mother's determination not to use the rod before her son reached twelve months was regarded as unusual. Most mothers agreed that as parents they required obedience early, and if it could not be secured by mild and gentle means, they used the rod. A mother was happy when she could report, if not an amenable small child, at least one who had been quite obstinate but was now well subdued.[28]

Other first words were similarly illuminating. Young Joseph Cooke "edified" his mother when, just fourteen months old, he looked at his hands one day and said "dirty."[29] The mothers took care to bathe their infants every day and keep them in fresh frocks, caps, and diapers. Children were trained as early as possible to control bladder and bowel movements. "Chair," like "dirty," figured largely in the vocabulary early acquired. Some mothers used a syringe to clear the baby's bowels regularly every morning. Once the child was on its feet, it was vigorously encouraged to signal its need to use the small chair, which had a chamber installed beneath it. Eighteen to twenty-one months was considered very late for babies not to be out of diapers, both day and night.

Juliette Cooke watched with pleasure as seven-month-old Joseph occupied himself busily with his playthings on the floor, seeing his intellect daily expanding. Little ones were given blocks with pictures stuck on with poi, rag and wooden dolls, stuffed toys, perhaps a tin tea set or drum, a little wagon to pull around the yard, picture books made by their mothers, complete with animals and flowers of America. Despite all the anxiety and care, babies and toddlers were also a source of happiness, talkative, playful, affectionate, and greatly loved. Her baby Elizabeth, wrote Laura Judd, was fat as a chief; "her *father* thinks her a *nonesuch*." And so it was for many small children.

Babies' smiles were cherished as evidence of love, first steps noted with joy. But the mothers feared the strength of their love, fearful that God would take back what they too selfishly prized. "Our dear little David has always been a very lovely child, and the affections of our hearts are very firmly fixed upon him; I sometimes fear lest there be an idolatrous attachment," wrote Sarah Lyman of her fourth baby. Baby Joseph was a great comfort to Juliette: "I am fearful that I shall idolize him and thus render it necessary for [him] to be early removed." Sybil Bingham's sixth baby, she thought, was so lovely that she wondered if he would live—it was thought that it was the most beautiful babes that were most at risk of premature death.[30]

And babies did die—a few of birth defects (heart malformation, obstructed bowel passages), others from dysentery, croup, whooping cough, erysipelas, "dropsy of the head," often with teething thought to be the precipitating factor. "We began, I fear, to feel too much as if he were secured to us," said one bereaved mother. Said another, "I tried to hold him with a loose hand to feel that he was only a lent blessing. But alas! my heart is strangely prone to excess in its affections." The deaths were heartrending. Some mothers feared that belief in the covenant, that young children of believers would be saved, induced carelessness about their babies' souls. But Abigail Smith, who had, in the end, five babies buried in her garden in Honolulu, clung to the promise of the covenant through her agony. Lucy Thurston consoled a bereaved mission mother with emphatic affirmation of the child's redemption: "A lamb of the first year without blemish. What a precious offering! Thank the blessed Savior for the rich experience which such scenes of unutterable tenderness and sublimity bring with them." Few mothers of large families escaped the trauma.[31]

If babies survived till their second birthdays, they had a fair chance of reaching maturity, and their moral and spiritual welfare now became the overwhelming preoccupation of their mothers. From the age of two, until either they sailed for America or reached the age of early adolescence in the islands, the children were faced with an increasingly structured day. Education and use of leisure time were directed at shaping firmly their personalities and behavior in the desired direction. If the toddlers had a nurse, or much contact with domestic servants, efforts to wean the child from a liking for Hawaiians were got under way. At eighteen months little Gerrit Judd supposedly dictated a letter through his mother telling of his small grass hut in the taboo yard. He had, he said, "such a wicked heart that he sometimes went without permission into the natives' yard, although they taught children very shameful things and he knows it is wrong and grieves Mother and displeases the Saviour." But he did not, of course, hate Hawaiians: He pitied them. "I have many playthings, but native children haven't any. I have a basket of clothes but native children haven't any and I have parents to teach me and take care of me and I have a nice trundle bed to sleep in, but native children have not any." A not-too-subtle style of socialization was in progress, and mothers noted with relief as their children began to call less often for their nurses.[32]

For the mission children, their world was shrunk to the mission premises, to the nuclear family. Constant maternal surveillance was now required to reproduce Americans in their parents' image. Unlucky first and second children were those most likely to take the brunt of their mother's zeal for education, partly because the mother herself had more time, partly because these children were lonely and more in need of extra mental stimulus. At twenty-three months, little Gerrit Judd had learned almost all of the alphabet, large and small letters, and could repeat "Now I lay me down to sleep"; two months later he could read and spell such words as cow, ox, boy, dog, and pig and knew who built the ark and who was the first man. By the time Sarah Lyman's first son, David, was nineteen months, he recognized more than one hundred and fifty pictures, and her second child, Henry, at two years and nine months, could read every word in Barnum's primer and point to all the prominent places on the map of the United States. All this prowess led to a notable achievement: On his fourth birthday he began reading, systematically, the entire Bible.[33]

The regimen was not always pleasurably received. When little Sanford Dole, having advanced through books with sentences to short stories, was presented with his large volume of the Bible bound in calfskin, he burst into tears at the prospect ahead. Fidelia Coan wept and prayed when four-year-old Munson showed listlessness, restlessness, and inattention when faced with his books, and she inquired of another mission mother whether she should break him in, willing or not. Some mothers counseled soft means, such as giving children some reading which truly interested them *(The Child Companion* or

The Child at Home) or credit marks or some treat. Others took direct action. When Curtis Lyons, at two, stubbornly refused to read a word in his primer which he had learned the previous day, Betsey whipped him; by three, he was reading very well. Little Henry Lyman's mother similarly had no qualms about dunking him, in exasperation, in the water tank of the bathhouse for not concentrating better.[34]

As further children appeared, the mothers found some answer to the problem of stimulus to concentrated study by the introduction of regular hours for schooling each day, sometimes together with other mission children. Lucy Thurston was perhaps the most impressive organizer, using the clock and bell to advantage. The working day began at 8:00 A.M. with a bell for half an hour's study; at 8:30 the bell rang again for household chores; a bell at 9:00 A.M. summoned the children again to the schoolroom, and so it passed all day. The Thurston children had become so well accustomed to the regimen that even if Lucy was absent, lessons were not interrupted. She taught the children grammar, geography, history, arithmetic, philosophy, and chemistry. Asa taught them singing and Latin, which he did at the end of every meal.

Sighed Mary Ives, "But ah we have few Mrs. Thurstons among [us]. I tremble when I think of my own deficiencies. My children will reflect most surely the image of their model." Most mothers found establishing their home education system difficult. Caroline Bailey was perhaps representative when, as mother of four sons aged eight, seven, three, and an infant, she outlined her program. After breakfast for one and a half hours, she carried out domestic chores and worked in the garden, the three older boys working with her or playing. (The boys, alas, were no prodigies and loved play much better than their books.) From nine o'clock she kept school for two hours—"if with the interruptions of tending a babe it is proper to call it a school"—and between eleven o'clock and dinnertime the boys bathed in the bathhouse while she worked or sewed. If she could manage it, the boys did more lessons in the afternoon under general supervision, reading, writing on a slate, or sewing.[35]

Moral and spiritual growth, not just book learning, was the central goal of education. Not a chance was neglected of impressing Christian values on children in the schoolroom. Little Sophia Bingham's first composition at the age of six followed typical lines: "I must learn to praise the Lord, though I am a very little child. . . . I must not be naughty and grieve my parents. . . . I must keep my hands and feet still when I go to bed. . . . I must learn to stay with Ma. . . . I must be good and learn to hear what is right. And go in the right path. And love the little baby."[36] Formal lessons and set work could not, however, take up all the child's day, so a strenuous effort had to be made to ensure that leisure hours were not only supervised but devoted to morally beneficial pursuits. Unstructured play was suspect, especially after the age of seven or eight; life was earnest, and the children needed to learn this lesson as swiftly as possible. The children's whole life must be based on an understanding of the hierarchy of power in which they found themselves.

It was not difficult to discern the child's subservient place in the family by observing, first of all, what children ate and wore. The mission infants were weaned onto *pia,* made with milk and sweetened with molasses, and this continued to form a large part of the children's diet, since with flour so scarce, only adults were permitted bread in most households. One thrifty mother made her children eat a pint bowl before every meal in order to reduce their appetite for the board's supplies. Together with local vegetables and milk, perhaps poi, this represented their main diet; chewing sugarcane was their favorite sweet, or bananas and guavas when available. Children's clothes were often made-over garments first owned by a parent or older sibling, and boys' pants were of cheap denim, with tucks that left bright blue bands as they were successively let out. As further children appeared in a family, others slept two or even three to a bed, and on a couch or the floor when there were visitors. Children were not to be pampered in this regard.[37]

If there were a few hours of play for children when some informality prevailed, it was gained because of the sheer pressure of work on the mother, not from any conviction of its value. Uplifting reading was the alternative to schoolwork favored by mothers, although there was widespread disapproval of fiction. *"We do not need story books, but useful books,"* they stated emphatically in orders to the American Board. Children could read missionary adventures, practical works, the accounts of pious lives. Eventually the moral tales of the American magazine the *Youth's Companion* were tolerated. If the children were not sitting reading, the preferred alternative was some constructive craftwork, most commonly patchwork or knitting, which was taught, out of desperation for alternative sedentary pastimes, to boys along with their sisters.[38]

As they grew older, children added to their infant toys with perhaps a hoop taken from a cask to drive with a stick and a jackknife for whittling boats, kites, bows and arrows, soldiers, or guns. Some had pets, a kitten, a kid (less often a dog), and the taboo yards often sported a swing and a flower garden in which girls planted seeds from America. Trouble lay in the fact that toys encouraged children in "fictitious play," which encouraged in turn lying and deceitfulness. Impromptu dramas were quashed in the act by most parents, unless perhaps they were a straight playing-out of a biblical event. It was no surprise to the Bishop children when Delia Bishop, from an array of toys in the depository which included a coveted Noah's ark, selected an iron skillet they could use as a gluepot. Games of chance, like checkers, were dismissed as a total waste of precious time.[39]

For that milestone of a child's year, a birthday, the offerings were meager and practical. Many parents joined the child in a day of fasting and prayer. On James Chamberlain's eleventh birthday in June 1846 Maria took the child upstairs, prayed with him, and made him the present of a pocket testament. Only gradually did it become customary for some families to acknowledge Thanksgiving, the Fourth of July, or New Year's Day with a special meal, and Christmas did not figure as a festival in their puritanical calendar. In the late 1840s, for the first time, some families exchanged presents and dined amply. Significant days in the mission child's life were marked by prayer, not feasting, presents, and jollity.[40]

For the most part, children did not move outside the trees and grounds of the mission yard without a parent to accompany them. Fathers might occasionally take an older child to the mountains to fetch wood or food. Mothers conducted children on short walks, invariably turning such forays into a botanical or geological expedition to be followed by the pressing of plants, the classification of rocks. Amazingly seldom was swimming in the sea a common pursuit: Mothers could not swim, the sea terrified them, and they feared the morality of sons and daughters bathing together. Bathing normally entailed splashing about in the tub, perhaps half of an oil cask, in the family bathhouse, within sound of their mothers. The Thurston and Bishop children were among the few who did swim frequently, after Lucy decided that sea bathing was nature's own provision for recreation. The mothers and children would walk to a rocky cove, where all donned flannel gowns to bathe, to be followed by a dowsing with brackish water to wash off the salt.[41]

As children grew older, the obvious way for the profitable expenditure of time was the performance of household chores. This brought mothers to the crux of their initial problem: How could children work without contact with Hawaiian domestic servants, who clearly helped children when wives were ill but ought not to do so in regular contact? Mothers' fears were compounded by persistent suspicion that children concealed a greater knowledge of the Hawaiian language than they were supposed to have. Yet it was not good for children's characters that others performed all the work for them; even if their parents' American homes had hired help, everyone in the family had worked as well. Mission children from the East, accustomed to servants, were returning to America with lazy "oriental habits," but parents in the Sandwich Islands Mission aimed to produce *"true men and women."* If mothers dispensed with household labor, however, they lost the assistance on which their mission work was based.[42]

In March 1845 Mary Clark wrote a little gloomily to Lucia Lyons that in addition to her former labors she had now taken a new burden onto herself for the benefit of her children—doing all their own work such as cooking, washing dishes, cleaning the house, and retaining help only for outside work. Alvah, the oldest boy, washed the large floors, made the fires, and fetched the wood, rather hard work for the lad. Lucia Lyons similarly set her children to domestic chores, while the Armstrongs directed the boys to the milking and the Tinkers, staunch abolitionists, likewise. Mary Tinker admitted that the plan cost her much self-denial, but she thought it would do her good. The Thurston children, also, had a spell of rotating the chores week by week, the cooking, the dairy, washing the dishes, being nursemaid, a plan which daughter Persis primly described as "better adapted to our family than the former one. It promotes industrious habits, and we better know how to value the comforts of life, after having labored to attain them." Most children were goaded to at least some work with unflattering comparisons with industrious New England boys, but the interaction with Hawaiians needed increased vigilance.[43]

The fear that Hawaiians would undermine their children's sexual purity remained the abiding terror. Since mission children reached puberty earlier in the islands, parents were especially concerned about the appropriate timing of information about "the connexion of the sexes" which mission children were, in their isolation, hopefully unlikely to learn from outside sources. Even young children raised

questions about certain passages of Scripture and were turned aside
with an anecdote, although mercifully many believed that the seventh
commandment referred to impure conversation or unmarried people
of the opposite sex occupying the same bed. Mothers, it was urged,
should keep a watchful eye for the judicious time to impart information, preferably too early rather than too late, and though the mother
should speak with delicacy, there should be no "disguise or mys-
tery."[44]

Clarissa Richards was amused to overhear her small son William saying to his brother Charles, "Boston, in America, is a very large place. I
believe it is a Continent—there are many beautiful houses and hills,
and mountains. The people are *polite* natives. There are no black
natives there Charles." Other mothers, however, were alarmed at the
inferences their children might draw from their separation from
Hawaiian society, fearing the effects on the children's characters. If the
children could not get to know Hawaiians, they could scarcely develop
human warmth or sympathy for them and could become "selfish and
circumscribed" in their affections. American children, back home,
after all, were encouraged to visit the sick and poor and join juvenile
benevolent societies. Some mission children accordingly accompanied
parents on visits to the sick, helping beforehand to prepare *pia* and
tea. The Gulicks, Lyonses, and Coans, among others, hired their own
children for tasks in order that the child could acquire money to
donate to charity. Structured and controlled situations of interaction
were, therefore, self-consciously introduced.[45]

For Salvation and Usefulness

When, at a Maternal Association meeting in 1841, the question was
raised whether any children of the mission were known to be serious,
one sister remarked that "she thought them unusually wild." Despite
this profound maternal investment in their offsprings' good behavior,
children were remarkably often quite naughty. One mother complained of her children's "rude rough manners" which seemed to lead
to nothing but contention all day long. Children of different families
fought vigorously during General Meeting, causing embarrassment to
the mothers, each of whom tended to blame the other child. There
were children of "peculiarly uneasy and restless dispositions" whom

any mother found hard to control. Impertinence, lying, damaging property, saying "by George," stealing fruit, practicing spitting—all came to light from time to time. At the Honolulu mission where a number might congregate, raids on the lump-sugar barrel in the mission depository and the breaking of windows in the disused printshop were not unknown, Even good girls were caught peering in at the window for Dr. Judd's taboo dispensary to watch with due horror the art of bleeding. These misdemeanors were all sins, either because they were forbidden by the Bible or because they were in defiance of a mother's ruling and hence against the biblical injunction of filial obedience.[46]

When children were refractory, various tactics were employed to instill obedience. When five-year-old Caroline Armstrong told a lie, she was put in the bedroom with only bread and water to eat until she showed herself penitent. Public humiliation might be adopted to contain unruly behavior, as when young Hiram Bingham's father drew a picture of the child's enraged face to pass around the breakfast table (though Sybil sadly confessed, "I am disposed to take the blame to myself"). An older girl might be given an essay to write, such as Elizabeth Judd's on rudeness: "Rudeness is a very bad trait in a little girl's character." Physical punishment, however, was promptly resorted to, perhaps a slap on the mouth for whining or impertinent complaining, but the rod for worse misdemeanors. Fathers in particular could lay on the whip with dexterity and frequency, though a warning voice was occasionally raised by mothers that too great severity could lead to deceit, to hardening in sin. The Lymans had a refined approach. The guilty child was sentenced to be punished the following day, when he was sent to the garden to select his own stick (a rawhide whip for serious cases), hoping desperately for his mother's rather than his father's ministrations. Prayer followed the beating.[47]

The long-term aim of the mother was to bring about obedience, not by force or in exchange for some privilege, but as an act of the child's own will. Children dutifully sang the hymn, "O that it was my chief delight to do the things I ought," reflecting the path mothers longed to see them follow. To bring children within the fold of good American childhood was to induct children into their parents' metaphysical basis of morality and character. Sadly, the children were not converted early. It was no consolation that newly arriving mission wives thought well of their children, thought them well advanced in

studies, suffering nothing in comparison with American youth, free
from the vulgarity so common at home. Children must find new
hearts, a deep personal relationship with their savior.[48]

When ten-year-old Gerrit Judd died from "inflammation of the
bowels" (an appendicitis) in 1840, he calmly took his farewells of parents, siblings, teachers, and friends, urging his companions to prepare
to meet him in heaven. This was a gratifying end, and others used it
to advantage. Amos Cooke, having sat some hours with the corpse
laid out on a board in the Judd's front room, went home to write to
two other mission boys, Lorrin Andrews and Asa Thurston, charging
them to take care, while Marcia Smith wrote to Halsey Gulick, "Halsey, are you ready to die? Shall eternal life be your portion or everlast-
ing death? You must not delay your choice." Mercy Whitney related
the deathbed scene in detail for her absent son Henry's benefit, so
that he could see how uncertain was life and that others younger than
himself could suddenly die. Mercy's reminders of the miseries of hell,
in fact, could be particularly descriptive. To son Samuel she once
wrote: "O to have your portion in the lake which burns with fire and
brimstone—the thought is dreadful!" And to daughter Maria, errant
at the age of eight: "God may in anger cut short your days and send
your soul to hell, as a reward of disobedience: and O, how can you
endure the thought, of living forever and ever in a lake of fire, with
none but devils and wicked spirits for your companions?" Another
dying mission lad on his sickbed admitted that he had always dreaded
hell, since, on a visit to the mountains on the big island of Hawaii, it
was pointed out to him that the volcano was the most dreadful
emblem of hell in the world.[49]

Every means was adopted to make the child's spiritual conversion
probable. As each year of their lives passed, children were encouraged
to spend more and more time in spiritual exercises. They were supposed to pray alone immediately on rising and retiring; there were
also family devotions night and morning. Parents took every possible
opportunity of talking of faith, and they watched for signs of spiritual
awakening. Maria Chamberlain wrote in March 1840: "The children
are somewhat tender; M. A. [Martha Ann] though at times quite
wayward frequently weeps when I converse seriously with her and
makes many good resolutions—James wished that God would make
Satan fast in hell so that he might not come into his heart and make
him do wrong." She was not interested in children's questions. When

one son asked, "Who made God?", she replied brusquely that it was the child's duty to have faith in what was plain, not to seek out mysteries. Mary Castle was sympathetic with the delicacy of children's spiritual growth and gave reflective, gentle answers, but Samuel Castle would reply more typically to every innocent "Why?" with the same answer: "Because it is written."[50]

Life-threatening illnesses were an appropriate opportunity to press children to turn to Christ, for parents faced the insupportable thought of children dying in their sins and becoming lost souls. When Mary Jane Armstrong, aged eight, was delirious for sixteen days on end, Clarissa felt anxious not so much for her recovery as for evidence that the child was converted. The trouble was that when the girl had her reason, she declared herself too sick to pray or talk. Her mother prayed, with success, that her daughter would not be taken without a new heart. Harriet Parker, a child of eleven, went through great distress "in view of the depravity of her heart" when she was very ill with measles. Her mother had rarely seen such anguish and thought her distress so deep that "it seemed a disease of itself." But the child turned to Christ. "The light has dawned in the heart of the child— Blessed Jesus Blessed Jesus," wrote Mary Parker in her intimate notebook. "Her face is that of an angel and her heart is all love."[51] One by one, most children during their teens found appropriate sentiments for showing themselves followers of Christ. The day a child joined the church was the highlight of the parents' year. There had been years and years of anxiety to be lived through before that miraculous day arrived.

Christian children were trained for usefulness in this life as well as a happy eternity after death. The anxiety of parents did not end with their children's personal conversion, despite the relief the commitment brought to their spirits. What, precisely, was to be the means by which mission children would earn an honest and dignified livelihood when schooling was done? In 1842 a school at Punahou, near Honolulu, was opened for older children, offering a broad, liberal curriculum modeled on principles adopted by Mount Holyoke and Oberlin. Boys were prepared for entry to a college in the United States or to act as "teachers, merchants, mechanics, farmers, or sailors." Girls, as well as boys, were to be prepared in such a way that they might "enjoy the advantages for the highest usefulness in whatever station Divine Providence may place them." Their education would be solid, not "merely ornamental." The guidelines stated "that girls must be taught to render themselves independent of the assistance of others as far as circumstances will permit."[52]

From the commencement of the mission, parents had brooded on their children's prospects for employment in maturity: Abroad, as at home, it remained their duty to provide for the future of their offspring. Their support for the establishment of Punahou was an indication that parents were willing to keep their children in the islands "in the expectation that the time is at hand when God designs to open before them a field of usefulness." But Punahou offered what was termed "a good share of book knowledge" without solving the second problem. By the late 1840s the issue was far from resolved. In a civilized land, Levi Chamberlain explained to the American Board, one's children were surrounded by equals; they stood a fair chance of doing as well as their neighbors by industriously cultivating the land. This was not the case in the islands. The Hawaiians were not the mission children's equals, not fit companions, nor should the children marry them. The mission young could not get a livelihood from the soil, or from a trade, and few parents wanted to see them go to sea or sail off as adventurers to California or the northwest coast. The threatened solution—that seasoned missionaries would pull up roots and return with their large families to America—forced the American Board to contemplate drastic changes in the material basis of the mission's organization, changes which would allow missionaries the chance to make material provision for their young. It was an alteration which would profoundly influence the future of the mission party in the islands.[53]

"What are we all to do?" Mary Parker asked Maria Chamberlain. "I think that you and I are working ourselves out of existence, at least we do only exist; as to leisure, 'tis a thing without a name." The gender division of labor, which rendered female missionaries subordinate in the work perceived as important and made the pressures on their lives so comprehensive, took a toll of the wives' physical and mental well-being. Newcomers to the islands described all missionaries as worn and drooping, showing "the wasting inroads" of the tropical climate and hard toil on their constitutions. But none had any doubt that it was the fading health and energy of the wives which was most marked. Those on the mission ground watched women of one reinforcement after another arrive with "blooming countenances," the picture of health, which was replaced within a sadly short time by pallid cheeks, wrinkles, and prematurely gray hair. Husbands themselves, comparing their wives with the robust women of the foreign community at large (despite their regimen of rich food, late nights, and wine), attributed the cause to mission mothers' conscientious maternal care.[54]

The mission wives' constitutions had been weakened in the first instance by poor management of their physiques, particularly during childbearing. Their effort to sustain American styles of living was a drain on their energies. But their efforts to reproduce their young in their own image had proved the death knell—not only to their ambition for a generous involvement in mission work, but for their physical and mental well-being. Whether they engaged fully or tangentially in teaching work, the nervous strain was considerable for mothers. Complained Caroline Bailey: "This is one thing that breaks down ladies here so fast. It is the *constant* care which presses, by day and by night. If one goes to Meeting, their children must go with them, if one goes visiting, their children must be of the party, and so of everything else, thus keeping up the pressure. I often think if I could leave them for a day or two with a trusty person, it would help me wonderfully."[55]

Women like Sarah Lyman complained of appalling nervous headaches which left them prostrate and scarcely able to sit up in bed, banished to a dark room. Mercy Whitney had pains in her head so acute that her thoughts became confused and wandering. Clarissa Richards described a period of insomnia when she got no more than one-third of her usual sleep: "No one can tell of the misery my wakefulness has occasioned me. It seems at times that the activity of my brain is such that my head will burst—and I am obliged to have something chained across the top of my head to keep the cranium from flying away." Delia Bishop, once so energetic, developed "dyspepsy" and a violent throbbing in the pit of her stomach when she tried even to write. Wrote Juliette Cooke: "I am sadly careworn. I live in the midst of so much noise, my head seems weak from the confusion of ideas—I feel sometimes that I am prematurely old." One night she woke Amos saying she could not breathe and was on the brink of palpitations: He threw water on her face. Charlotte Baldwin developed asthma of a nervous origin. Sybil Bingham once described herself as a run-down watch—before long, the mainspring would fail.[56]

The solution offered by mission husbands was that wives must cut down on their mission labor. Quite properly a wife, said one in a eulogy to a dead mission sister, came to the islands not merely to be a missionary's wife but to be a missionary herself, but the burden of combining all her duties was excessive: Wives were called upon to exercise self-denial by reducing this labor, her "meat and drink," within the compass of her ability. When Titus Coan observed Fidelia's pallid cheeks, he urged her "to give up a part of those arduous toils which in this enervating climate too often press our females towards an early grave." An adjustment in the gender division of labor or a weakening of ethnocentric rigidity were not considered.[57]

For the women frustration, despondency, sometimes stoicism, were the outcome. "I sometimes feel that I am a double exile, first from my country, and then from the people among whom I sojourn," wrote Lucy Thurston. Were she so distracted with care as she had been in recent months, said Sarah Lyman on one occasion, "I should desire not to live on missionary ground." Lucia Lyons wrote, "There is so much to discourage. . . . My heart fails me and I do not know what oar I shall pull next but I feel that it will be a feeble pull." Lucia received a letter from a depressed Caroline Bailey: "I feel that I am next to a cipher—perhaps I am one."[58]

Wifehood and motherhood would have to suffice as models to sustain identity. Every hour, said Laura Judd, that she might reasonably claim of her husband's aid in domestic care, from which she excused him, she regarded "as so much public work done by myself, and feel great pleasure in it." As for motherhood, raising a family was after all a worthy task. Parnelly Andrews assured Fanny Gulick that she should have consolation in the possession of her fine children. In turn, Fidelia Coan recalled in a letter to Fanny that her own dear mother had spent most of her life training a family of eight children: "Whatever others may think she used to comfort herself with the remark of an old divine that one who had given to the world a family of children possessing good moral character had not lived in vain."[59]

Maria Chamberlain, newly delivered of her fifth baby, asked a sister at home: "Perhaps the question may rise in your mind what good can you do for the natives, now that you have so many children? Something doubtless by way of example. By being sober, loving our husbands, loving our children; being discreet, chaste, keepers at home, obedient to our own husbands; virtues which converts from heathenism would be slow to learn without living examples set before them."[60] Mission wives like Maria knew that cultural change, shifts in perceptions of proper behavior, of belief systems, did not occur simply as a result of formal instruction. Every contact with Hawaiians, every act of theirs which Hawaiians observed, might prove the catalyst for change. Yet the final defeat which the mission wives experienced was to realize that however stoically and miserably they sustained their inferior role, however tension-ridden was their effort to combine some teaching with child care, the effects on Hawaiian women were unsatisfactory. The American wives attempted to recreate Hawaiian women in their own image also. The attempt was doomed to failure.

CHAPTER SEVEN

Devoted Missionaries

In all the vicissitudes of the five past years, I
have not for a moment desired to retrace my
steps; to be *obliged* to do so would be my
greatest earthly affliction. I only mourn my
exceeding unfitness for the work, and unfaithfulness in the cause of my blessed master. . . .
   Still I am not without evidence that my
efforts, poor and feeble as they are, are not
altogether in vain. I do not *know* that I have
been the means of saving *one* soul. I do not
feel greatly desirous of such evidence in this
world, perhaps I could not bear it; but I do
hope to be the instrument of much good to
many; I hope that in eternity I shall stand
before the throne with a great company of
Sandwich Island mothers and children, who
have attained that blessedness through my
instrumentality.
                        —Laura Judd, *Mother's Magazine,*
                        July 1833

American mission women in the islands deplored their restricted
access to what they termed direct mission work. And yet, as most realized, their influence through a myriad minor if less glorious activities
was highly significant; new cultural ways were not only transmitted by
direct formal instruction. A man visiting a mission aunt in the 1830s
wrote a telling tribute to her influential presence. There was nothing
in this wilderness, he said, which she could not do, from scolding,
working, washing, baking, praying, making dresses, catechizing, and
planting to driving stray pigs from the garden. "She exercised," he
continued, "an influence from her energy and practical virtue which
bordered on absolute authority. As I walked with her through the village, her presence operated as a civilizing tonic. . . . As she appeared,
tobacco pipes disappeared, idle games and gambling were slyly put

by, Bible and hymn books brought conspicuously forward and the young girls hastily donned their chastest dresses and looks."[1] Subjectively, as they daily compared their mission experience with those youthful expectations they could not entirely relinquish, the wives regarded themselves as failures. Viewed from the outside, they were powerful representatives of an alien, evangelical culture.

Utterly ethnocentric as the American women clearly were, they nevertheless offered Hawaiian women something valuable. Faced with a new order which remorselessly invaded their world, Hawaiian women were offered by the mission wives an introduction to a range of skills and a model of feminine behavior which could provide them with a competency to survive and negotiate their changing environment. What American wives offered Hawaiian women was no less than what they offered their own children: the cultural forms of New England society, taught alongside the definition of Christianity in which that culture was embedded. Hawaiian women were to be educated in formal Western style, were to be taught the basis of proper femininity, to be pious and chaste and domestically oriented. For this agenda, mission wives strove and suffered, as they did for their own young, whom, so they thought in their more charitable moments, Hawaiians resembled.

The notable convert, Kaahumanu, had been astute enough to recognize the ambitious contours of the mission wives' quest. One Sunday morning early in her days of faith, she was carried by her attendants into the chapel at Waimea for the service at which Samuel Whitney was preaching. Her bearers placed their chiefly charge in a chair at the front of the chapel, level with the minister, and, like him, facing the congregation. Mercy and Samuel were offended: The proud chief had placed herself symbolically on the same level as God's own representative. The mission couple chided Kaahumanu, who, admitting her ignorance, made a revealing request: She "begged them to tell her how to conduct herself at home, at church, in the house, eating and drinking, lying down or rising up." Kaahumanu expressed a clear perception of the quality of change required of her. Her career was triumphant, and her end was hallowed. Kaahumanu, a satisfied Mercy Whitney could write to Christian supporters back home, was truly a light in the midst of darkness. Her apprenticeship had borne fruit.[2]

Nonchiefly Hawaiian women had less incentive than chiefly women to pursue comprehension of another culture so intimately. But the goal which American wives sought was in any case unrealizable in a decade, or a generation. Hawaiian women were not children but fully fledged members of a different culture. The transformation of Hawaiians into Americans, which alone would satisfy mission wives, was a mirage to be sought in vain. Mission wives created unease and sometimes outright pain in the objects chosen for their charity, as they created unease and pain, frustration and unhappiness, for themselves. They came to Hawaii believing that Hawaiian women were sunk to the lowest place of abjection; they came to enable these women to "lift up their heads" and enjoy the fruits of a higher social status.[3] In fact, mission wives attacked and undermined those very aspects of Hawaiian culture which offered Hawaiian women some measure of autonomy in their own system. Meanwhile they were powerless to re-create for Hawaiians the conditions which gave American women the degree of informal power which they themselves knew.

Piety and Learning

For the entire period of mission activity in the islands, the central goal of interaction with the Hawaiian people was to assist them to achieve genuine piety. This was the keystone for the construction of the good man and the good woman, the basis on which the proper ordering of ideas and behavior could rest. The mission wives' task was to introduce Hawaiian girls and women to an understanding of genuine experimental Christian spirituality, which sprang from the heart and fed on a personal relationship with their maker. Such spirituality would be sought through the intimately related means of conducting separate gatherings for religious instruction or prayer meetings (in addition to hearing male preaching in mixed church sessions) and the teaching of the formal skills of Western learning. Through literacy children and women would gain direct access to the Bible, thereby acquiring the wider understanding on which Christian character and personality were seen to rest. Whether missionary wives directed their spiritual instruction at women and girls in the 1820s and 1830s, however, or after the remarkable revivalist movement, the "great awakening," of the 1840s, they reported the same uphill battle to encourage genuine religious belief.

The practice of mission wives conducting separate meetings with Hawaiian women proved highly acceptable to Hawaiian churchgoers, mirroring as it did the sexual separation of the traditional religion. As the first missionaries had anticipated, women's meetings allowed space for female initiative which missionaries might well have suppressed in mixed gatherings. Theodotia Green, for example, described how at her station, when the female prayer meeting became too large to meet in a private house, the women themselves took the initiative in building a meeting house: Each woman supplied a share of grass, timber, or mats, and quite quickly two hundred women were gathered in a neat, new building with the chief woman conducting prayer and pious exhortation. At such gatherings, not only could chiefly women take a leading role but nonchiefly women took their turn to read from the Bible, ask questions, pray in extemporary prayer sessions, sing hymns, and recite the catechism and weekly verses from the *Daily Food.* Some female meetings were restricted solely to church members who pledged themselves to specific reform goals—to leave off "vile practices" and follow "whatever is lovely and of good report." Sometimes the meetings were for inquirers in the faith, and hundreds could clamor to attend, not all for the "right" reasons, alas.[4]

The main problem faced by mission wives was seldom indeed the overt issue of "heathen" worship. Idols were in fact hard to come by when mission wives packed boxes of curiosities for the edification and amusement of the family back home, boxes into which they stowed in undifferentiated fashion *kapa* and mats, calabashes and *kahili,* shells and rocks. Mercy Whitney, on request, had discovered the basketwork of two old feather idols, "awful looking things" for a deity she commented, but no doubt they would astonish the "civilized community" back home. Once a shocked Sarah Lyman came upon a god made of earth, a small stone, a pepper pod, roots, and beans—a sight which usually surprised Hawaiian women themselves. Sometimes the high chiefs obligingly supplied relics. When Kaahumanu ordered an ancient *heiau,* or altar, demolished, she gave the timber to the missionaries to make into canes and contribution boxes to send home. Kapiolani, having sent a woman up a cliff to raid caves on a precipice for idols, handed them to a mission wife, saying "Send them to your friends in America." The casual attitude of mission wives to ancient sacred sites was illustrated by Lucy Thurston's practicality. She kept her milk pans and butter in the cool entrance to a sacred cave near her house.[5]

Idol worship might be a thing of the past, yet old styles of thinking persisted. There would be anxious queries from Hawaiian women on propriety: Would God be angry if they prayed when, unbeknownst to them, there was a man in another part of the house who overheard? In 1834 some people were discovered converting Bibles into playing cards, and drinking rum made from sugarcane and potatoes, because they were afraid of being prayed to death by witchcraft. Concern about disease and death led to "superstitious doings" in some way connected with "medical prescriptions," especially among elderly people. Missionaries reported the occasional appearance of a man, or a woman, claiming divine power, who convinced hundreds that they could heal diseases miraculously and that others could pray people to death. Yet even more difficult than such practices was the prevalent belief that good works would earn church membership and guarantee salvation. True piety, mission women reiterated, came not from show but from the heart. It pained the wives to hear that Hawaiian women believed they had earned their way to church membership by such good works as learning to sew and iron, praying forty times a day, or fasting five days in succession. Faith was the essential factor.[6]

When Sarah Lyman observed that two women, discovered peeling taro, could not read or write, she felt that "their prospects for eternity were as dark as their circumstances were miserable in this life."[7] Sarah thus made an explicit link between piety and literacy. Instructing Hawaiian girls and women in the skills of formal Western education was the essential adjunct to deepening their purchase on spirituality. In counseling Hawaiian women, mission wives made little distinction between meetings explicitly intended for religious instruction and attendance at school. The mission press turned out, along with the Bible, the rudimentary texts for reading, writing, arithmetic, natural history, geography, astronomy, and the moral sciences which formed the "common branches" of an elementary education. To educate women, old and young, was to bring them, whatever their rate of progress, more surely within the means of grace. While this formal instruction was a task mission wives engaged in fitfully, it nevertheless formed a keystone of their proselytizing endeavor.

There were many fortunate aspects of regular access to schooling. One was the introduction of the notion of dividing time into complex periods devoted to different uses. The school run by two Honolulu wives signaled its opening each day by the raising of a flag, reading "Superb," reclaimed from a wrecked ship. Others acquired a bell; some used a conch shell which could be used as a horn. Education similarly enabled wives to rid their pupils of such outlandish notions as that a woman gave birth to the Hawaiian islands; that an eclipse occurred when a god ate the sun or the moon; that an earthquake occurred when the man who slept beneath the earth turned over. One could deal patiently with adults who had difficulty working out the cost of four oranges at two cents apiece or with women who appeared unable to count how many children they had borne—"very many" was a common answer.

Many adult women showed themselves keen to learn. It was not so with the young. Mission teachers in the 1820s and 1830s had considerable difficulty keeping children in school. The only means, in fact, was by interesting them, turning education into a diversion which could compete with their usual pastimes, since even parents who were glad to attain literacy themselves put scant pressure on their young to follow suit. The children were untamed, said Laura Judd, and impossible to catch. "Their parents said they were like the goats on the hills, and had as little idea of subjugation." Sarah Lyman set out one day to collect children for the school in a nearby village but could find only three out of sixteen pupils; by the time she had argued with one mother to root out a child from his hiding place, one of her three had absconded. Too exhausted to continue, she returned home heavy-hearted. A few teachers resorted to bribery, gifts of clothing and books, but the children ran off after the bounty was distributed. Unless a chief, like Hoapili on Maui, ordered attendance, teachers could only try improved methods, perhaps the new infant teaching scheme of the United States. They sent for apparatus, though with little optimism. When children were disorderly, it was difficult to know what to do. An offender who had lied, pilfered, smoked, or engaged in "promiscuous bathing" might be put in the center of the room while others marched around singing a hymn suited to the occasion. Once Sarah Lyman tied a boy up at home for several hours. (She was known, too, to put errant children in the cellar.) If they tried to separate the sexes, the boys stopped coming. Children who were whipped tended never to return.[8]

It was not surprising, then, that those inspecting schools found more gray-haired pupils, and those with babes in arms, than children under the age of twelve. Mission records indicate that of those adults, as many were women as men. By 1833, there were twenty thousand readers in the islands, most over the age of fifteen, and an equal proportion were male and female. At first, before equipment or books were available, Hawaiians learned to write on banana leaves, smooth stones, and wet sand, and they brought bags of seeds for counting lessons. Wives sat up nights constructing maps for teaching geography, using red, yellow, and blue paints; for geometry they made cones and pyramids from taro. Before reading materials appeared, much teaching was by memory, a feat in which adults were adept from their long practice of preserving genealogies, chants, and traditions. After a single hearing of the first chapter of Matthew, two women astounded Lucy Thurston by reciting the names from Abraham to Jesus. Even quite elderly women might repeat with facility the psalms, the Sermon on the Mount, a whole chapter of John. They had, however, in the mission wives' view, the habit of reading or committing to memory without attending to the sense. Wives needed to explain everything obscure in their lessons a.id catechize them very minutely.[9]

Despite this painstaking effort, many a mission wife shared Mercy Whitney's despair when, one depressing day, she exclaimed: *"Can there be any real, experimental religion among the Sand. Islanders?"* In truth, the Hawaiians mystified the mission wives. No sooner did ground appear to be gained than evidence of ignorance or sin reappeared. One wife realized that though she could speak Hawaiian, she had not sufficient fluency to understand how Hawaiians really thought, how to analyze their characters. One needed to name every trifling particular about conduct, for Hawaiians believed they had acted morally when they observed a rule but in fact did not have sufficient judgment to sense the *spirit* of the law. Women might even come to the mission wife claiming the most heinous crimes, including infanticide, and seem unmoved except in their race to see who would be first to tell her terrible story. Instruction in Christian faith and doctrine, and the literacy necessary to extend a personal spiritual inquiry, were clearly insufficient. Structural change in Hawaiian society must be sought.[10]

While the mission struggled to establish true religion, the efficacy of the church and school, essential though they were, was called into question. Individually and collectively, missionaries voiced one central goal which would underwrite all their labors: the reform of the family. The moral sense of members of congregations and classes was formed in that one basic, essential institution which, in cultural terms, impinged increasingly on the missionaries' own consciousness. Surely the total absence of orderly family life was the stubborn obstacle in the way of the success of the gospel. Missionaries struggled against the current, trying to save one here and one there from a flood of iniquity which was in fact nourished in the family. Neither children nor adults appeared to find reinforcement for decent behavior in the one place where altruistic and uplifting relationships were essential. "It is impossible to conjecture who are husbands and wives, parents and children from their appearance assembled on the sabbath or at any other time," one missionary wrote. "Nothing of that courtesy and attention is shown to each other by persons not intimately related as in the Christian population."[11]

Rather than in state, church, or school, the main thrust of the reform endeavor should be shaped around the family life of Hawaiians. The Hawaiian wife and mother would be targeted as the agent for regeneration; the main reliance, then, would be upon instilling "moral and religious culture" in the females. The meaning of marriage and chaste sexuality would be made plain; the role of housewife and mother would be elucidated; then the influence of the Hawaiian woman, at the center of her well-regulated family, would ripple outward, redeeming wayward children, errant husbands, and, finally, the whole kingdom, for godly living.

Purity and Propriety

The missionaries waged their principal campaign in the battle to reform the Hawaiian family over the maintenance of monogamous marriage. The first rules governing marriage were established by the mission in 1826. Christian rules on consanguinity or affinity were to apply; thus intermarriage of siblings in upper-strata marriages was outlawed immediately, along with polygamy and polyandry. Marriages which had already been entered into, "heathen" style, if not repugnant to scriptural rules, were to be considered permanent (lest everyone rush to change partners); but from that date onward, future marriages should be formalized, in the presence of witnesses, by a missionary or chief. Divorce would be permitted on grounds of adultery or willful desertion, provided that mediation had failed to mend the rift; both parties could remarry.[12]

The question of polygamous marriages caused the mission particular difficulty, because this issue applied mainly to the chiefs. Missionaries urged chiefs to choose the spouse nearest in age to themselves and to separate from the rest. One chiefly woman on Hawaii, sister of Naihe, confessed to having had no fewer than forty husbands, several at the same time, as did Kokupuolii—a custom, unless the highborn women were wives of the king. Samuel Whitney asked one unconverted male chief whether having seven wives did not give him some anxiety. "Yes, much," came the reply. "My mind is with them all the time. I cannot sleep, for fear some other man will get them." After much persuasion, he agreed to live with his "old wife" and take care of her and their son.[13]

Marriages increasingly conformed to the missionary prescription, at least in terms of the ritual for entry. Chiefs' marriages provided an opportunity for feasting and spectacle, with silk dresses, uniforms and swords, scarlet umbrellas, processions, and throngs of witnesses. By contrast, Clarissa Armstrong described the wedding of two commoners at which the groom was dressed in an old shirt, a piece of *kapa,* and an old hat, the bride in a dirty undergarment with a piece of cotton tied around her and a Hawaiian plaited bonnet. "It was ludicrous to see them, he with his great bare legs, and she bare feet—yet it was solemn." On one occasion in Honolulu nineteen couples presented themselves at the altar, one groom in a blue cloth coat with bright buttons (which the lucky owner rented to bridegrooms), one bride in a nightcap, another with her head in a white handkerchief knotted on top, a green veil thrown over the whole.[14]

Efforts to introduce Hawaiians to the proprieties of the wedding ceremony paled in comparison with the task of persuading them to the meaning of the union itself. Hawaiians, the mission complained, entered marriage far too early and without proper consideration. No man thought it necessary to wait until he had a house, a farm, a shop, or even a whole suit of clothes, in order to take a wife, nor did the women regard these qualifications as essential when they sought or accepted the hand of a husband. A mission treatise of the 1840s endeavored to point out the difficulties of youthful marriage, made more pressing because adolescents ranging in age from twelve to seventeen frequently presented themselves to be wed. During youth, the mind and body were not ready for God's work, so young people should resist acting impulsively. Young men, moreover, should not marry old women, or young girls old men: If the married pair were close in age they would be better suited and happier together. The mission pressed couples to think seriously whether they loved each other. They should know each other well and feel committed to one another personally. No woman should be tempted by a stranger from another place, for example, impressed perhaps by fine clothing. Only when they were convinced of similarity in their thoughts, needs, and affection should they marry. Then, the commitment publicly celebrated, they should settle into the "God-given vocation" of matrimony and live together until death.[15]

"Marriage is honourable in all, and the bed undefiled, but whoremongers and adulterers God will judge," preachers would thunder from a favorite Hebrew text. Irregular sexuality, nevertheless, continued to abound. Sexual trafficking between sailors and Hawaiian women could be opposed by mission and government alike, but with shipping increasing in Hawaiian ports by the year, prostitution was poorly controlled. Some said that as much as three-quarters of the money taken in Honolulu shops was "the wages of licentiousness."[16]

The sin of adultery, more threatening because more prevalent, clung to the people like leprosy, the missionaries complained with regularity. They believed that chastity in America arose from, first, public opinion, second, modesty and reserve, and, third, ignorance among the young. How could there be such ignorance, asked one wife, when it had been normal for aged Hawaiian women to spend time instructing children, especially little girls, in "all those lewd and sinful practices, against which a christian parent would guard his offspring, with the utmost persevering vigilance?" Children indulged in sex play as early as two or three years. With adults and children sleeping on the same mat at night, there was obviously no privacy for "any act in the performance of which nature itself dictates and craves seclusion from the common gaze."[17]

There was so little disapproval of sexual irregularity that there was consequently little fear of loss of character if discovered. Impurity lurked even among church members, but in the church community there existed so little watchfulness that people were not suspected of deception until their sin became public. Under the influence of the mission, the government instituted laws against adultery with imprisonment or hard labor as the penalty. Some said adultery built the road system in Hawaii.[18]

At the mission station itself lesser measures could be set in train. Church members beyond doubt guilty of adultery were suspended, and at Waimea their number included Deborah Kapule who sustained a liaison with a young married man. Mission wives sought to keep at least their domestic servants on the straight and narrow, though this effort involved them in considerable perplexity. On one occasion Clarissa Richards dismissed from her household a young lad for having "improper intercourse" with the wife of Kehai, but then she discovered that Kehai himself was committing adultery with a nurse girl in Julia Spaulding's home. The sorting out of justice was tricky in such cases.[19]

Finally, to counteract adultery, mission wives undertook an energetic campaign to keep people clothed. It was perhaps not surprising that adultery abounded, many thought, when unclothed bodies everywhere provided incitement to erotic impulses. On Laura Judd's first morning in Honolulu she had gone into the kitchen to find a cook, "clad much in the style of John the Baptist in the wilderness," frying taro. Tearful and shocked, she vowed to use all her influence "to increase the sale and use of American cottons." The difficulty was deep-seated. Hawaiians appeared to consider clothing as ornamentation, for display, rather than as "a covering for their deformity." A few wives were perceptive enough to see that there were niceties of distinction among Hawaiians, who in fact always concealed their genitals with their hands if with no other covering. Others reiterated that Hawaiians had no sense of propriety which might make them shrink from nudity. The wives struggled to keep women dressed in the vicinity of the mission, at least, and encouraged them at first to wear a cotton or calico slip, around which they wound the traditional *pau* of *kapa,* perhaps a colored handkerchief around their necks. The next step, more ambitious, was to sew dresses, *holoku,* patterned on nightgowns, which fell from a tight yoke and long sleeves, appropriate, it appeared, for the mature Hawaiian women's form.[20]

Having got bodies clothed was not of course the end of the matter: It really was unfeminine for heads to be bare. The wreaths of flowers worn round head and neck were unsuitable and wasteful of time. The substitute was the bonnet, braided from the sugarcane or coconut leaf, vigorously promoted as the proper adjunct to the cotton dress. But problems abounded here as in all aspects of dress. Women, for example, wore bonnets when a taboo was declared by a chief (with punishment perhaps a shaved head), but promptly removed them when the taboo was lifted. Where women submitted to bonnets, they loaded them with bows of dyed *kapa* ribbon and extended the brims to enormous proportions. Leg-of-mutton sleeves, padded with *kapa*, ballooned out voluminously.[21]

Out of sight of the mission house, moreover, women and men discarded Western clothing, and the elderly often did not bother to adopt it in the first place. One wife wrote that Hawaiian women did not like the mission wives to see them naked because they knew the Americans disapproved, but if wives took them by surprise at their houses, "nothing is more common than to see the children either entirely naked, or with a strip of native cloth a few inches wide about the loins: and not unfrequently are adults found in the same condition." Continuing unabashed acceptance of scanty clothing, even in public, was not uncommon. One Sunday morning some female chiefs of Honolulu squeezed themselves into corsets for church; desperately uncomfortable, they undressed themselves outside afterward and walked home, quite unself-consciously, with their stays over their arms. Since the Hawaiian *kapa* tended to disintegrate when wet, Hawaiians who emerged from service into a heavy shower might innocently undress in similar fashion, despite the new materials, and walk off carefully protecting their precious clothes.[22]

If marriage was concerned with the regulation of sexual accessibility, it was also, however, concerned vitally with proper authority and proper feeling between husbands and wives. These were difficult concepts to impart, not readily conducive to civil or legal codes, but essential nevertheless. The delicate balance involved in the definition of submissiveness of wife to husband almost defied explanation in terms of chiefly Hawaiians. Missionaries had no choice but to accept the enormous power of chiefly women, despite continuing uneasiness. One missionary, describing the school he conducted for *konohiki*, or headmen, in his district, explained: "Some, by the way, are women; for Paul's injunctions are not observed on the Sandwich Islands. Women often usurp reins of government over large districts." The problem of marital deference was more general in the population, however.[23]

The American missionaries always looked askance at the marriage of Christian believers and nonbelievers, but particularly so when the nonbeliever was the wife. The problem here was the proper submission that a wife owed to husbandly authority: "In the marriage contract," the mission asserted, "the woman surrenders herself to the authority and control of the husband in a sense materially different from the surrender of the husband to the wife (though the husband's authority cannot contravene the authority of Christ which is always paramount)." It was this consideration that led them to oppose, also, older chiefly women's marriages to youths where there was a great disparity in rank, age, or influence, "for the wife would probably surrender her superiority reluctantly if at all." If the older partner were a male chief, the tension would not be so severe: "There is not the same danger of unwelcome usurpation, or competition for supremacy."[24]

The message was by no means an uncomplicated one: The concept of submissiveness was not, after all, unproblematic for the mission wives themselves, as the reminder that the Christian conscience was the ultimate arbiter of authority hinted. Missionaries were gratified when a wife tacked "wahine" onto her husband's name rather than retaining her own after marriage—"Hoapili wahine" rather than Kalakua, for instance. They warmed, too, to see couples (as happened on rare occasions) walking arm-in-arm, signifying companionship. Yet the more common observation was similar to Abigail Smith's when one day she sighed and thought how little one married couple would know of true conjugal happiness. As the newly married pair left the chapel, the bridegroom left the bride to follow along behind him, as he walked home "in the pride of unconscious superiority." Couples simply did not seem to comprehend proper marital deportment. Mission wives wanted to indicate that, under overarching male authority, men should be companions to their wives and treat them with loving care.[25] Wives were enjoined in turn to "reside in proper conduct under their husbands" and avoid quarreling and fighting.

Hawaiian women were, however, offered compensatory avenues for the extension of their personality and skills, through participation in church and charitable activities. A twofold plan was set in train. First, Hawaiian women should be weaned away from coarse and inappropriate pastimes. Then, secondly, their attention should be directed to more fulfilling pursuits. Commenting on a boxing craze in the local village, a mission report recorded that the "females, too, at the other end of the village are assembled for female fights, that is, *pulling hair, scratching* and *biting.*" Some women continued to spend time swimming and surfing, in card playing, gambling, "furious" horse riding, dancing, and traditional games of skill and chance. Women (and children too) smoked along with their menfolk and, before temperance ideas spread, drank alcohol (either imported or, more often, manufactured locally) when it could be procured.[26]

It was undeniable that the indiscriminate use of both drugs had serious implications for women's health and physical safety. Hawaiians swallowed smoke, which had a stupefying effect on them similar to drunkenness, and their houses were easily combustible. Acts of violence, including domestic violence, proliferated when drunkenness became widespread. It was, however, the inappropriateness of the activity as much as its potential dangers that motivated mission wives to campaign for reform. Maria Chamberlain tried on one occasion to shame her scholars out of their foolish smoking habit by telling them that it resulted in nothing but bad breath and a desire to drink often and then spit on the mats. "Moreover," she concluded, "young ladies in America do not smoke. Old men and old women and rum drinkers do."[27]

The main thrust of reform for the wives concerned with Hawaiian women was to find substitutes of a proper feminine kind, at the same time offering women space for personal enterprise and leadership. At Maria Ogden's school at Waimea in 1829, the objects she put to use for seats and writing tables for the women were "those boards, on which the natives used to spend much of their time, sporting in the surf." Her inspiration was both practical and symbolic. One change could give rise to another. Western clothing itself helped get women out of the water. As one missionary observed, Western dress was less convenient for women to wear in the water, compared with the earlier "native girdle," and it was certainly "less decorous and safe to lay it entirely off on every occasion they find for a plunge or swim or surfboard race."[28]

School, church, and social reform were to offer women new avenues of leisure and personal gratification. Sabbath School picnics, tea meetings, and school examinations were a time for huge social gatherings, speeches, and feasting which women could work for. "The maids and matrons adorned themselves with all the glory of the fields and shops, and they, with the other sex, have been making all manner of animal diagrams, evolutions and involutions," reported one missionary. The table of food was "loaded like a freighter." The scholars' exercises might last all day, but the crowd of spectators seldom tired of it. Social occasions might also be humble affairs, with mission wives offering, after a sewing class, "an entertainment" with plain cake and guavas. Choirs were similarly useful, though wives made the constant complaint that Hawaiians had no ear for music. (Mary Parker, for one, could hardly keep from laughing sometimes, they sang so laboriously. "Nature seems not to have designed them for the best singers.")[29]

The personal counsel of mission wives proved essential. Hawaiian women were begged to change their ways; in particular, wives were urged to combine their interests more closely with their husbands'. When Hukona, one of Clarissa Richards' servants, was guilty of "delinquency" while assisting Fanny Gulick, Clarissa insisted that the woman should remain with Fanny "and that she live quietly with her husband and submit herself cheerfully to his authority and theirs." She could return to visit the Armstrongs, and her relations, after Fanny's confinement, but Clarissa did not want Hukona to feel that her services were indispensable: "If she does not love her husband, nobody wants her." The constant "gadding about" of Hawaiian mothers and wives, as well as the men, was a source of anxiety for its implications for settled family life. "It is an every day occurrence for the mother to leave husband and several children and go roaming for months through Maui and Oahu; not unfrequently she casts her infant upon its grandmother," one missionary reported. Often husbands did not even know of their peregrinations, let alone expect to be asked for permission.[30]

It was the kinship network, the "relations," that many missionaries realized was the stumbling block to submissive wifely behavior. Their own culture upheld dutiful deference of young unmarried daughters to the authority of parents until marriage. Hawaiian women, however, sustained links with their family of origin which superseded their ties with their husbands throughout their lives. Hawaiian women were involved in strong bonds of reciprocity with their kin, for material, emotional, and physical support, and such demands frequently drew wives from the marital home. The functional value of this reciprocity totally escaped the Americans' understanding—who felt nothing but annoyance, for example, at Hawaiians' habit of sharing their bounty with their kindred. If a mission wife gave her Hawaiian domestic servants a whole hog or goat, "they would boil it up and share it with their friends," the Americans noted with disapproval, "and then perhaps go without any meat for days on end." Similarly if servants were given more clothing than was absolutely necessary, they promptly gave it away to someone more needy, or perhaps more easygoing, than themselves and certainly could not refuse a request for fear of being called stingy.[31]

Mission wives emphasized by contrast the discrete, overriding autonomy of the conjugal family. Presents and dutiful services to kin were proper. Alienating essential material resources, or accepting the control of kin over family behavior, were not. Thrift and saving would be unknown until those families which prospered could retain their bounty free from the predatory visitations of kin.

Domesticity and Motherhood

Teaching the real meaning of wifely submissiveness was intimately related to the encouragement of women to lead a domestic-oriented existence based on an American-style gender division of labor. Mission teaching was explicit. It was the husband's responsibility to work out-of-doors, farming, building the home. Wives should maintain the house and all within it: "It is wrong to neglect work and to leave the husband to keep the household. It is right to remain within the house and to work without daydreaming, providing food, clothing and all that is essential for life together." If current housekeeping was a very light affair, this stemmed from the insufficient customary labor which fell to a woman's lot. If women's labor was to be expanded beyond the weaving of mats and the making of *kapa* (an inferior product in any case), housework would have to be created for them, however much the plain style of domestic living militated against the plan.[32]

That the home might be seen principally as a place of shelter for sleeping and eating, rather than as a site for day-long occupation for family togetherness, was a notion unwelcome to missionaries. They denounced as oppressive of women the chiefly fashion for three houses—one for the husband, one for the wife, and one common to both. But pure horror was the mission's response to the one-roomed Hawaiian dwelling, offering, amidst the smoke of a *kalo* fire, hospitality to parents, children, extended kin, and domestic animals, without partitions even to separate sleeping quarters. Furnishings were spare: a few mats for the floor, on which all slept, *kapa* for bed coverings, calabashes for food and water. Any other possessions acquired by better-off Hawaiians, such as nets, canoe paddles, saddles, would be piled in a corner; if a rare bedstead (costing as much as $40) had been acquired, it would occupy perhaps one-third of the floor space, but this was an object to be looked at rather than used. Missionaries strove to persuade the people "to live like human beings," to build better houses, make tables and seats, use separate dishes and eating utensils, put fences around their houses, and cultivate a garden. (One of Clarissa Armstrong's first tasks was to plant a garden since "it would be a great thing if I could make these poor creatures love the beautiful works of God.")[33]

The imaginary wants of many people in America were quite too numerous, thought Ursula Emerson; she believed in simple living, "but here the people live much too close to nature and too far from civilization and refinement." The diet of Hawaiians was a case in point. Only chiefs learned to like bread and cake, custards and puddings. Otherwise, little was encouraging. Just a few straggly cabbages and onions appeared here and there to mark the domestic garden. Dogs continued to be eaten. Imagine, said Juliette Cooke in disgust, women used not to be *allowed* to eat dog. Hawaiians ate "crabs, worms, and every sort of thing that lives in the form of shell-fish." Some innovation occurred: Lucky Hawaiians might make tea in a large washbowl, stirring in molasses with their fingers. For the most part, fish and poi continued to be their staple diet, eaten by a swift rotary action of two fingers. On their visitations to inspect homes, mission wives gave out good advice, arriving as they did unannounced in their hope of catching out the unwary. But many Hawaiian women were unashamed to be found in disarray, or even asleep mid-morning, while more often it was not the bustling housewife but the halt, the sick, or the aged who occupied the premises. The Hawaiian home remained stubbornly unconducive to the performance of a day's housework.[34]

While missionaries dreamed of ways to introduce a cash crop which would offer Hawaiian men a place in the marketplace economy, wives pressed for an avenue to household production for women. Central to this aim was their effort to induce Hawaiian women to undertake sewing and knitting—which not only provided sorely needed clothing but also generated occupation—followed by the tasks of laundering, ironing, mending, and preserving the product. The most concerted effort was the attempt to initiate cloth making in the homes. In 1834 Lydia Brown was sent to the islands expressly to spearhead this effort. "It is certainly of the utmost importance to make employment, and to create a necessity for it, for the people of the Islands," the American Board reasoned. "And it is very desirable to exert every influence on them that will be likely to produce among them industrious, orderly families." [35]

Lydia Brown found women at her first station of Wailuku remarkably keen to learn and swiftly adept at the skills of carding, spinning, knitting, weaving, doubling, and twisting. Within a matter of months they had produced ninety yards of perfectly respectable cloth, as well as knitting "decent" stockings which a few undertook to wear. Lydia began rejoicing that new habits of industry would soon have important bearing on their moral character. But it was not long before the experiment faltered. She had to concede that imported cloth was cheaper, more readily obtained, and finer in texture than the Hawaiians' own industry could produce. Meanwhile individual Hawaiian women became fine craftswomen, but this was a pleasure, a hobby, not the earnest labor of the good housewife producing for her own. [36]

Pressure to reform the family continued with an effort to induct Hawaiians into the responsibilities of parenthood. The persuasion of Hawaiian women to devote more time to child care, however, was yet another frustrating task. When the missionary looked out of the window, what sight met the eyes but Hawaiian boys and girls roaming from morning to night, both sexes together, under no parental control, almost naked: "Sporting on the sandbeach, bathing promiscuously in the surf, or following the wake of some drunken sailors, and learning all their profaneness, obscenity, and swaggering behavior." The mission unanimously was of the opinion that all that had ever been written on the subject of maternal influence had been quite inadequate. While sustaining the uncertain hope that their own children's conduct, viewed at a distance, would spur on Hawaiian mothers to greater effort, mission wives organized local Maternal Associations to spell out the necessary qualities for successful mothering, as well as for care of husbands and homes. They selected groups of the most "enlightened" Hawaiian mothers to visit and speak to women about the management of their children; where they perceived deficiencies, offenders were to be pointed to their duty. [37]

Instruction began with a sharp attack on fertility control. Distanced as the wives were from any perceptive understanding of Hawaiian society, there could only be speculation that Hawaiian doctors knew means of "producing barrenness" in women of childbearing age. Abortions, those "base and inhuman practices," also certainly occurred, though they were usually passed off as spontaneous miscarriages. (While missionaries undoubtedly exaggerated its extent, infanticide had existed but declined in frequency with the massive mortality from introduced diseases of the 1830s and 1840s and with the sterility which resulted from venereal diseases.) The missionaries described the problem in high moral indignation. There was the issue of traditional sexual easiness: "Females became *effete* by reason of excess—the fountains of life are drained and dried up often in both sexes by intercourse at a very early age." There was the second problem of venereal disease, introduced by sailors and spread because of "licentious habits," which also caused infants to be born "tainted in the blood" and sickly. The contrast between declining Hawaiian fertility and the burgeoning mission families became blatant.[38]

Wives were more confident about their ability to pass on the right advice about childbearing. "A woman heavy with child should stay at home quietly in the house," they advised. "Do not go far away. Do not do exhausting work. It is not true that the child will lie straight at birth, if the mother keeps going and going." Attendants should not *lomilomi* the abdomen during labor nor grasp it firmly; births must be managed as were the Americans' confinements. But Hawaiian wives often delivered infants themselves, examining the placenta to be sure it was complete, getting up immediately to bathe themselves and their newborn babies. Lucy Thurston told of a woman who arrived at Kailua from her mountain home, gave birth in an astonishingly short time with only her brother present, appeared at Lucy's house the day following, and walked home three days later. It was all quite irregular.[39]

The high infant mortality among Hawaiian babies was attributed to the laziness and lack of affection of mothers. Nothing they did was correct. Undeniably a range of Western and indigenous infections produced signs of ill health, including the skin eruptions which afflicted many Hawaiian infants and which defied Hawaiian, as they did American, medical treatments. In fact anything that was not customary for Americans was deemed wrong for Hawaiians. Dwight Baldwin declared that the death of the infant son of Kauikeaouli and

Kalama in 1842 was the result of inept Hawaiian nurses adhering to wrongheaded Hawaiian practices. Laura Judd, at the birth of Kinau's fourth child, showed the better way. On the morning after the boy's birth, sixteen men presented themselves at Laura's door and set out for the royal home each with a bowl, the water, soap, a napkin, flannels, petticoats, diapers, caps, ready for the bathing and dressing of the noble babe.[40]

Anomalies, so it seemed, were legion and advice flowed freely. The baby needed a mother's first milk to clear its bowel of meconium—not a full feeding from another nursing mother with a well-established supply—lest its delicate stomach be injured. The baby needed soft clothing to keep it warm, and it ought not to be left naked. A baby's head must be washed along with the rest of its body; it was not true that water would run into the baby's head through the fontanel and kill it. A little baby should not be taken out in the rain, or exposed to strong wind or the heat of the sun, nor should it sleep outdoors at night. The mother alone should care for it; the baby should not be left for hours at a time with someone else. Fish and poi were not "genuine" food for babies. Mother's milk alone was suitable, and a little soft food when the baby grew teeth. No baby should be fed from another's mouth, with food mixed with another person's saliva.[41]

The Lyonses were angered one day in 1833 when a church member came several miles on a "very singular" errand: to beg from other church members their young baby to rear. "The parents were perfectly willing to give up, yea give away, their little one of not more than a month old." The Lyonses advised the parents against the transaction, and the applicant went away very disappointed. Beyond everything else related to child care, missionaries urged that this task be undertaken by the biological mother. The giving away of children was unnatural, a "grievous outrage upon maternal instinct." It could not be controlled among chiefs, who pleaded "state policy," nor fully among ordinary Hawaiians. Indeed, a mother might even give away her own child and take another to feed in its place and find merit in doing so. The most the missionaries could do was insist that if such a transaction had taken place, the adoptive and not the biological parents present the child for baptism.[42]

When it came to sorting out which adults were to be held responsible for the physical and moral well-being of older children, the issue of adoption loomed even larger. Sarah Lyman expressed common exasperation at the practice when, at a Maternal Association meeting at Hilo, she failed dismally to compile a neat list of mothers and children. Thirty women attended, but it proved impossible to discover exactly how many children they had, as "the own mother, grandmother, aunt, nurse, and perhaps someone else will all lay claim to one child."[43]

When pressed, Hawaiian mothers explained that as children grew more independent, it was impossible to keep them if the parent tried to exert control over their movements. Children simply rolled up their mats under their arms and moved to a related household. And children brooked no physical chastisement. One child told his mother that if she hit him he would jump off a precipice. Another mother described how, when she picked up a rod, her child spat in her face, bit and scratched her, tore her clothes, and ran away for several days. If the father was a church member and attempted to discipline a child as instructed, the mother, who was a nonbeliever, would set up a wail as though the father were killing her child. Hawaiian women, reminded of their duty, calmly replied: "You have repeatedly told us so before—we know that is right, but we are so accustomed to our old ways, we soon forget what you say to us." In any case, the women were convinced that there was so wide a difference in the dispositions of Hawaiian and American children that theirs could never be made to act like the mission young: Clearly they were just born different.[44]

True family feeling, the mission wives assured one another, did not exist among the Hawaiians. As Paul had said, the heathen were "without natural affection." A mission woman could tell the heroic tale of a Hawaiian wife supporting her husband for long hours in the water, trying to keep him from drowning; another could witness the tears and homesickness of lads, taken into boarding school, who blurted out their love for their mothers. They heard of a mother who plunged into the surf in an attempt to save her child from being killed by a shark; they knew of Hawaiians carrying on their backs and in their arms the old, the sick, and the young to save them from a tidal wave which swept away a village. None of this impinged much on the American consciousness. The Hawaiians did not show the right family feeling, the proper behavior.[45]

While the major thrust of reform endeavor centered on the family, there were some within the mission who urged an alternative project:

selecting particular children and insulating them (as they attempted to do with their own young) from the influence of the Hawaiian family in sex-segregated boarding schools. This was in some sense reverting to the pioneers' policy, but with a marked difference. The Hawaiian children in mission care would be kept apart, in a "total institution," distant from their homes. Coming and going between family members would be kept to a minimum. Everything she had accomplished in day schools was like trying to write on sand, thought Fidelia Coan, when she put her influence behind the boarding school. The "stormy elements which warred in the bosom of almost every family" appeared otherwise to obliterate all her successes.[46]

Lorrin Andrews, principal of the Lahainaluna Seminary, had turned his attention to boarding schools for children as a result of his first year's experience with the mature male students under his supervision. Unhappily, scholars repeatedly fell foul of the administration because of irregular sexual liaisons so widespread that it became useless even to dismiss individual men. One year the entire examinations had to be canceled because of "fornicators" and "adulterers." Moreover, the shocking revelation came to light that Lahainaluna graduates out in the schools were using their newfound status to gain sexual favors from female pupils. "We must begin with children," Andrews maintained, "or most of our labor must be lost as far as civilization and mental improvement are concerned." As for the Hawaiian ruling group, some felt the same was true. Chiefs' children showed not the slightest inclination to be educated alongside plebian children, and a boarding school appeared the most hopeful way of introducing them to notions of good Christian leadership, though there were others who preferred that chiefly children should forget their rank.[47]

The Cookes were delegated to run a boarding school for chiefs' children. Lahainaluna was converted in 1837 to a boarding school for nonchiefly boys and, at a discreet distance, the Wailuku Female Seminary similarly opened its doors to nonchiefly girls aged from six to ten years. The boys were headed for government employment, the girls to be their wives, due to exert "an extensive salutary female influence."[48]

At Wailuku, under the principal Miss Maria Ogden, Hawaiian girls received the training in true womanhood that the female missionaries had tried to offer adult women. Their daily schedule revealed much. Girls rose before dawn for prayers, set the tables, cleaned their rooms, washed, combed their hair, and came down to breakfast at the sound of the bell. They sewed from 7:30 to 9:00 A.M., studied till midday, and again after lunch from 2:00 to 4:00 P.M. Another hour's sewing preceded supper at 5:00 P.M., followed by a Scripture reading and prayer. On Saturdays the scholars scoured the dining room, school-room, tables, basins, aprons, plates, knives, and forks; they washed and ironed their clothes, neat uniforms of sensible cottons. They learned at the school the basic elements of formal education com-bined with an apprenticeship in female arts and crafts. Trained in such rigorous style, Wailuku graduates often prospered and married, as hoped, the Lahainaluna youths, but suffered from the secondary place allotted them in the mission scheme of things. One mission wife noted in 1845 that generally among Hawaiian teachers there was a feeling that girls were not "wealth to the nation" since it was the boys whose education was more important in terms of future employ-ment.[49]

The boarding-school scheme remained in any case very limited in application. The majority of parents were not interested in sending children off to boarding schools; the expense of running more than a few was beyond the mission's means; men who had come as ministers and missionaries to a foreign station scarcely wanted to coop them-selves up unheroically for years on end with a handful of children; wives were unable to sustain such intensive labor. Boarding schools only ever catered for a small number of children, and the outcome was always problematic. "You know it is difficult to raise a Hawaiian above the level of general society, and still harder to *keep* him above it," wrote Fidelia Coan five years the wiser, reviewing the graduates of her own small boarding school. Like reform of the family, reform of the child in isolation did not answer all the needs of the mission agenda.[50]

Rare Successes, Rarer Praise

By the late 1840s, the mission had to admit to some change. One could observe among Hawaiians more common use of clothing, some thatched, mud-walled cottages, some separate sleeping places parti-tioned off for children, a scattering of home-built furniture, wooden bowls and spoons. There was greater use of tools, of farm implements and beasts of burden. Some couples walked arm-in-arm to church; more than a few families took the Hawaiian-language newspaper, and generally paid for it. Yet essentially the scene was discouraging. The people remained far from being pious, civilized human beings; they were "rough unpolished blocks from a miserable quarry." Time might be annihilated by the magnetic telegraph, space by the power of steam, but the moral being—"the *minds, habits, thoughts, feelings, sympathies, affections*"—of a heathen nation defied swift reform. Missionaries had utilized school and church, they had developed a new agenda for family living, but success had eluded them. Women and men alike turned attention to the political and economic structures of Hawaiian society which they now believed undermined the fundamental reforms which were essential.[51]

From the beginning, the Americans had believed that to be efficient Christians, Hawaiians needed basic civil rights. "Still dear America with all thy faults thou art the sweetest land (to me) on earth," wrote Juliette Cooke one Fourth of July. When she compared America with the despotic government of Hawaii, "I cannot help groaning for this poor people and saying in my heart may the Lord ease them of their burdens and make them his free men." People remained subject to the whims of chiefs, could be sent hither and yon to provide labor, were taxed disproportionately, had goods confiscated. How could one encourage Hawaiians to industry, asked Fidelia Coan, when the most productive were the most likely "to tempt the cupidity of the rulers"? The nation could not be civilized and enlightened until incentives to hard work and thrift were strengthened. Despite increasingly progressive civil rights legislation, the situation remained anomalous. The overpowering central need became obvious: Hawaiians must be allowed in law to own their own land. The "Great Mahele," as the massive change in land tenure commenced in the late 1840s was known, was seen as the beginning of essential change. Ordinary Hawaiians, along with foreign-born citizens, for the first time were to be permitted to hold land in fee simple. Despite the advantages in land tenure retained by royalty and the chiefly elite, the economic organization of the islands appeared to the mission to be established on constructive new lines.[52]

The scenario was optimistic. Hawaiians, once owners of small farms, would happily work hard because they would receive the fruits of their labor; hence the family would be properly clothed and fed, men would build better houses, and parents would rear their own young who would hope to inherit. A legitimate means of acquiring goods would remove the need of women to barter sexual services and men's need to steal. A godly, industrious, healthy citizenry could then emerge, one that could discover "some of that ingenuity which made many a Yankee rich." To the "moral suasion" applied so assiduously for decades, economic and political reorganization would lay the basis for a new Christian Hawaii. And to assist this reformed populace in benevolent progress would be not only the aging missionaries but their children, who would form a "moral nucleus" for the white population.[53]

Meanwhile, mission wives faced an increasing burden of labor that was totally unexpected and certainly uncongenial—that of nurse. Hawaiians kept dying, prized converts, pious chiefs, church leaders, and all. Would they even live to populate the new Hawaii? "Surely this people are melting away like dew," wrote one wife. "My soul is pained for this dying nation," mourned another. "What the Lord designs to do with this nation," thought a third, "his providence must disclose, but it sometimes seems to me as if he was about to sweep it away." Influenza, measles, whooping cough, and smallpox decimated the population in turn. Mercy Whitney described the deathlike stillness which reigned in her village during one influenza epidemic when she alone was on her feet and able to minister to anyone. Lucia Lyons, during another, took child after child into her home to nurse, only to keep the deathwatch. The mission concluded, "God has hid himself in thick clouds and darkness. He has been doing his strange work."[54]

One happy day, a Hawaiian woman who sat by the cradle of Maria Chamberlain's baby, brushing the flies off his face, kindly praised Maria's and the other missionaries' activities. Formerly, she said, Hawaiians knew nothing about taking care of children, but gave them away to others to nurse. They knew nothing about domestic happiness; husbands and wives quarreled, committed adultery, drank, lied, and stole. "Now we have put off all those things; we wish to obey the word of God to live together with love to take care of our children and have them wear clothes as the children of the missionaries."[55]

Such praise was rare; mission wives did not even believe it to be true. They had sought the path to a righteous goal in all good faith. Somewhere, somehow, they had lost their way.

CHAPTER EIGHT

Family Fortunes

> Missionaries were charged with accumulating
> wealth, and it did come about that lands
> given by the chiefs to the mission with a gen-
> erosity which recognized the benefits the
> nation had received at their hands and which
> lands were afterwards distributed among some
> of the missionary families, became in later
> years of great value and enriched their owners;
> and it is true that some of the missionaries
> upon reasonable grounds left the mission and
> engaged in secular pursuits, and were pros-
> pered; this is all true and let us rejoice that we
> have this illustration of the Master's words
> that every one that hath left houses or breth-
> ren or sisters or father or mother or children or
> lands, for His name sake, shall receive a hun-
> dred fold.
> —Sanford Ballard Dole, presidential address
> to the Hawaiian Mission Children's Society,
> 1888

The early 1850s ushered in a period of significant change in the lives of mission families. On the one hand, the Great Mahele had opened up the right of foreigners, along with Hawaiians, to purchase land, and hence the basis was laid for the economic development of the islands on capitalistic lines. On the other, the home missionary plan coincidentally offered the missionaries diversified means of sustaining their families in the islands, while the possibility now existed for a livelihood completely independent of the American parent body. The ramifications of these twin developments influenced markedly the lives of the mission party in the second half of the nineteenth century. In their deliberations over the material directions which it was proper to take, missionaries in the late 1840s and early 1850s reiterated that they could never forget the needs of the Hawaiian church and nation, "the child of our adoption." As they had clung to Hawaiians' interests, which were woven into their very existence, through all weathers, so they desired to spend their lives raising Hawaiians to "a higher rank."[1]

It was the future of the children of their loins, however, which for the most part appeared the more pressing obligation, many of whom by the early 1850s had not only reached full maturity but looked down from a greater height on their parents. The children were numerous, their parents' desire for their future livelihoods acute, and most missionaries welcomed the change in their circumstances for that reason. "It is pleasant to be situated so that we can do good, and yet, not be objects of charity, or live on the charity of the churches," Clarissa Armstrong had told her brother when Richard Armstrong took up his government post as minister in charge of education in 1848. Some missionaries were apprehensive at the thought of change, looking to their graying hair and spectacles to excuse their feelings of inadequacy at the thought of generating income by pursuits more proper for thrusting youths. But those who disliked the common-stock system, or the salary system which replaced it, and who had felt like beggars on the receiving end of slightly grudging handouts, welcomed the changed circumstances. To them, the possibilities, materially at least, were exciting.[2]

The New Materialism

Troubles in the mission began, however, immediately with the division of mission property, houses, lands, and herds, which the American Board handed over for judicious allocation among those currently in occupation who expressed a firm intention of remaining for life in the islands. The American Board's plan had been that ministers should seek all their support, or part of it, from their Hawaiian congregations, while recognizing that some would supplement their keep with the modest means of American pastors: They might keep some cows, or plant a small crop, or purchase some further minor holding. Anything which smacked of bargain or trade solely to get rich, rather than to supply honest wants by the sweat of their brows, the board angrily opposed. Within the mission, too, there were those ready to denounce any intrusion of the "money-making and soul-neglecting world" which thought only of its own profit. Some mission families acquired the choice premises, others were envious. Some missionaries pressed for acquisition of properties vacated by others, raising the ire of the board. There was an undignified and heated demarcation dispute over a piece of land between the Honolulu and Punahou missionaries, in which many "unkind and unchristian" things were said.[3]

There were worse eventualities than disputes over mission property. Many missionaries, unhappy with the prospect of further years of parsimonious living off a poor and fast-dwindling Hawaiian parish, made a yearly case for continuing American support. They had growing families to educate and get established in life, and they faced in the islands sudden enticing opportunities. Some would seize them. As early as November 1849, Maria Chamberlain, newly widowed, complained to Rufus Anderson's wife Eliza that the mission was greatly changed from its earlier pursuit of "disinterested benevolence." Henry Dimond, for example, now stood behind a counter in the town, retailing goods. Two years later Maria informed Rufus directly that, though she did not want to turn accuser of the brethren, some were purchasing land in a way she found shocking when she recalled the instructions given her mission band on its departure all those years before. The Emersons, Gulicks, and Armstrongs were implicated; missionaries constantly accused one another of becoming worldly, while each man in turn claimed himself to be acting honorably. Even the sisters, she reported next, were infected with the new materialism: Ursula Emerson and Mercy Whitney no longer provided mission families in Honolulu with butter, but sold it for the highest price they could find.[4]

A few other individual missionaries supported Maria's evaluation of the situation. Securing houses, lands, herds, merchandise, and a temporal inheritance for their children seemed to absorb parents' minds; at meetings they even perverted Scripture to justify their course. Titus Coan, for one, lay much of the blame on the American Board, which seemed in a mood to overlook "the most palpable plodding and engrossing worldliness" if it saved money for the American churches. But the board believed that the distinction it made about acceptable economic behavior was not only critical but easily recognizable. In 1851 Rufus Anderson protested at what he viewed as a deterioration in propriety and discipline. The new provisions relaxed no one's paramount responsibilities to spiritual interest, nor was anyone at liberty to become "a legislator, mechanic, surveyor, land-broker or specula-tor, trader, banker, or money-maker." The missionaries' private and family interests would be most effectively secured by seeking to estab-lish the Kingdom of God in the islands. What good was their connec-tion with the board if this was not their grand object? What good would it do for the board to arrest a homeward drift by missionaries if only to give stronger stimulus for worldly provision for their children in the islands? No one in America had the slightest intention of changing the mission into a "mere secular community," certainly not into a "colony."[5]

For missionaries bent on capital accumulation, the way out was to sever all ties with the board and seek an entirely independent liveli-hood. Some, Gerrit Judd, Richard Armstrong, and Lorrin Andrews, were already in government employment by the end of the 1840s. More now departed for fresh fields. Samuel Castle and Amos Cooke converted their mission trading concern into a business embracing all comers. Edwin Hall joined the government printing service and pro-ceeded from there to develop the firm of E. O. Hall and Sons. Wil-liam Rice left to manage the Lihue sugar plantation; Elias Bond devel-oped a plantation at Kohala. The impetus to trade arising from the California gold rushes favored commercial development at just the right time. Other missionaries remained connected with the American Board under the new scheme, though often only partially supported from America. The obvious means of securing capital, however, for both groups, was through land dealing.

"Naturally," observed historian Jean Hobbs in her 1935 study of land dealings in nineteenth-century Hawaii, "as thrifty New En-glanders would be expected to do, they [the missionaries] acquired land and with their interests bound up in the future of the country bent their energies toward achieving a sound prosperity."[6] Viewed from this perspective, viewed from the perspective of most mission-aries themselves, the acquisition of land seemed a prudent, Christian decision, accompanied in the case of those like John Emerson with a sincerely held attachment to the good of Hawaiian smallholders as well as the good of the mission children. Viewed from the perspective of later protagonists for the Hawaiian people, the missionaries' land dealings could only appear distinctly problematic.

All missionaries who had served at least eight years in the islands, who did not already own five hundred and sixty acres of land, were allowed by the government to buy up to that amount at fifty cents below current prices. Moreover, land was often given by chiefs to missionaries, indicated by the description of sale for "one dollar and services rendered." But missionaries also purchased land on the open market—not just for their occupation, but to sell for a profit. Some, of course, were much less skillful at this style of speculative wheeling and dealing than others and made little. Most showed a net profit, though, either in substantial holdings or in money amassed. Standing out against the tide were Lydia Brown, Maria Chamberlain, and Mercy Whitney, who, as spinster and widows, acquired no land.[7] Abner Wilcox, Jonathon Green, and Lorenzo Lyons acquired modest holdings and did not alienate them. Maria Ogden was given only thirty-eight acres and sold them to Edward Bailey for $50. Of the many who dealt in land, in the sense that a great deal more passed through their hands than they retained but made no great profit, some had alienated land cheaply to their children at a low price. (John Paris, for example, who acquired in his lifetime some twenty-four thousand acres, sold at least ten thousand acres to his children.)

An outstanding group showed hefty gains from land dealing, either in land retained or in financial profit. William Alexander made $12,974 from such trading, Claudius Andrews $12,441, Peter Gulick $10,791, and Lowell Smith $10,000. Edward Bailey made the massive profit of $77,586. Richard Armstrong ended his life owning 2,966 acres of land, Elias Bond 2,363 acres, John Emerson 2,597 acres, John Paris 11,746 acres. Gerrit Judd finally made $12,379 from land dealing and owned 3,696 acres of land.[8] Compared with the extent of land which missionaries might have acquired, few gains were excessive. Such dealing as occurred, however, scarcely matched the American Board's injunction against a "worldly spirit."

Fractured Friendships and Rapid Aging

The change of the mission organization to home missionary status, and the withdrawal of the American Board from official connection with the mission in 1863, did not markedly alter the material situation for mission wives; only perhaps Mary Rice and Mary Castle lived long enough to enjoy wealth. Of forty-one women who lived their lives out in the islands, or at least until old age, twenty-three lived to

see in the decade of the 1880s and six witnessed the dawn of the new
century. For these women who had survived the vulnerable childbearing years, twenty-eight saw out their promised span of three score
years and ten, and nineteen saw their eightieth birthdays. Of the
thirty-nine who were married women, twenty-four outlived their husbands, twelve living in a widowed state for twenty years or more. (Six
widowed men remarried in their later years.) The somewhat less
straitened circumstances of some households did not become trans-
lated into noticeably more comfortable living: Profits were made to
invest in the children, not in luxuries for themselves. The new situation was scarcely less alienating for many women. Many of the foreign
group at large became distinctly more affluent, with carriages and
ostentatious living conditions. Within the mission itself, the reorganization had left many fractured friendships. Clarissa Armstrong for one
mourned in 1859 the creeping in of "cold contemptuous treatment"
of fellow Christians. The Johnsons and the Wilcoxes at Hanalei were
immersed in a petty feud, the Dimonds' injuries rankled, the Cookes
tried to carve off a slice of Maria Chamberlain's back yard, so that
Maria refused as much as a ride in the Cooke's carriage. Maria Kinney
refused to speak to the Damons because of Samuel's free remarks on
her character, nor would she associate with the Smiths. The Judds continued under heavy suspicion of worldliness. "Pride, luxury, ease,
envy, and tale-bearing too much abound. Doubtless there are secret
chambers where the saints meet their God but I have not yet found
them," Titus Coan informed Fidelia about the Honolulu scene in
1856.⁹

   Widows like Mercy Whitney, Maria Chamberlain, and Rebecca
Hitchcock, struggling alone, soon felt the absence of their breadwinner and handyman, despite their salary equivalent to that paid to the
single women: It was not sufficient to keep the roof over their heads
repaired without stringent effort. Maria took in boarders, while she
watched adobe walls crumble, the pump fail, the well bucket break,
and tradesmen charge a dollar per day for labor amidst the California
gold-rush boom. Meanwhile, she needed a bathhouse and a place
built for poultry and a pig. Rebecca Hitchcock accepted her sons'
help, despite the awful sense of being "an *expense* rather than a *profit*
to her sons." At least the presentation of some false teeth gave her joy:
"The great luxury of masticating my food has been enjoyed for about
3 months, as also the ability to read aloud, and speak plainly," Rebec-

ca reported to the board. She went at long last to live on son Edward's plantation, where she read the Bible and prayed with his Hawaiian laborers.[10]

On Kauai, Mercy Whitney tried to live on her $150 annual allowance, supplemented with a *kalo* patch purchased with her own money, determined to keep independent if at all possible. She observed with amazement the technological miracles of the new age: How short seemed the distance between the United States and the islands! To her sister Emily she wrote in 1863: "Well, prophecy is being fulfilled, and the ends of the earth will soon meet. The President's message was recd at Honolulu, printed, and in the hands of the people, in 14 days after it was delivered in Washington. Such improvements as are now being made, I did not 40 years ago, ever expect to see. But those who come after us and are on the stage of action some 40 or 50 years hence, will witness still greater improvements. We live in an age of wonders." Mercy died at the station she had served for fifty-two years.[11]

The mission marriages stayed strong to the end. If ever a match was made in heaven, it was the Alexanders', said one of their sons at the couple's golden wedding anniversary in 1881. Yet life for the women, whose spouses remained alongside them, was by no means always financially affluent and was, besides, decidedly mundane. One morning in Hilo in November 1852, Fidelia Coan set out to write a letter, but the forenoon passed "between beggars, borrowers, buyers, sellers, and callers." She became an unenthusiastic potterer about the house, recognizing easier circumstances by requesting some paper hangings from America, a sofa and new chairs, and a harmonium. Fidelia took in boarders from time to time, wearing out her nerves and strength. "Will there ever be an end to this boarding business until there is an end of me?" she exclaimed one day after nine straight months of "women and children, visitors and boarders." The departure of her last child, once the source of so much tension, simply depressed her further: "Nature weeps and bleeds. It is not so hard to go from home as to have home go from you. . . . If our children are well off when absent from us, we will be satisfied for their sakes." Lucia Lyons at Waimea occupied herself and made a little money by taking in some girls, often white or part Hawaiian, as boarding scholars till the last left in 1879, the only thing, it seemed to her, she could do in her circumstances. Her husband pitied his able wife's isolation, mostly with just her daughter for adult company. "It is certainly very trying to live so. I endure it much better than Elizabeth and Mother—to live so is a great grief to them."[12]

At Hilo, Sarah Lyman, too, kept the routine household affairs ticking over, weeping in her heart as her children scattered, praying to the God who understood perfectly "the height and depth, the length and breadth of a mother's heart, a mother's trials." She grieved over the nature of her children's early years. God knew how she had tried to make home as sunny as possible, but there had seldom been much sunshine in her heart. Aging rapidly, in her journal she wrote out, somewhat surprisingly, a quotation she found pertinent: "The fact is I don't know anything and don't do anything, but just get through the day somehow, wondering what all this strange unfamiliar state of things will end in." Laura Judd in Honolulu sustained a more vigorous style, dreaming that if she had an unmarried adult daughter to keep house, she would set up a milliner's shop, keep boarders, set up school, write a book. She engaged in cautious matchmaking for her daughters, kept a close eye on the Hawaiian royal family, and entertained Lady Jane Franklin on her visit in 1861. The mission wives found Laura more acceptable in her later maturity. "She seems to know her bearings better than formerly, and to vibrate less between popularity and piety," one said. Enfeeblement came relatively early, in 1872, with a stroke which removed her power of speech.[13]

Laura Judd wrote her book of reminiscences, as did Lucy Thurston after her. Lucy had a breast tumor removed without anesthetic in 1854 and kept a girls' school for a spell. She wrote to the board on behalf of Asa in 1866 requesting extra funds to repair their cottage which had dry rot, sinking pillars, doors which would not open, and a roof which leaked in all five rooms. Lucy nursed Asa till his death in March 1868, and then frankly requested extra funds for some comfort in her widowhood, including a carriage. Once she had gone contentedly in a chair strung on two poles, but at seventy-three years, no longer. She complained in no uncertain terms when, on Asa's death, the *Missionary Herald* ceased to arrive: "Mr. and Mrs. Thurston stood shoulder to shoulder through all the ups and downs of pioneer missionary life. For 48 years they received and read together the Missionary Herald. Then Mr. Thurston slept in death. Mrs. Thurston lived on. But with silent dignity she is made to understand that the Missionary Herald is no longer to be laid upon her centre table. The man has gone, *only woman* remains." Lucy made a will, leaving her house to her widowed daughter Mary, provided Lucy herself was well cared for and that if Mary married her husband "must be to Mary what the Prince Consort was to Victoria in her kingdom." (There was also some real estate for division in North Kona: "I advise the heirs to hold on to this land as I have done till the value of real estate is raised.") A visitor, Charles Nordoff, saw Lucy Thurston in 1873 as a "bright, active, lively old lady" with a shrewd wit, who drove herself to church on Sundays and had decided views on passing events. It puzzled him how she could have lived fifty years in the tropics without losing an atom of "the New England look"; clearly her appearance revealed the strength with which the missionaries had clung remorselessly to their habits of dress, living, thought, and the "ruthless determination which they imported, with their other effects, around Cape Horn."[14]

Politics and Progeny

There was little change in mission attitudes toward women's proper place in its activities. Women were admitted as voting members of the Hawaiian Missionary Society, established in 1851 as the governing body of the mission, and by the mid-1850s Charlotte Baldwin, the spinsters Lydia Brown and Maria Ogden, and the widows Mercy Whitney and Elizabeth Rogers were on the membership list. Women voted in elections of officers; their ballots changed little.[15] It was Clarissa Armstrong who nursed the deepest regret about the women's lot in the mission experience and she who sustained in later years efforts, frustrated as they were, to engage in work with Hawaiians. After Richard died in 1860, Clarissa felt more forcibly that Lowell Smith, the strong figure in the Honolulu parish, wanted to eject her from her customary classes: "Poor natives! Sin holds them back. Wicked men hold them back. Alas, how many who profess to love Christ hold them back . . . because their prejudices say, women should not lead men to Christ. Better let them stay away, than that a woman should tell [a] poor ignorant native how to get a passport to heaven . . .: let women keep silent—they may teach women, but never tell men, however ignorant, hungry or thirsty men may be, never a woman point them to Christ . . .![16]

Lowell Smith, Clarissa heard, had even told some Hawaiians that she was *pupuli* (bad), not in her right mind. She was edged also out of her women's meeting and watched with disguised pleasure the dwindling numbers. The "hydra head of bigotry and prejudice" caused the door of usefulness to move on its hinges and shut, she concluded by 1865. News of Northern women moving South to teach freed black men in the Civil War thrilled her. She confided in Lucia Lyons: "Naughty women, to presume to teach men! Some of *our* good ministers, drilled in N. England Theology, would tell them what Paul says. . . . If there is any reproach attached to ladies for teaching men 'niggers' they may clear themselves by saying that Paul did not forbid women from speaking in a tobacco barn, if he did in a church." Perhaps in this wonderful age, even Lowell Smith's bitter opposition to women would be overturned. Clarissa had the pleasure, too, of hearing of female temperance lecturers. Her fellow spirit, Mary Castle, welcomed two such women to Honolulu in the 1880s and helped form the Woman's Christian Temperance Union, with its platform of female suffrage, in the islands.[17]

For mission wives, it was the success of their children which provided their greatest satisfaction in their later years. "The children of the missionaries seem destined to possess the land," wrote Mary Parker in 1859, "not I hope by dispelling or driving out the Canaanites." Separated so often by distance, whether because children were studying or working in the United States or living elsewhere in the islands, mothers resorted to their powerful pens to counsel, warn, admonish, and reassure. Despite Punahou School, older children continued to be dispatched home for a college education in the face of Rufus Anderson's expostulation that the youth he met were already perfectly well educated. "Were I at present at the Islands," he wrote in 1851, "with my present views, I think I should send no *daughters* home; nor *sons* either, unless there were strong reasons, in the young men themselves, in favor of their receiving a highly liberal education." But no fewer than twenty-two mission children met in Williamstown for Henry Lyman's graduation in 1857 (the "Cannibal Convention," as some dubbed it). There were sufficient numbers living in New York in 1865 to form a society. Boys and girls graduated creditably, sometimes brilliantly, from Yale, Williams, Andover, Princeton, Oberlin, and Mount Holyoke.[18]

Some lads drifted to the California goldfields where, on a Sabbath morning, a group of mission sons could be found in clean clothes, reading the Bible together, as a result of their mothers' pleas. Others joined up for the North in the Civil War: Nathaniel Emerson, James Chamberlain, Munson Coan, Samuel Conde, three Forbes boys, Henry Lyman, and, most notably, the forceful Samuel Chapman Armstrong, who led a black regiment and stayed to found the Hampton Institute in Virginia as a manual training school for blacks. Mission daughters left colleges and moved south to teach the children of newly freed slaves: Jenny Armstrong, Sarah Coan, Mary Green. A number of daughters stayed in the States to teach, often marrying ministers; their brothers became college teachers, doctors, lawyers, scientists.[19]

If once mission mothers had been chary of pressing children to return to the islands, the new economic possibilities changed their attitudes. After 1850, some children reached maturity, in fact, without even a period of Americanization in their parents' homeland. A new frontier existed in Hawaii with opportunities to be exploited, and who better placed to benefit than the mission young who had been born and bred there? The children characterized themselves as uniquely prepared for the task of protecting Hawaiians against both unprincipled foreigners and oppressive ruling caste alike. It was to mission children, promised Asa Thurston Jr. in 1853, born in monarchical Hawaii but of republican principles, that Hawaiians could look as defenders and protagonists. Back to the islands they came, so many mission offspring, economic ambitions and a sense of mission nurtured in their breasts, to seek livelihoods in the land of their birth.[20]

Increasingly through the 1850s, 1860s, and beyond, the important presence of mission children became marked. Numbers of daughters took up teaching work, especially in privately run secondary schools. Hattie Coan and Emma Smith served at Punahou, Lydia Bingham and Lizzie Johnson at the Kawaiahao Female Seminary, Mary and Carrie Parker at the reform school for boys at Palama, Ellen Holden in a Hilo school for Hawaiians, Ella Paris in an English school in Kona, her sister Mary in a boarding school on Molokai. Other daughters married and turned to their mothers for advice. The oldest Castle girl, Mary, married to Edward Hitchcock, marooned on a plantation, was one who found full-time domesticity and motherhood a strain when she was hard pressed by a restless overactive son. She told her mother: "I know the fault must be mostly in me. I long for a resting place, not of body, but of mind and soul, and it seems to me that I shall never reach it. . . . It is, I think, this continual indoor life, as much as anything else, that takes away all one's life and energy. Why, if Edward was confined in the house one half of the time that I am, he would be stupid, and sleepy, and good for nothing."[21]

Mission sons, too, found openings in the islands: government posts, positions in mercantile and commercial establishments, professional work. The Henry Parker who once crept backward now strove forward to the pulpit of the Kawaiahao Church. Sereno Bishop, Anderson Forbes, and Joseph Green similarly engaged in religious pursuits. The most ambitious sought their fortunes on the land—in the plantations which appeared the only lucrative means to discover more than a modest livelihood. The movements of mission sons in just one year, 1865, indicate the search which had been set in train. Charles Judd purchased a ranch at Waimanalo, Oahu, from the Armstrongs; the husband of Elizabeth Judd bought the "Oahu Plantation" at Kualoa; the Chamberlain's plantation at Waialua began grinding; Joseph Emerson became manager of a plantation at Kaneohe, Oahu; Edward Bailey and his sons contemplated starting a sugar plantation at Wailuku; Samuel Alexander moved to Wailuku to engage in the sugar business though, not forgetting "higher claims," he assisted his father in the pulpit on Sundays. It was a fluid situation, and not a few sons failed. Others, however, prospered: the Alexanders and Baldwins (backed by Castle and Cooke money), the Wilcoxes, Elizabeth Judd Wilder's husband.

The lucrative partnership of William Alexander and Henry Baldwin was cemented by a significant tie: William married Henry's sister Abigail, and Henry in turn married William's sister Emily. Thirty-four mission children married within the mission fold—four in the Alexander family alone, three in the Lyman family, two in the Chamberlain, Clark, Cooke, Green, Rowell, and Wilcox households. Rarely did they marry those of Hawaiian or part-Hawaiian descent. Many mission betrothals, as well as a host of friendships and liaisons of an economic nature, were formed within an unusual association which older mission children formed in June 1852: the Hawaiian Mission Children's Society. The impetus had come from a gathering to farewell one of the Gulick boys, Halsey, who was about to depart for the new mission in Micronesia;[22] conspicuously few mission children went to foreign missions, but the Gulicks were shining exceptions. The "cousins," as the enthusiastic participants called themselves, pledged to raise money;

even the younger members braided watch chains (boys) and hemmed handkerchiefs (girls) for the cause. The toils of their parents were uppermost in their minds. "What a glorious privilege that we have such a *heritage*," thought founding member Persis Thurston Taylor, who had returned, said one mission wife, with the polish of mind and manners such as only New England could produce. Persis was the corresponding secretary, her brother Asa president, Caroline Armstrong vice-president, Orramel Gulick recording secretary, and Henry Whitney treasurer. Said Orramel Gulick: "If we who have been cradled in the lap of missions, whose earliest recollections take us back to the scenes of our parents' labors for this people, who have been from our earliest years familiar with the trials and blessings of the missionary life, if we the children of missionaries have not the missionary spirit, where shall the church and the world look for an exhibition of that spirit?"[23]

If the missionary spirit was not often to be manifested in the second generation in terms of personal service on a foreign field, it was to be shown in support for benevolent Christian causes abroad, but in Hawaii above all. Within a very short time the "cousins," who for the most part had been mere acquaintances or even strangers, met as friends and allies. The daughter of Rufus Anderson encountered the group some ten years later, when members were preparing the Punahou schoolhouse for their general meeting with American and Hawaiian flags and with wreaths bearing the mottos of "Unity," "Harmony," "Excelsior." Membership grew by leaps and bounds, as exiles abroad were contacted and as spouses and a few close associates were cautiously admitted. The second generation of the mission faced the new Hawaii from the security of a network of mutual support, solidarity, and affection based on common experiences of the past and common convictions about the future. By 1872 the membership, six hundred strong, represented a leading and influential component of the foreign population of the islands. Sereno Bishop, retiring president, pointed out that they now formed a distinct body of whites of tropical birth. As a rule, European colonists' children degenerated in tropical lands, failures in manhood and virtue. They, on the other hand, had "preserved unimpaired the virtue, intelligence, and thrift of our ancestral race, avoiding degeneracy and maintaining progress." The mission children inherited from their parents, said Albert Lyons some eighteen years later, a richer bequest than gold—namely "the fruits of their work in the material prosperity which the Christian civilization they established here has made possible." Prosper they did, some of them impressively so.[24]

For Lucy Thurston, the Mission Children's Society seemed, perhaps, an offshoot of that other important earlier sodality, the Maternal Association. Another mission wife, Mary Rice, reflected in the late 1880s that it was not so strange that some of the mission children became rich when one considered "the habits of temperance, economy, and diligence in which they were trained." Other missionaries felt sad, however, at the price—namely the plight of Hawaiians, displaced from their habitual occupation of the land and rapidly displaced, too, by Asian laborers, in the work force of the new capitalist entrepreneurs. "The country is being drained to fill up a few seaports," wrote Titus Coan, "and to work a few plantations where the mower and the reaper gather in the harvest of death." Where once children played and families lived, luxuriant grasses now waved in silence and solitude. Missionaries had dreamed of small farming households, charming villages, a prosperous yeomanry. Instead, ordinary Hawaiians became marginalized economically and socially, just as in turn the ruling Hawaiian elite eventually became superseded politically. The missionaries' Hawaiian protégés suffered, ironically, from the economic individualism to which missionaries themselves, in all good conscience, gave birth.[25]

Hawaiian Christians kept the faith in terms of their own religious construction of reality. In 1853 the Hawaiian church sent Hawaiian missionaries to the Marquesas Islands, where Americans had earlier failed. Eliza Anderson, wife of the American Board secretary, called by ten years later to tell Hawaiian women, once again, to be keepers at home, transforming their humble dwellings into centers of love for homecoming husbands and domesticated children. Christians showed their mettle perhaps in other ways, quietly and patiently supporting from their meager resources religious and community needs, as death took its sad toll on their number. It was not Hawaiian church leaders, however, who shaped the character of the new Hawaii. Among those, for the most part men, who did, mission children were to the fore. In business, church, and state, in all positions of responsibility, and in every organization of any standing, the "cousins" were found as leaders, officers, or members; so the second generation congratulated themselves by the turn of the century, having duly manifested a sense of momentary solemnity at the lowering of the Hawaiian flag upon American annexation in 1898. On the centenary of the landing of the first missionaries, many could agree that it had been the missionaries, their children, and their grandchildren who had been responsible for Hawaii's character, for her "Christianization, her civilization, her Americanization, her preservation from other designing nations until the time was ripe for her incorporation into the United States to fulfil her destiny as the military and naval defense outpost to the Pacific Coast, as the commercial half-way station between the Occident and the Orient."[26]

This situation did not match the original vision the mission wives had in mind when they made their eager commitment to foreign mission service. Fear of the threat of Hawaiian culture for their young had first kept these women from the full engagement they had sought. Ironically, their young had assimilated American culture so fully that they in turn helped conquer economically the Hawaiian society which their parents sought, once, to save spiritually.

Agendas and Consequences

Mission wives had come to Hawaii with their husbands as part of a separate female agenda: the conversion and reform of ignorant sinners in a pagan, distant society. They had not been camp followers but independent recruits, part of an evangelical outreach which had emerged from the material and ideological transformations of north-eastern America in the early nineteenth century. With the males of their group, their goals had been to redeem, for disciplined, pure, and holy ways of living, a society held to be degraded and disordered when judged by the rigid values of their American culture. The presence of American mission wives broadened the model of Christian concepts of proper behavior by providing not only insight into adult female roles but insight into the ordering of marriage, parenting, and family life, with all its material and sentimental implications. Wives, in addition, actively promoted American Christian culture, always more constrained by the complexity of tasks which was their due, but significant figures nevertheless in the process of acculturation of Hawaiian subjects. An account of the mission in Hawaii which leaves unexplored the importance of the wives' attempts to transmit new notions, along with the men's, leaves unrecognized the intricate nature of the mission's task and unappreciated the range of adaptive strategies pressed upon Hawaiians of elite and commoner class alike.

In the annals of missiology, the success of the mission to Hawaii was remarkable: On paper, results seemed swift and decisive. Mission wives' own assessment of their experiences, however, differed markedly from received wisdom. They felt, by contrast, a pervasive disappointment in the outcome of their venture, amounting in rare cases to bitterness at the restrictions on their careers. Wives did not articulate resentment at their frequent childbearing, which was accepted as inevitable. The demands on women for American-style housekeeping, and the responsibility mothers were forced to assume for childrearing, however, were experienced as oppressive, though few could attribute blame to anything other than the novel circumstances of their situation. The assumption of a domestic burden first prevented as active a participation as the men's in the public mission work. Further, however, the notion of the sex-specific nature and role of women was used deliberately to restrain mission wives from extending the boundaries of female participation in a direction which conflicted with male dominance. For women who had sacrificed a good deal to reach a mission field, the situation could only be regarded with ambivalence.

The defeat of this female mission endeavor was effected in part by patriarchal notions of male dominance; yet nowhere were such ideas embedded more usefully than in many mission women's consciousnesses themselves. The glorification of American motherhood which arose simultaneously with women's loss of significant economic functions in the household economy implied better conditions of childrearing in many cases; it also implied the formulation of proper femininity in such a way as to confine married women just as securely to the domestic sphere. Mission wives embraced the enhanced importance given to motherhood. Any hope that a few more stalwart souls might have withstood the pressure was negated by another factor in their worldview, one shared by their menfolk: their intense ethnocentricity, amounting in late twentieth-century evaluations to racism. The wives believed, like the abolitionists they were, in the equal value of all souls in the sight of God and in the redemptability of all men and women. Faced with the power of an alien culture on their own young, however, the Americanization and conversion of mission children took precedence over the teaching career for which the women yearned. In the last analysis, it was the wives' own cultural rigidity, combined with a division of labor that advantaged the men, which proved the stumbling block.

One could not describe the wives' own evaluation of their plight without, however, considering the character of their enterprise in less subjective terms. Mission wives were extremely influential, whether on their own terms or not, and contributed substantially to the religious conversion and reorientation of Hawaiian culture in the first half of the nineteenth century. This cultural encounter, assessed in terms of Hawaiian women, could be described at best as uneasy. With a self-confidence amounting to arrogance, with the insensitivity and self-righteousness which were the unpleasant face of the mission wives' endeavor, Hawaiian women were to be brought, no matter what the cost in suffering, into American ways. On the other hand, Hawaiian women were in any case already exposed to foreign influences. And whereas those other encounters might be less tense, an unfortunate outcome in terms of venereal disease, the ill effects of drugs, and the proletarianization of the Hawaiian work force were proceeding apace. Mission wives did offer Hawaiian girls and women an opportunity of value—an introduction not only into the metaphysical system but into the skills and knowledge of that Western society which increasingly dominated their world.

Such Hawaiian women as were "successful" in nineteenth-century Hawaii served an apprenticeship in the American mission program. Yet ultimately the American women's activities could prove of only marginal value to the majority of Hawaiians who survived the ravages of imported diseases. American prescriptions of true femininity were based on an economic organization which it proved impossible to replicate for Hawaiians. The notion of the male breadwinner, the small farmer or artisan, supporting a wife and family in modest comfort was a dream which faded before it could emerge. The wives' own ambitions for their children had been basic to this failure, though in a fashion the women were incapable of realizing. The mission women had come to Hawaii to "do good"; their children "did well." The mission wives had offered Hawaiian women a competency in skills with which to negotiate a new social system, yet the rigid application of American ways drove both groups of women into an unhappy encounter. Eventually the depopulation of the islands, combined with the substitution of Asian for Hawaiian labor in capitalist enterprises, negated the possibility that a material basis for the fuller adaptation to American culture could soon develop.

American Christians attempted to eulogize the lives of surviving mission women, using their experience to appeal to others of their sex to show forth the missionary spirit. Of Lucy Thurston an American cleric wrote in the *Church Missionary Register* in 1868 that she had taught Hawaiian men to love their wives, Hawaiian women to love their husbands, Hawaiian children to obey their parents, as she taught all to honor the Lord. "So she carried into the huts of that dark land those blessed words—Love, Virtue, Home, Jesus, Heaven."[27] Indeed, Lucy and her compatriots had made such an effort. They died unconvinced of victory, however, and with good reason. There were few at home or abroad who could comprehend their plight. Their children and grandchildren, and those of their protégés, lived on to confront, from a position of uneven political strength, the consequences.

NOTES

All letters are held in the Hawaiian Mission Society's archive under "Missionary Letters" and all journals under "Missionary Journals" unless otherwise stated.

INTRODUCTION

1. P. Bidwell, *Rural New England at the Beginning of the Nineteenth Century* (New York: A. M. Kelley, 1972 [1916]); D. North, *The Economic Growth of the United States, 1790–1860* (New York: Norton, 1966).

2. Nancy Cott, *The Bonds of Womanhood: "Woman's Sphere" in New England, 1780–1835* (New Haven: Yale University Press, 1977); T. Dublin, *Women at Work: The Transformation of Work and Community in Lowell, Massachusetts, 1826–1869* (New York: Columbia University Press, 1979).

3. K. Sklar, *Catharine Beecher: A Study in American Domesticity* (New Haven: Yale University Press, 1973); L. Kerber, "Daughters of Columbia: Educating Women for the Republic, 1787–1805," in E. McKitrick and S. Elkins (eds.), *The Hofstadter Aegis* (New York: Knopf, 1974); G. Lerner, "The Lady and the Mill Girl: Changes in the Status of Women in the Age of Jackson, 1800–1840," *Midcontinent American Studies Journal* 10 (Spring 1969): 5–14; A. Douglas, *The Feminization of American Culture* (New York: Knopf, 1977); B. Welter, "The Feminization of American Religion: 1800–1860," in M. Hartman and L. Banner (eds.), *Clio's Consciousness Raised: New Perspectives on the History of Women* (New York: Harper & Row, 1974); M. Ryan, *Cradle of the Middle Class: The Family in Oneida County, New York, 1790–1865* (Cambridge: Cambridge University Press, 1981); B. Welter, "The Cult of True Womanhood 1820–1860," *American Quarterly*

18 (1966): 151–174; C. Smith-Rosenberg, "Beauty, the Beast, and the Militant Woman: A Case Study of Sex Roles and Social Stress in Jacksonian America," *American Quarterly* 23 (October 1971): 562–564.

4. *Panoplist and Missionary Magazine,* February 1819, p. 67; see Cott, *Bonds of Womanhood,* p. 33, and P. Kaufman, *Women Teachers on the Frontier* (New Haven: Yale University Press, 1984).

5. W. Cross, *The Burned-Over District* (Ithaca: Cornell University Press, 1950); W. McLoughlin, *Revivals, Awakenings and Reform: An Essay on Religion and Social Change in America, 1607–1977* (Chicago: University of Chicago Press, 1978), chap. 4; J. Andrew, *Rebuilding the Christian Commonwealth: New England Congregationalists and Foreign Missions, 1800–1830* (Lexington: University of Kentucky Press, 1976); N. Cott, "Young Women in the Second Great Awakening," *Feminist Studies* 3 (1975): 15–29.

6. C. Smith-Rosenberg, "The Female World of Love and Ritual: Relations Between Women in Nineteenth Century America," *Signs* 1 (Autumn 1975): 1–29; C. Lasch and W. Taylor, " 'Two Kindred Spirits': Sorority and Family in New England, 1839–1845," *New England Quarterly* 36 (1963): 23–41; Cott, *Bonds of Womanhood,* chap. 5; G. Lerner, *The Grimké Sisters from South Carolina: Rebels Against Slavery* (Boston: Houghton Mifflin, 1967); E. DuBois, *Feminism and Suffrage: The Emergence of an Independent Women's Movement in America 1848–1869* (Ithaca: Cornell University Press, 1978); K. Melder, *Beginnings of Sisterhood: The American Woman's Rights Movement, 1800–1850* (New York: Schocken, 1977); B. Hersh, *The Slavery of Sex: Feminist-Abolitionists in America* (Urbana: University of Illinois Press, 1978).

7. R. Berkhofer, *Salvation and the Savage: An Analysis of Protestant Missions and American Indian Response, 1787–1862* (Lexington: University of Kentucky Press, 1965); W. McLoughlin, *Cherokees and Missionaries 1789–1839* (New Haven: Yale University Press, 1984). For a study of the first London Missionary Society mission in the Pacific, see N. Gunson, *Messengers of Grace: Evangelical Missionaries in the South Seas 1797–1860* (Melbourne: Oxford University Press, 1978).

8. P. Smith, *Daughters of the Promised Land: Women in American History* (Boston: Little, Brown, 1970), p. 182; J. Brumberg, *Mission for Life: The Story of the Family of Adoniram Judson* (New York: Free Press, 1980); *Missionary Herald,* November 1825, pp. 360–361; C. Beecher, *A Treatise on Domestic Economy* (New York: Schocken, 1977 [1841]), p. 13.

9. Andrew, *Rebuilding the Christian Commonwealth,* R. Anderson, *History of the Sandwich Islands Mission* (Boston: Congregational Publishing Society, 1870), pp. 99–101; Hawaiian Mission Children's Society (HMCS), *Missionary Album* (Honolulu: HMCS, 1969).

10. "A Lady," *Conversations on the Sandwich Islands Mission* (Boston: Massachusetts Sabbath School Union, 1829), p. 6.

11. The following description of traditional Hawaiian society is derived from D. Malo, *Hawaiian Antiquities* (Honolulu: Bishop Museum Press, 1980 [1898]); J. Ii, in D. Barrere (ed.), *Fragments of Hawaiian History* (Honolulu: Bishop Museum Press, 1983); S. Kamakau, in D. Barrere (ed.), *Ka Po'e Kahiko: The People of Old* (Honolulu: Bishop Museum Press, 1979); S. Kamakau, *The Works of the People of Old* (Honolulu: Bishop Museum Press, 1976); M. Sahlins, *Social Stratification in Polynesia* (Seattle: University of Washington Press, 1958); I. Goldman, *Ancient Polynesian Society* (Chicago: University of Chicago Press, 1970); E. Handy and others, *Ancient Hawaiian Civilization* (Honolulu: Kamehameha Schools, 1933); E. Handy and M. Pukui, *The Polynesian Family System in Ka'u, Hawai'i* (Rutland: Charles E. Tuttle, 1972); W. Ellis, *Polynesian Researches: Hawaii* (Rutland: Charles E. Tuttle, 1974 [1842]); A. Fornander, *An Account of the Polynesian Race,* 3 vols. in 1 (Rutland: Charles E. Tuttle, 1969 [1778–1885]).

12. The sexual dichotomy embedded in traditional Polynesian religious constructs has been treated recently in F. Hanson, "Female Pollution in Polynesia," *Journal of Polynesian Society (JPS)* 9 (3) (September 1982): 335–382; S. Ortner, "Gender and Sexuality in Hierarchical Societies: The Case of Polynesia and Some Comparative Implications," in S. Ortner and H. Whitehead (eds.), *Sexual Meanings: The Cultural Construction of Gender and Sexuality* (Cambridge: Cambridge University Press, 1981).

13. See G. Daws, *Shoal of Time: A History of the Hawaiian Islands* (Honolulu: University of Hawaii Press, 1968); R. Kuykendall, *The Hawaiian Kingdom, 1778–1854,* vol. 1, (Honolulu: University of Hawaii Press, 1938); C. Ralston, "Hawaii 1778–1854: Some Aspects of *Maka'ainana* Response to Rapid Cultural Change," *Journal of Pacific History* 19 (1–2) (1984): 21–40; H. Bradley, *The American Frontier in Hawaii: The Pioneers 1789–1843* (Gloucester, Mass.: Peter Smith, 1968); M. Sahlins, *Historical Metaphors and Mythical Realities: Structure in the Early History of the Sandwich Islands Kingdom* (Ann Arbor: University of Michigan Press, 1981).

14. H. Bingham, *A Residence of Twenty-one Years in the Sandwich Islands* (Rutland: Charles E. Tuttle, 1981 [1847]), p. 169; Anderson, *History of the Sandwich Islands Mission,* p. 33.

15. Kuykendall, *Hawaiian Kingdom,* p. 100; Daws, *Shoal of Time,* p. 104. See also B. Smith, *Yankees in Paradise: The New England Impact on Hawaii* (Philadelphia: Lippincott, 1956).

16. For a thorough examination of women's history, see B. Carroll (ed.), *Liberating Women's History: Theoretical and Critical Essays* (Urbana: University of Illinois Press, 1976); C. Smith-Rosenberg, "The New Woman and the New History," *Feminist Studies* 3 (1/2) (1975): 185–198; N. Z. Davis, " 'Women's History' in Transition: The European Case," *Feminist Studies* 3 (1976): 83–103; J. Kelly-Gadol, "The Social Relations of the Sexes: Methodological Implications of Women's History," *Signs* 1 (1976): 809–823.

17. M. Whitney to C. Ely, 25 June 1828; F. Coan to M. Robinson, May 1836; F. Coan to E. Anderson, 20 January 1837; F. Coan to T. Coan, 15 December 1836.

18. F. Coan to M. Robinson, 24 October 1836; J. Cooke to M. Montague, 23 November 1841; S. Lyman, "Journal 1830-1863," May 1863.

CHAPTER 1

1. L. Thurston, *Life and Times of Mrs. Lucy G. Thurston* (Honolulu: The Friend, 1934 [1882]), pp. 3 and 248; L. Thurston to M. Howe, 21 February 1828.

2. Thurston, *Life and Times,* pp. 242-247; L. Thurston to M. Howe, 21 February 1828.

3. D. Kirkpatrick, *The City and the River: The Story of Fitchburg, Massachusetts* (Fitchburg: Fitchburg Historical Society, 1971), pp. 122-123; Thurston, *Life and Times,* p. 6.

4. Thurston, *Life and Times,* pp. 7 and 13.

5. Judd Family, *Fragments: Family Record of the House of Judd* (Honolulu: privately published, 1903), pp. 26-28.

6. Ibid., p. 27.

7. G. Judd, *Dr. Judd: Hawaii's Friend* (Honolulu: University of Hawaii Press, 1960).

8. Judd, *Family Record,* p. 28; *Mother's Magazine,* July 1833, p. 111; Judd, *Dr. Judd: Hawaii's Friend,* p. 38.

9. For birth dates and places see HMCS, *Missionary Album.*

10. C. Lyman to parents, 20 September 1822.

11. Gunson, *Messengers of Grace.*

12. R. Anderson, "Introductory Essay to the American Edition," in W. Ellis, *Memoir of Mary Ellis* (Boston: Crocker & Brewster, 1836), p. viii.

13. Background information on the male missionaries is from C. Phillips, *Protestant America and the Pagan World* (Cambridge: Harvard University Press, 1969), p. 298; D. Baldwin to ABCFM, 25 February 1832, ABCFM-Hawaii papers; HMCS, *Missionary Album,* biographical entries; ABCFM, "Letters of Candidacy," ABCFM-Hawaii papers. See also numerous autobiographical and biographical publications on the male missionaries, such as J. Paris, *Fragments of Real Missionary Life* (Honolulu: The Friend, 1926).

14. D. Dole, "Testimonial request for Daniel Dole," in ABCFM, "Letters of Candidacy," ABCFM-Hawaii papers.

15. E. Rothman, *Hands and Hearts: A History of Courtship in America* (New York: Basic Books, 1984); see also M. Norton, *Liberty's Daughters: The Revolutionary Experience of American Women, 1750-1800* (Boston: Little, Brown, 1980).

16. See W. Alcott, *The Young Wife, or Duties of Women in the Marriage Relation* (New York: Arno Press, 1972 [1837]), pp. 69–78.

17. M. Kittredge to E. Clark, April 1823; E. Clark to M. Kittredge, 19 September 1824; F. Church to T. Coan, 10 February 1832; T. Coan to F. Church, 18 February 1832; M. Kittredge to E. Clark, 13 December 1824; T. Coan to F. Church, 12 June 1833.

18. L. Andrews to ABCFM, 1 August 1827, ABCFM, "Letters of Candidacy"; B. Munn to ABCFM, 23 March 1836, ABCFM, "Letters of Candidacy"; B. Munn to ABCFM, 6 April 1836, ABCFM, "Letters of Candidacy."

19. L. Andrews to ABCFM, 1 August 1827 (postscript), ABCFM, "Letters of Candidacy"; L. Andrews to ABCFM, 17 September 1827, ABCFM, "Letters of Candidacy."

20. B. Munn to ABCFM, 23 March 1836, ABCFM, "Letters of Candidacy"; B. Munn to ABCFM, 8 August 1836, ABCFM, "Letters of Candidacy"; C. Knapp, "Journal 1836–1846," 1 April 1837.

21. D. Baldwin to ABCFM, 27 March 1829, ABCFM, "Letters of Candidacy"; D. Baldwin to ABCFM, 24 August 1830, ABCFM, "Letters of Candidacy"; D. Baldwin to ABCFM, 21 September 1830, ABCFM, "Letters of Candidacy"; D. Baldwin, to ABCFM, 16 October 1830, ABCFM, "Letters of Candidacy."

22. D. Baldwin to ABCFM, 29 October 1830, ABCFM, "Letters of Candidacy"; D. Baldwin to ABCFM, 2 December 1830, ABCFM, "Letters of Candidacy"; M. Alexander, *Dr. Baldwin of Lahaina* (Stanford: Stanford University Press, 1952), pp. 8–9; M. Noyes and Church Committee, Testimonial for C. Fowler, 30 November 1830, ABCFM, "Letters of Candidacy."

23. H. Humphrey to E. Fitch (Yale College), 8 September 1819.

24. M. Partridge to J. Brewer, 4 February 1819.

25. M. Partridge to J. Brewer, 30 August 1819.

26. M. Partridge to E. Dow, 20 September 1819; M. Partridge to W. and L. Partridge, 27 September 1819; M. Partridge to E. Partridge, 25 September 1819; M. Whitney to Rev. J. and E. Dow, 4 November 1819.

27. L. Coan, *A Brief Sketch of the Missionary Life of Sybil Moseley Bingham* (n.p., n.d. [1895]), pp. 5–6; excerpt from Sybil Bingham's journal, 14 September 1820, in *Missionary Herald,* August 1821, p. 249; Coan, *Brief Sketch,* pp. 5–6.

28. L. Menton, " 'Everything That Is Lovely and of Good Report': The Hawaiian Chiefs' Children's School 1839–1850" (Ph.D. thesis, University of Hawaii, 1982), p. 59; C. Knapp, "Journal 1836–1846," 16 March 1837; M. Alexander, *Amos Starr and Juliette Montague Cooke: Their Autobiographies . . .* (Honolulu: privately published, 1941), p. 47; J. Montague to A. Cooke, 2 November 1836; J. Cooke to M. Montague, 12 December 1836.

29. R. Armstrong to ABCFM, 17 September 1831, ABCFM, "Letters of Candidacy"; H. Ludlow, "Clarissa Chapman Armstrong," in H. Haydn,

American Heroes on Mission Fields (New York: American Tract Society, 1894), pp. 256–258.

30. C. Chapman to Ludentia, 25 September 1831.

31. J. Cooke, "Journal Aboard the *Mary Frazier* 1837," 23 March 1837; Anderson, in Ellis, *Memoir of Mary Ellis*, p. xiii. See also ABCFM, "Answers by the Sandwich Islands Missionaries to Questions in the Circular of March 15, 1833 sent to the Missionaries of the ABCFM," typescript, HMSCL; ABCFM, "Agreement Signed at New Haven, 18 November 1822 by Ashbel Green, Charles Stewart and Betsey Stockton, Approved for the ABCFM by Jeremiah Evarts (Sec.)."

32. L. Chamberlain to ABCFM, 11 March 1824, ABCFM–Hawaii papers; L. Chamberlain to ABCFM, 15 October 1825, ABCFM–Hawaii papers.

33. S. Ruggles to ABCFM, 4 May 1836, ABCFM, "Letters of Candidacy"; [H. Kellogg] to ABCFM, 25 December 1835 and 4 January 1836, ABCFM, "Letters of Candidacy"; C. Knapp, "Journal 1836–1846," 17 March 1837; J. Hopkins to ABCFM, 5 April 1836, ABCFM, "Letters of Candidacy"; H. Smith to ABCFM, 4 April 1836, ABCFM, "Letters of Candidacy"; S. Ruggles to ABCFM, 4 May 1836, ABCFM, "Letters of Candidacy."

34. M. Parker, "Journal (C), Intimate Notebook," 29 September 1829 and [January] 1830; M. Parker, "Journal (B), Intimate Notebook," [1830]; M. Parker, "Journal (B)," n.d. [August 1832?] and September 1832. Mary Parker wrote to Charlotte Baldwin in Hawaii thirty years later a strongly affectionate letter thanking Charlotte for the last letter, which was "the voice of friendship and love, and *that* my heart"; please write again, she asked, telling "Dear, dear C." to describe all her joys, sorrows, hopes, and fears; could Charlotte come and visit?"; M. Parker to C. Baldwin, 27 January [1864]; HMCS, *Jubilee Celebration of the Arrival of the Missionary Reinforcement of 1837* (Honolulu: Daily Bulletin Steam Print, 1887), p. 197.

35. A. Bishop, "Account of the Early Life of Elizabeth Edwards Bishop," 1828; L. Goodale to Elizabeth, n.d; see E. Bishop [Edwards], "Journal, Fragments 1819–1820," 11 October 1819, 28 August 1822, 30 August 1822, 3 September 1822; E. Bishop to L. Thurston, 27 April 1823.

36. J. Spaulding, "Autobiographical Sketch," ABCFM–Hawaii papers; M. Frear, *Lowell and Abigail: A Realistic Idyll* (New Haven: privately published, 1934), p. 14; M. Whitney to Mrs. White, 3 February 1840; P. Taylor, address to "brothers and sisters," 23 October 1895, Children of the Mission; P. Thurston to P. Andrews, 27 December 1841, Children of the Mission; M. Lyon to ABCFM, 26 November 1841, ABCFM, "Letters of Candidacy."

37. W. Castle, *Life of Samuel Northrup Castle* (Honolulu: Castle Foundation, 1960), pp. 14–15; S. Castle to ABCFM, 12 August 1842, ABCFM, "Letters of Candidacy"; M. Smith to ABCFM, 19 August 1836, ABCFM, "Letters of Candidacy."

38. O. Emerson, *Pioneer Days in Hawaii* (New York: Doubleday, 1928), p. 16.

39. J. Cooke, "Journal Aboard the *Mary Frazier* 1837," 23 March 1837. Juliette said of Harriet McDonald, of New York City, "she has some city ways, but they are not very disagreeable to me." Approximately one in five white women in Massachusetts were teachers at some time in their lives, although less than one percent of young people attended college, and few were women. See R. Bernard and M. Vinovskis, "The Female Schoolteacher in Antebellum Massachusetts," *Journal of Social History* 10 (March 1977): 332–345.

40. E. Damon, *Father Bond of Kohala* (Honolulu: The Friend, 1927), p. 37; C. Knapp, "Journal 1836–1846," 18 March 1837; D. Dole to ABCFM, 28 October 1839, ABCFM, "Letters of Candidacy."

41. C. Lyman to E. Lyman, 9 November 1821.

42. F. Church to T. Coan, 23 March 1831; T. Coan to F. Church, 29 March 1831.

43. F. Church to T. Coan, April 1831.

44. F. Church to T. Coan, 14 June 1831.

45. T. Coan to F. Church, 23 June 1831.

46. E. Damon (ed.), *Letters from the Life of Abner and Lucy Wilcox 1836–1869* (Honolulu: privately published, 1950), pp. 12–13; Thurston, *Life and Times,* pp. 12–13; E. Doyle, *Makua Laiana: The Story of Lorenzo Lyons* (Honolulu: Advertiser Publishing, 1953), p. 3; L. Judd, "Friendship Book, 1826," HMCSL; S. Bingham to ABCFM, 23 October 1819; C. Lyman to E. Lyman, 9 November 1821.

47. Of seventy brides in the period 1819 to 1850, wed for the first time in the United States prior to going to the mission, the average age was 25.16 years and the median age 25.33 years. Brides ranged in age from 18 years (Betsy Curtis Lyons) to 38 years (Rebecca Johnstone). Thirty-three were between the ages of 18 and 24 years, thirty-one brides were between 25 and 29 years, and six were 30 years or older. The average age of grooms was 27.77 years, the median 28.14, a calculation which includes some second marriages after the death of a first wife. In eight matches, brides and grooms were the same age; in forty-six marriages, the groom was older than the bride (in the range of 1 to 11 years); in sixteen marriages, the bride was older than the groom (in the range of 1 to 5 years). Statistics calculated from HMCS, *Missionary Album.* The studies of Daniel Scott Smith on the village of Hingham found the average age of marriage for New England women rising to 23.7 years for the marriage cohort 1781–1800 and to 26.4 years for men; D. S. Smith, "The Demographic History of Colonial New England," in M. Gordon (ed.), *The American Family in Social-Historical Perspective* (New York: St. Martin's Press, 1973), p. 406. Maris Vinovskis, in *Fertility in Massachusetts from the Revolution to the Civil War* (New York: Academic Press, 1981),

suggests little change in Massachusetts, at least, in the first half of the nineteenth century (p. 49).

48. ABCFM, *Instructions of the Prudential Committee of the ABCFM to the Sandwich Island Mission* (Lahainaluna, Maui: Mission Press, 1838), p. 65.

49. Frear, *Lowell and Abigail*, p. 21.

CHAPTER 2

1. Bingham, *A Residence of Twenty-one Years*, pp. 53–54; *Panoplist and Missionary Magazine*, November 1819, pp. 527–528; Andrew, *Rebuilding the Christian Commonwealth*, p. 31.

2. ABCFM, *Instructions of the Prudential Committee*, p. 25.

3. Ibid., p. 31.

4. S. Castle, "A General Review of the Mission Work in Hawaii," in HMCS, *Jubilee Celebration*, pp. 11–12; Thurston, *Life and Times*, p. 22; S. Bingham, "Journal on *Thaddeus* and First Years in the Island 1819–1823," 8 November 1819; S. Ruggles and N. Ruggles, "Journal on Board the Brig *Thaddeus*, 1819–1820," 24 February 1820 (entry of N. Ruggles).

5. M. Whitney to brothers and sisters, 4 February 1820; S. Bingham, "Journal on *Thaddeus*," 26 November 1819; S. Bingham, "Journal on *Thaddeus*," 22 March 1820 and 30 November 1819.

6. Thurston, *Life and Times*, p. 30; S. Bingham, "Journal on *Thaddeus*," 30 and 31 March 1820; M. Loomis to Utica friend, 14 May 1820; S. Bingham, "Journal on *Thaddeus*," 30 March 1820.

7. Bingham, *A Residence of Twenty-one Years*, pp. 86–88; L. Holman, *Journal of Lucia Ruggles Holman*, Special Publication 17 (Honolulu: Bishop Museum, 1931), p. 7.

8. Bingham, *A Residence of Twenty-one Years*, p. 107.

9. Holman, *Journal*, p. 38.

10. L. Thurston to Mary Howe, 21 February 1828.

11. S. Bingham, "Journal on *Thaddeus*," 11 April 1820; Bingham, *A Residence of Twenty-one Years*, p. 95; N. Ruggles to L. Holman, 20 April 1820; M. Whitney, "Journal 1821–1860," 21 and 25 July 1820.

12. Bingham, *A Residence of Twenty-one Years*, p. 108; M. Loomis, "Journal 1819–1828," 21 June 1820; Thurston, *Life and Times*, p. 44; Holman, *Journal*, p. 28.

13. S. Ruggles and N. Ruggles, "Journal on Board the Brig *Thaddeus*," 8 May 1820, entry of S. Ruggles; Thurston, *Life and Times*, pp. 46 and 49; L. Thurston, letter dated 31 August 1820, copy in ABCFM file, ABCFM–Hawaii papers.

14. M. Loomis, "Journal 1819–1828," 17 February 1821; S. Bingham, "Journal on *Thaddeus*," 7 July 1820; M. Whitney, "Journal 1821–1860," 21 April 1821.

15. M. Whitney, "Journal 1821–1869," 21 April 1821; S. Ruggles and N. Ruggles, "Journal on Board the Brig *Thaddeus*," 29 May 1820; S. Bingham, "Journal on *Thaddeus*," 12 February 1821; Thurston, *Life and Times*, p. 71.

16. Holman, *Journal*, pp. 32–33; M. Loomis, "Journal 1819–1828," 1 October 1821. See also H. Bingham to ABCFM, 2 November 1820, ABCFM–Hawaii papers.

17. *Missionary Herald*, February 1823, p. 28; Thurston, *Life and Times*, p. 47; S. Worcester to Bingham, Thurston, and others, 8 June 1820, ABCFM–HEA papers.

18. M. Loomis to Utica friend, 14 May 1820.

19. S. Bingham, "Journal on *Thaddeus*," 8 August 1820 and 14 March 1822.

20. M. Whitney, "Journal 1821–1860," 28 March 1823; M. Loomis, "Journal 1819–1828," 23 August 1820.

21. S. Bingham, "Journal on *Thaddeus*," 13 July 1820 and 31 June 1820; Sandwich Islands Mission, "Journal of the Sandwich Island Mission Begun on Brig *Thaddeus*, Capt. Blanchard, 23 October 1819," June 1820, typescript HMCSL, pp. 52–53; M. Loomis to Utica friend, 14 May 1820; Bingham, *A Residence of Twenty-one Years*, p. 106.

22. M. Loomis, "Journal 1819–1829," 18 October 1820; D. Chamberlain to ABCFM, 6 October 1820, ABCFM–Hawaii papers.

23. M. Whitney, "Journal 1821–1860," 28 April 1821; M. Loomis, "Journal 1819–1828," 12 November 1820; S. Bingham, "Journal on *Thaddeus*," 13 February 1821.

24. *Panoplist and Missionary Magazine*, January 1817, p. 32; M. Whitney, "Journal 1821–1860," 8 July 1820; M. Loomis to Utica friend, 14 May 1820; M. Loomis, "Journal 1819–1828," 4 November 1820.

25. *Missionary Herald*, August 1821, p. 249.

26. M. Loomis, "Journal 1819–1828," 14 December 1820; S. Bingham, "Journal on *Thaddeus*," 15 February 1821; *Missionary Herald*, February 1823, p. 42 [mistake for p. 41].

27. M. Whitney to cousin Mrs. Ely, 30 April 1836; D. Chamberlain, "Journal 1819–1820," 24 April 1820 and 1 July 1820; E. Loomis, "Journal 1819–1827," 20 January 1821; D. Chamberlain, "Journal 1819–1820," 1 July 1820; E. Bishop, "Journal, Fragments 1823," Saturday, 6 [?] 1823; see also *Missionary Herald*, July 1825, p. 213.

28. Thurston, *Life and Times*, p. 55.

29. M. Loomis, "Journal 1819–1828," 6 February 1821.

30. Thurston, *Life and Times*, p. 57; O. Gulick and A. Gulick, *The Pilgrims of Hawaii* (New York: Fleming H. Revell, 1918), p. 89.

31. C. S. Stewart, *Journal of a Residence in the Sandwich Islands During the Years 1823, 1824, and 1825* (Honolulu: University of Hawaii Press, 1970 [1830]), p. 171; C. Richards to parents, 21 May 1823.

32. *Missionary Herald,* February 1823, p. 40.
33. Thurston, *Life and Times,* pp. 64 and 67–70.
34. *Missionary Herald,* October 1823, p. 319.
35. L. Chamberlain, "Journal 1822–1849," 11 December 1823.
36. Bingham, *A Residence of Twenty-one Years,* pp. 183 and 192.
37. S. Bingham, "Journal 1822–1849," 20 November 1823; Bingham, *A Residence of Twenty-one Years,* p. 164.
38. Ibid., pp. 164–165; W. Ellis, "Journal, Oahu 1823," 9 March and 16 May 1823, South Seas Journals 5, LMS.
39. *Missionary Herald,* July 1825, p. 210.
40. L. Chamberlain, "Journal 1822–1849," 3 February 1825; Bingham, *A Residence of Twenty-one Years,* pp. 255–256.
41. M. Whitney, "Journal 1821–1860," 6 August 1820.
42. Thurston, *Life and Times,* p. 56; M. Loomis, "Journal 1819–1828," 3 March 1822; C. Richards, "Journal from Lahaina, 1824," 12 May 1824.
43. Stewart, *Journal of a Residence,* p. 236; M. Whitney to N. Ruggles, 27 October 1823; M. Loomis, "Journal 1819–1828," 8 April and 3 October 1822; S. Bingham, "Journal on *Thaddeus,*" n.d., 1822; M. Loomis, "Journal 1819–1828," 8 April 1822.
44. Sandwich Islands Mission, unpublished minutes of the General Meetings 1819–1828, typescript, HMCSL, p. 5 (insert), 12 September 1823.
45. M. Loomis to N. Ruggles, 11 August 1823; M. Loomis, "Journal 1819–1828," n.d. [1–3 June 1824].
46. S. Bingham, "Journal on *Thaddeus,*" 16 February 1823.
47. Bingham, *A Residence of Twenty-one Years,* p. 159.
48. L. Thurston to Miss A. Parker, 31 January 1822, ABCFM–Hawaii papers; E. Loomis, "Journal 1819–1827," 19 February, 3 March, and 9 May 1821.
49. M. Loomis, "Journal 1819–1828," 3 March 1821 and 1 September 1822.
50. Stewart, *Journal of a Residence,* p. 119.
51. E. Loomis, "Journal 1819–1827," 13 September 1822; H. Bingham and S. Whitney, "A Few Hints in Great Haste to Sister Holman," n.d. [August 1820]; Smith, *Yankees in Paradise,* p. 134; S. Reynolds, "Journal 1824–1845," passim.
52. W. Beal, "William Beal's Writing Book 1823," ms., HMCSL.
53. L. Chamberlain, "Journal 1822–1849," 16 February 1824.
54. S. Bingham, "Journal on *Thaddeus,*" 15 February 1822.
55. D. Tyerman and G. Bennet to ABCFM, 9 August 1822, ABCFM–Hawaii papers.
56. Sandwich Islands Mission, unpublished minutes of the Sandwich Islands Mission 1819–1828, typescript, HMCSL, p. 16.
57. L. Thurston to W. Goodell, 23 October 1834. See N. Gunson, "The Deviations of a Missionary Family: The Henrys of Tahiti," in J. W. Davidson

and D. Scarr, *Pacific Island Portraits* (Canberra: Australian National University Press, 1973), pp. 31–54.

58. H. Bingham, A. Thurston, and E. Loomis to ABCFM, 20 March 1823, ABCFM–Hawaii papers.

59. W. Ellis, "Journal, Oahu, 1823," 20 March 1823, South Sea Journals 5, LMS.

60. M. Whitney, "Journal 1821–1860," 22 May and 17 September 1823.

61. Thurston, *Life and Times,* p. 77.

62. Bingham, *A Residence of Twenty-one Years,* chap. 10.

63. Kalakua, "Hoapili Wahine's statement respecting Captain Buckle's purchasing a mistress to accompany him on a sea voyage," ms., South Seas Letters 6, LMS.

64. W. Richards to ABCFM, n.d. [October 1825], copy, South Seas Letters 6, LMS.

65. *Missionary Herald,* February 1827, p. 40.

CHAPTER 3

1. Thurston, *Life and Times,* p. 134.

2. Nearly half of the ordained missionaries and their wives lived alone at stations; R. Anderson to missionaries at the Sandwich Islands Mission, 19 July 1848, p. 16, ABCFM–Hawaii papers.

3. M. Ives to mother, 27 May 1837.

4. M. Ives to aunt, 21 January 1838; Lyman, *Her Own Story,* p. 46; C. Richards, "Journal from Lahaina, 1824," 24 April 1824; L. Judd, *Honolulu: Sketches of the Life, Social, Political and Religious, in the Hawaiian Islands from 1828 to 1861* (Honolulu: Hawaiian Star-Bulletin, 1928 [1861]), p. 19; F. Coan to T. Coan, 12 March 1839; C. Richards, "Journal from Lahaina, 1824," 24 April 1824.

5. F. Coan to M. Robinson, 12 March 1839.

6. HMCS, *Jubilee Celebration,* p. 50; J. Alexander, *Mission Life in Hawaii: Memoir of Rev. William P. Alexander* (Oakland: Pacific Press, 1888), p. 37; M. Ward to Mr. and Mrs. Stockton, 24 October 1829.

7. F. Coan to Samuel and Abigail Church, 8 December 1836.

8. M. Whitney, "Journal 1821–1860," 19 February 1835.

9. J. Cooke, "Extracts from a Journal, 1837," June 1834; ABCFM, *General Letters to the Sandwich Islands Mission 1831–1840* (letter Rufus Anderson to missionaries, 15 March 1833), pp. 1–2; J. Cooke to mother M. Montague, 8 June 1839.

10. J. Cooke to M. Montague, 21 December 1838; J. Cooke to brother Charles Montague, 3 July 1840; M. Whitney, "Journal 1821–1860," 15 May 1829; M. Whitney to brother Oliver Partridge, 10 November 1832.

11. J. Cooke to M. Montague, 27 December 1839.

12. M. Alexander, *William Patterson Alexander in Kentucky, the Marquesas, Hawaii* (Honolulu: privately published, 1934), p. 202.

13. J. Cooke to M. Montague, 4 July 1840; F. Coan to S. and A. Church, 8 December 1836; F. Coan to M. Robinson, 8 June 1838; M. Chamberlain to sister Ann, 19 October 1833.

14. M. Whitney to sister Pamela, 21 November 1829; L. Judd to F. Gulick, 6 November 1838.

15. M. Parker to F. Gulick, 31 December 1834.

16. M. Parker, "Journal (A), Voyages to Hawaii and the Marquesas 1832–1833," 31 March 1833.

17. F. Coan to M. Robinson, 11 November 1835.

18. C. Armstrong to R. Armstrong's sisters, Mary and Jane, 25 October 1834.

19. S. J. Lyman, *Sarah Joiner Lyman of Hawaii: Her Own Story* (Hilo: Lyman House Memorial Museum, 1970), pp. 56–57.

20. M. Patton to sister, 19 May 1828.

21. Alexander, *Dr. Baldwin of Lahaina,* p. 34.

22. P. Taylor, *Kapiolani* (Honolulu: Robert Grieve, 1897); Stewart, *Journal of a Residence,* p. 165; Thurston, *Life and Times,* pp. 137–138. Persis Thurston Taylor wrote that Kapiolani was, "unlike any other Hawaiian woman I ever saw, truly attractive in the neatness of her dress and the refined cordiality of her manners"; Taylor, *Kapiolani,* p. 5.

23. J. Cooke to cousin Thankful Smith, 30 August 1839; Judd, *Honolulu,* p. 5; Judd Family, *Fragments: Family Record of the House of Judd* (Honolulu: privately published, 1903), p. 58; J. Cooke, "Extracts from a Journal 1837," 5 July 1837; Thurston, *Life and Times,* p. 88; Wight, *Memoirs of Elizabeth Kinau Wilder,* p. 7.

24. M. Dibble to Mary, 9 September 1828; J. Spaulding, "Autobiographical Sketch," ms., ABCFM–Hawaii papers; *Missionary Herald,* May 1826, p. 142.

25. M. Ward to M. Chamberlain, 12 April 1832; M. Ives, "Journal of a Voyage to Hawaii, at Hana and at Kealakekua, 1837–1841," 8 April 1838; M. Whitney to sister Maria, 20 October 1842; M. Whitney to C. Ely, 22 November 1833.

26. Lyman, *Her Own Story,* pp. 89–90; Thurston, *Life and Times,* p. 155.

27. J. J. Jarves, *Scenes and Scenery in the Sandwich Islands* (Boston: James Munroe, 1844), pp. 20ff; M. Whitney, "Journal 1821–1860," 11 August 1834.

28. L. Lyons, "Station Report of Waimea, Hawaii," May 1841; Wyllie, *Answers to Questions,* p. 70.

29. C. Armstrong to Reuben Chapman, April 1836.

30. Judd Family, *Fragments IV: Family Records of the House of Judd* (Honolulu: Honolulu Star-Bulletin, 1928), p. 13.

31. S. Reynolds, "Journal 1824–1845," 14 August 1828 and 5 May 1829.

32. Judd, *Honolulu,* p. 78.

33. Judd, *Fragments,* p. 60.

34. M. Chamberlain to sister Isabella, 25 December 1833; M. Chamberlain to F. Gulick, 25 September 1835; C. Armstrong to R. Chapman, 1 December 1837.

35. L. Judd to N. Ruggles, 26 February [ca. 1830]. Clarissa Richards wished Juliette Cooke could live in the country and yet "carry all the city privileges" with her; C. Richards to J. Cooke, 31 August [ca. 1843]. Mercy Whitney found her retired situation at Waimea more pleasant after a visit in the "bustle and confusion" of Oahu; M. Whitney, "Journal 1821–1860," 16 November 1829.

36. Damon, *Father Bond of Kohala,* p. 98.

37. L. Ely to E. Bishop, 14 January 1825.

38. H. Hitchcock to sister Jenny, 23 November 1823; Doyle, *Makua Laiana,* p. 94; E. Bliss to L. Lyons, 24 July [1823].

39. M. Ogden to M. Patton, 15 May 1828.

40. Maternal Association of the Sandwich Islands (MASI), "Records 1834–1841," Annual Meeting, 2 June 1841.

41. L. Smith to J. Cooke, 5 May [1838].

42. C. Richards to M. Chamberlain, March [1838]; M. Whitney, "Journal 1821–1860," 20 January 1828; C. Armstrong, "Journal 1831–1838," 18 June 1838.

43. C. Bailey to M. Ives, 21 October 184; H. Hitchcock to ABCFM, August 1836, ABCFM–Hawaii papers.

44. J. Cooke, "Journal 1837–[1839?]," 9 November 1837; Judd, *Honolulu,* p. 37.

45. C. Diell to Mrs. W. Gilman, 26 June 1835; F. Coan to Mrs. H. Hill, 30 August 1837; F. Coan to L. Lyons, 18 May 1839; F. Coan to T. Coan, 24 June 1848.

46. S. Bingham to N. Ruggles, 3 May [1831?].

47. M. Parker to L. Lyons, 2 July [late 1830s?].

48. M. Parker to F. Gulick, 12 January 1836.

49. C. Richards to N. Ruggles, 10 May 1831.

50. T. Green to N. Ruggles, June 1830; A. Cooke, "Journal 1833–1871," 14 March 1840; M. Parker to M. Chamberlain, 23 [1834?]; C. Armstrong, "Journal 1831–1838," 24 June 1834.

51. R. Armstrong, "Journal on My Voyage to the Sandwich Islands 1831–1834," 7 December 1831; T. Green, "Journal letter written to her sister in Connecticut on voyage to the Sandwich Islands, 1827–1828," 1 December 1827; M. Parker, "Journal (A), Voyages to Hawaii and the Marquesas, 1832–1833," written to sister Betsey, 19 February 1833; T. Green, "Journal letter," 1 December 1827.

52. M. Whitney to C. Ely, 28 November 1844; M. Whitney to son S. Whitney, 26 November 1857.

53. J. Cooke, "Journal 1837–[1839?]," 24 and 28 September 1837; M. Alexander, "Journal 1831–1833," 18 and 21 January 1833; C. Armstrong to F. Gulick, n.d. [January 1833]; C. Armstrong, "Journal 1831–1838," 7 May 1832.

54. M. Clark to E. Clark, 19 July 1856; M. Clark to E. Clark, n.d. [1852]; M. Chamberlain, "Journal 1825–1849," 28 March 1846, 22 May 1846, 23 April 1840.

55. Frear, *Lowell and Abigail,* pp. 100–101; M. Whitney to Mrs. Whitney, 8 February 1840; A. Bishop to ABCFM, 18 December 1827, ABCFM–Hawaii papers; D. Dole to W. Rice, 14 May 1844; D. Dole to D. Greene (ABCFM), 1 July 1844, ABCFM–Hawaii papers; Maternal Association of Honolulu (MAH), "Records 1838–1845," 13 April 1842; M. Whitney to son S. Whitney, 26 November 1857.

CHAPTER 4

1. C. Baldwin, "Journal on Board the Ship *New England,* New Bedford, Massachusetts, for the Sandwich Islands, 1830–31," 5 August 1831.

2. M. Whitney to Dr. and Mrs. Winslow, 13 October 1849; S. Lyman, "Journal 1830–1863," 20 November 1836; M. Ogden to M. Chamberlain, 20 August [1831?]; S. Smith to J. Cooke, 2 November [?].

3. T. Coan to F. Coan, 14 June 1847.

4. J. Cooke to sister Fanny, 12 January 1840; F. Coan to M. Robinson, 8 June 1838; F. Coan, *Life in Hawaii: An Autobiographical Sketch* (New York: Anson D. Randolph & Co., 1882), p. 222; F. Coan to T. Coan, 22 February 1848.

5. Maternal Association of Honolulu, "Records 1838–1845," 6 January and 1 August 1841. See R. Bloch, "American Feminine Ideals in Transition: The Rise of the Moral Mother, 1785–1815," *Feminist Studies* 4 (2) (June 1978): 102–103. Bloch notes that the revised wifely ideal stressed "female rational capabilities, advocating more serious education for women, and urging greater equality in marriage."

6. S. Whitney, T. Coan, and S. Dibble to ABCFM, 18 May 1841, Bliss Case, Missionary Letters.

7. Lyons, Report of Lorenzo Lyons [May 1841], Bliss Case, typescript, p. 4; I. Bliss, "A Reply to Certain Charges," Bliss Case.

8. S. Whitney and others to ABCFM, Bliss Case.

9. J. Cooke to sister Fanny, 1 March 1841.

10. C. Armstrong, "Journal 1831–38," 20 November 1832; See B. Welter,

"The Cult of True Womanhood," which underestimates the effective agency inherent in the religious construct common in church circles.

11. Thurston, *Life and Times,* pp. 289–290; L. Thurston to L. Chamberlain, 9 September 1830.

12. L. Thurston to P. Taylor, 13 February 1851 (extract), ABCFM–Hawaii papers.

13. Damon, *Father Bond of Kohala,* p. 46.

14. M. Goodrich to N. Ruggles, 1 July 1829; C. Bailey to L. Lyons, 19 [?] 1838 or 1839; S. Bingham to N. Ruggles, n.d. [ca. 1825].

15. M. Patton to sister, 20 August 1828.

16. L. Chamberlain to ABCFM, 30 September 1828, ABCFM–Hawaii papers.

17. L. Chamberlain, "Journal 1822–49," 1 September 1828; N. Ruggles to L. Chamberlain, 17 September 1828; M. Ogden to sisters of M. Chamberlain, n.d. [1829].

18. Maternal Association of the Sandwich Islands Mission, "Records 1834–41," minutes of general meeting, 21 May 1840.

19. E. Damon, *Koamalu* (Honolulu: privately published, 1931), p. 106.

20. S. Reynolds, "Journal 1824–45," 30 March 1828.

21. E. Dole to sister S. Ballard, 25 October 1841, Dole papers.

22. T. Coan to F. Coan, 18 February 1845; T. Coan to F. Coan, 3 November 1846; T. Coan to F. Coan, 20 February 1849; T. Coan to F. Coan, 10 May 1841.

23. F. Coan to T. Coan, 21 May 1839; F. Coan to T. Coan, 11 December 1839; F. Coan to T. Coan, n.d. [23 July 1839]; T. Coan to F. Coan, 24 January 1844; T. Coan to F. Coan, 24 January 1844.

24. Frear, *Lowell and Abigail,* p. 153; A. Bishop to ABCFM, 14 January 1824; H. Hitchcock to ABCFM, April 1836.

25. T. Coan to F. Coan, 8 May 1848; L. Smith to R. Anderson (ABCFM), 2 June 1854, Dwight Case, ABCFM–Hawaii papers.

26. S. Dwight to R. Anderson, 9 June 1854.

27. J. Smith, E. Johnson, and D. Dole, "Report of the Committee in the Case of Reverend George B. Rowell of Waimea, Kauai . . . March 29, 1865," Rowell Case, ABCFM–Hawaii papers; M. Whitney to Mrs. R. Anderson, 9 August 1865, ABCFM–Hawaii papers; G. Rowell to R. Anderson (ABCFM), 29 May 1860, ABCFM–Hawaii papers.

28. M. Whitney to Mrs. R. Anderson, 9 August 1865, ABCFM–Hawaii papers.

29. E. Rogers to ABCFM, 12 February 1835, ABCFM–Hawaii papers; R. Anderson to brethren of the Sandwich Islands Mission, 16 September 1835, ABCFM–HEA papers; C. Armstrong to R. Chapman, April 1836.

30. A. Bishop to ABCFM, 17 December 1828, ABCFM–Hawaii papers;

L. Judd to N. Ruggles, 25 November 1828; A. Conde to F. Gulick, 25 October 1842.

31. L. Lyons to ABCFM, 18 September 1837, ABCFM–Hawaii papers; Doyle, *Makua Laiana,* pp. 101–102; L. Lyons, "Excerpts of Journal," held with journal of Betsey Curtis Lyons, 5 May 1837 and 14 July 1838.

32. Doyle, *Makua Laiana,* pp. 101 and 120. On 14 May 1881, he recorded in his journal, "Forty-four years today since my dear companion Betsey left me"; ibid., p. 211.

33. A. Conde to F. Gulick, 25 October 1842.

34. For details see HMCS, *Missionary Album* and Mission Journals.

35. M. Chamberlain to B. Lyman, 7 June 1867; for first birth, see E. Clark to ABCFM, 13 October 1828, ABCFM–Hawaii papers; for date of second birth, Maternal Association of the Sandwich Islands Mission, *The Names of Mothers, Members and Children* (Honolulu: Mission Press, 1835), p. 2.; M. Goodrich to M. Chamberlain, 17 January 1833.

36. D. Baldwin, "Medical Journal 1836–1843," 21 November 1839; M. Whitney to mother and sisters, enclosed in letter 22 October 1835; E. Whittlesey to M. Kinney, 14 July 1852.

37. M. Chamberlain to B. Lyman, 7 June 1867.

38. Damon, *Letters of Abner and Lucy Wilcox,* p. 113; Damon, *Father Bond of Kohala,* p. 101; R. Anderson to missionaries at the Sandwich Islands Mission, 19 July 1848, ABCFM–HEA papers. For changes in family size in New England see J. Potter, "The Growth of Population in America, 1700–1860," in D. V. Glass and D. Eversley (eds.), *Population in History* (London: Edward Arnold, 1965), pp. 639–643; D. S. Smith, "The Demographic History of Colonial New England," in M. Gordon (ed.), *The American Family in Social-Historical Perspective* (New York: St. Martin's Press, 1973), pp. 397–416.

39. C. Armstrong to R. Armstrong's sisters, Mary and Jane, 25 October 1834; Ludlow, "Clarissa Chapman Armstrong," p. 272.

40. C. Richards to F. Gulick, 18 January 1836.

41. D. Baldwin, "Medical Journal 1836–1843," report for 1836; M. Ives to parents and sister, 24 October 1842.

42. F. Coan to M. Robinson, 26 July 1837.

43. Sandwich Islands Mission, *Extracts from the Minutes of a General Meeting* (Honolulu: Mission Press, 1848), p. 7.

44. C. Armstrong to R. Armstrong's sisters, Mary and Jane, 25 October 1834; C. Armstrong to L. Lyons, 6 September 1839.

45. Frear, *Lowell and Abigail,* p. 189.

46. M. Chamberlain to B. Lyman, 18 August 1867; T. Coan to F. Coan, 10 May 1841; M. Whitney to mother and sisters, included in letter 22 October 1835; M. Whitney to N. Ruggles, 29 October 1836.

47. C. Armstrong, "Journal 1831–1838," 31 April 1832.

48. E. Bishop to L. Ely, 13 January 1824; E. Bishop, "Journal, Fragments, 1825–1827," 10 January 1825.

49. C. Armstrong, "Journal 1831–1838," 16 September 1838.

50. D. Baldwin, "Medical Journal, 1836–1843," 30 August 1837.

51. J. Cooke to M. Montague, 6 August 1839.

52. Damon, *Father Bond of Kohala,* p. 39.

53. E. Dole to mother, 22 May 1841; M. Whitney to Mrs. Whitman, 1 February 1845; M. Chamberlain to sister Jane, 31 December 1834; C. Armstrong, "Journal 1831–1838," 22 May 1834; E. Rogers to ABCFM, 29 August 1834, ABCFM–Hawaii papers.

54. M. Smith to L. Lyons, 28 July 1840; Damon, *Letters from the Life of Abner and Lucy Wilcox,* p. 166; S. Lyman, "Journal 1830–1863," 23 December 1835.

55. F. Coan to T. Coan, 20 September 1839.

56. S. Damon, "Reminiscences of My Son, Samuel Mills," Damon papers; T. Coan to F. Coan, 3 November 1836; T. Coan to F. Coan, 22 September 1839; M. Ives to Mary Ives' mother, 26 October 1842.

CHAPTER 5

1. A. Chapin and M. A. Chapin, "Journal 1830–1833," 21 May 1832; J. Emerson to ABCFM, 5 May 1833, ABCFM–Hawaii papers; Emerson, *Pioneer Days in Hawaii,* pp. 71–72; R. Hitchcock, "The Work on Molokai," in HMCS, *Jubilee Celebration,* p. 60; M. Whitney to E. Dow, 15 March 1828.

2. M. Parker, "Journal (A), Voyages to Hawaii and the Marquesas 1832–1833," 31 March 1833.

3. Emerson, *Pioneer Days in Hawaii,* pp. 72–73.

4. M. Whitney to Mrs. Walker, 30 January 1841; J. Cooke to sister Fanny, 12 January 1840.

5. L. Chamberlain, "Request for list of needed articles," 1 July 1838, Honolulu, in ABCFM, *Letters to the Sandwich Island Mission, 1831–1840,* p. 2.

6. Judd, *Honolulu,* p. 57.

7. Sandwich Islands Mission, *Extracts from the Minutes of a General Meeting,* 1844, pp. 21–22.

8. C. Armstrong, "Journal 1831–1838," 28 May 1832; M. Parker, "Journal (A)," 31 March 1833.

9. Emerson, *Pioneer Days in Hawaii,* p. 58; F. Coan to M. Robinson, 26 January 1838.

10. F. Coan to S. and A. Church, 8 December 1836; S. Lyman, "Journal 1830–1863," 11 October 1836; R. Hitchcock to mother, 10 November 1834.

11. Lyman, *Her Own Story,* pp. 59 and 66; C. Richards, "Journal from Lahaina, 1824," 10 April 1824; F. Coan to T. Coan, November and December 1835.

12. *Mother's Magazine,* April 1830, p. 90; M. Goodrich, "Journal of Voyage to Hawaii," 21 [May] 1823; S. Bingham to [Clarissa Richards?], 20 October 1836; W. Alexander, R. Armstrong, and B. Parker to ABCFM, 26 June 1833, ABCFM–Hawaii papers.

13. S. Lyman, "Journal 1830–1863," 24 January 1835.

14. C. Armstrong, "Journal 1831–1838," 24 June 1834.

15. Lyman, *Her Own Story,* p. 58.

16. M. Whitney, "Journal 1821–1860," 1 November 1830.

17. Emerson, *Pioneer Days in Hawaii,* p. 100.

18. M. Clark to E. Clark, 15 February [1852?]; L. Chamberlain to ABCFM, 15 October 1823, ABCFM–Hawaii papers; C. Richards, "Journal from Lahaina, 1824," 7 June 1824.

19. L. Thurston to W. and A. Goodell, 24 October 1834.

20. L. Brown to L. Chamberlain, 7 December 1837.

21. M. Parker, "Journal (A)," 31 March 1833.

22. Wight, *Memoirs of Elizabeth Kinau Wilder,* p. 57; Ludlow, "Clarissa Chapman Armstrong," p. 262; S. Lyman, "Journal 1831–1838," 26 December 1835.

23. E. Damon, *Sanford Ballard Dole and His Hawaii* (Palo Alto: Pacific Books, 1957), p. 8.

24. C. Armstrong, "Journal 1831–1838," 12 September 1834; A. Chapin to ABCFM, 24 September 1834, ABCFM–Hawaii papers.

25. C. Richards to M. Chamberlain, 6 September [1841?]; M. Chamberlain to F. Gulick, 22 August 1835.

26. Sandwich Islands Mission, *Extracts from the Minutes of a General Meeting,* June 1831, p. 17.

27. Bingham, *A Residence of Twenty-one Years,* p. 365.

28. K. Hoover, "The Hawaiian Anti-slavery Society," HMCSL, typescript.

29. C. Bailey to L. Lyons, 19 [?] 1839.

30. M. Whitney to C. Ely, 29 July 1839; J. Cooke to mother, 8 June 1839.

31. M. Whitney to N. Ruggles, 30 October 1834.

32. M. Whitney to N. Ruggles, 30 June 1837.

33. Alexander, *Dr. Baldwin of Lahaina,* p. 46; M. Ogden to M. Chamberlain, 20 August [1831?]; Lyman, *Her Own Story,* pp. 48–49; J. Cooke, "Journal 1837–[1839?]," 29 August 1837.

34. Lyman, *Her Own Story,* p. 58.

35. Coan, *Sybil Moseley Bingham,* pp. 64–65; S. Lyman, "Journal 1830–1863," 3 April 1841. See also N. Ruggles to M. Whitney, 22 April [1832?]; F. Coan to T. Coan, 14 June 1839; T. Coan to F. Coan, 29 May 1839.

36. Bingham, *A Residence of Twenty-one Years,* p. 335; M. Whitney, "Journal 1821–1860," 15 May 1829.

37. C. Richards to N. Ruggles, 25 June 1832; E. Spaulding to ABCFM, October 1832, ABCFM–Hawaii papers.

38. M. Whitney to her children, 26 February 1846; M. Whitney to sister Maria, 12 October 1847.

39. *Mother's Magazine*, April 1839, p. 90; Gulick, *Pilgrims of Hawaii*, pp. 188–189; R. Armstrong, *An Obituary Notice of Mrs. Angeline L. Castle* (Honolulu: Mission Press, 1841), p. 9.

40. E. Bishop to L. Thurston, n.d. [1827]; Thurston, *Life and Times*, pp. 91–92; *Missionary Herald*, January 1829, p. 24.

41. M. Whitney to Mrs. Judd, 23 December 1839; F. Coan to A. Church, 11 May 1839; M. Whitney to E. Goodrich, 20 April 1837.

42. C. Armstrong, "Journal 1831–1838," 18 November 1832; M. Whitney to M. Chamberlain, 24 June 1833; Bingham, *A Residence of Twenty-one Years*, p. 459.

43. M. Parker, "Journal (B), Intimate Note Books," 10 August 1833.

44. C. Armstrong, *Reminiscences of a Missionary Chair* (San Francisco: Murdock, 1886), p. 13; J. Alexander, *Mission Life in Hawaii: Memoir of Rev. William Alexander* (Oakland: Pacific Press, 1888), p. 80.

45. C. Armstrong to Armstrong's sisters, Mary and Jane, 25 October 1834; C. Armstrong, "Journal 1831–1838," 11 April 1834; C. Armstrong to S. Armstrong, 24 August [1887].

46. T. Coan to F. Coan, 3 June 1851; M. Smith to L. Smith, 5 March 1838; G. Nellist, *Women of Hawaii* (Honolulu: Paradise of the Pacific Press, 1929), p. 61.

47. C. Armstrong to R. Chapman and wife, 8 March 1848.

48. C. Armstrong to L. Lyons, 8 July 1880.

49. C. Armstrong to R. Chapman, April 1836.

50. C. Armstrong to R. Chapman, 27 August 1848.

51. C. Armstrong to L. Lyons, 8 July 1880.

52. F. Coan to T. Coan, 21 May 1839.

CHAPTER 6

1. Thurston, *Life and Times*, p. 129.

2. S. Lyman, "Journal 1830–1863," n.d.

3. *Mother's Magazine*, July [1833], p. 110.

4. Maternal Association of Honolulu, "Records 1839–1845," 6 October 1841.

5. Damon, *Letters . . . of Abner and Lucy Wilcox*, p. 106.

6. R. Armstrong, "Journal 1840–1858," 5 December 1842.

7. L. Smith to J. Cooke, 1 September [1837].

8. M. Whitney to Mrs. Hoadley, 20 May 1830; Maternal Association of Honolulu, "Records 1839–1845," 17 August 1842.

9. M. Chamberlain to sister Isabella, 29 October 1830; M. Whitney to C. Bidwell, 13 December 1828.

10. M. Parker to Mrs. L. Frisbie, April 1836; C. Armstrong to R. Chapman, April 1836; E. Bliss to L. and L. Lyons, 14 September 1838.

11. Sandwich Islands Mission, "Unpublished minutes of the General Meetings of the Sandwich Islands Mission 1819–1828," typescript, HMCSL, p. 51; M. Whitney, "Journal 1821–1860," 18 September 1828.

12. W. Richards to ABCFM, 7 December 1832, ABCFM–Hawaii papers.

13. L. Thurston to W. Goodell, 23 October 1834.

14. Thurston, *Life and Times,* pp. 127–128; L. Thurston to W. and A. Goodell, 24 October 1834.

15. S. Bingham to Eunice, December 1828, Bingham family papers; M. Whitney, "Journal 1821–1860," 11 November 1826.

16. F. Coan to M. Robinson, 8 June 1838; Judd, *Honolulu,* pp. 53 and 122; L. Judd to F. Gulick, 17 December [1836].

17. J. Cooke to brother Charles, 5 January 1842.

18. Judd, *Honolulu,* pp. 91–92; M. Smith to ABCFM, 12 October 1837, ABCFM–Hawaii papers; S. Lyman, "Journal 1830–1863," 20 February 1836; L. Wilcox to L. Lyons, 28 September [1839] and 10 December 1839; Maternal Association of the Sandwich Islands Mission, "Records 1834–1841," Minutes of General Meeting, 1840.

19. F. Coan to L. Lyons, 28 September 1838; F. Coan to F. Gulick, 3 December 1847.

20. S. Bishop, "Recollections of the Hawaiian Mission," in *Jubilee Celebrations,* p. 103; S. Bishop, *Reminiscences of Old Hawaii* (Honolulu: Hawaiian Gazette, 1916), pp. 21 and 30–31.

21. W. Richards to ABCFM, 4 September 1834, ABCFM–Hawaii papers (enclosed copy); M. Goodrich to N. Ruggles, 4 December [1834].

22. J. Evarts to missionaries at the Sandwich Islands, 27 October 1827, ABCFM–HEA papers.

23. ABCFM, *General Letters to the Sandwich Islands Mission,* 1851, letter of R. Anderson to missionaries, 14 July 1851, pp. 1–4.

24. M. Tinker to F. Gulick, November 1834.

25. A. Cooke to brother Charles, 11 November 1843.

26. C. Richards, "Journal from Lahaina, 1824," 4 February 1824.

27. Judd, *Fragments: Family Record,* p. 35; C. Armstrong, "Journal 1831–1838," 27 September 1834.

28. Damon, *Koamalu,* p. 111; F. Coan to M. Robinson, 7 December 1836; S. Lyman, "Journal 1830–1863," 29 October 1838; S. Damon, "Reminiscences of My Son, Samuel Mills."

29. J. Cooke to mother, 11 July 1839.

30. J. Cooke to mother, 21 December 1838; L. Judd to F. Gulick, 4 October [1831]; S. Lyman, "Journal 1830–1863," 7 March 1841; J. Cooke to mother, 6 August 1839 [1838]; S. Bingham to S. Bingham, 28 July 1831.

31. Coan, *Sybil Moseley Bingham*, p. 25; Frear, *Lowell and Abigail*, p. 186; Thurston, *Life and Times*, p. 157. Of the twenty couples who produced seven or more children, sixteen experienced the loss of at least one child; seven of these lost two children; one lost five out of seven. The thirty-eight fertile married women who remained in the islands, at least until the wife reached forty-four years, bore a total of two hundred and fifty-two children, of whom thirty-six died (just over one in every fourteen children).

32. Judd, *Fragments IV*, p. 70.

33. L. Judd to N. Ruggles, 26 February [1831]; L. Judd to N. Ruggles, 25 April [1831]; Lyman, *Her Own Story*, p. 80; S. Lyman, "Journal 1830–1863," 8 September 1838; Lyman, *Hawaiian Yesterdays*, p. 24.

34. Damon, *Sanford Ballard Dole*, p. 16; F. Coan to F. Gulick, 6 December 1843; Richardson, "Memoir of Her Grandmother," p. 5; B. Lyons to parents, Mr. and Mrs. S. Curtis, 15 August 1836; Lyman, *Hawaiian Yesterdays*, p. 26.

35. M. Ives to Aunt Rossiter, 25 December 1841; C. Bailey to L. Lyons, 2 November 1846.

36. S. Bingham, "Sophia's First Effort at Composition November 1826 Kailua," Bingham family papers.

37. Wight, *Memoir of Elizabeth Kinau Wilder*, p. 51.

38. S. Shepard to ABCFM, 12 November 1832.

39. Bishop, *Reminiscences*, p. 40.

40. M. Chamberlain, "Journal 1825–1949," 9 June 1846.

41. Bishop, *Reminiscences*, p. 39.

42. Maternal Association of the Sandwich Islands Mission, "Records 1846–1852," Minutes of General Meeting, 20 April 1849.

43. M. Clark to L. Lyons, 22 March 1845; M. Tinker to F. Gulick, 15 March 1838; P. Thurston to L. Lyons, 20 January 1838.

44. Maternal Association of the Sandwich Islands Mission, "Records 1834–1841," Minutes of General Meeting, 1841.

45. C. Richards to parents, 21 January 1830; Maternal Association of the Sandwich Islands Mission, "Records 1834–1841," Minutes of General Meeting, 1840; F. Coan to F. Gulick, 6 December 1843.

46. L. Judd to F. Gulick, 17 December [1836]; Maternal Association of the Sandwich Islands Mission, "Records 1834–1841," Minutes of General Meeting, 1839 and 1840.

47. C. Armstrong, "Journal 1831–1838," 27 December 1837; C. Miller, *Fathers and Sons: The Bingham Family and the American Mission* (Philadelphia: Temple University Press, 1982), p. 76; Wight, *Memoirs of Elizabeth Kinau Wilder*, p. 65; Lyman, *Hawaiian Yesterdays*, pp. 26–27.

48. M. Parker, "Journal (A)," 31 March 1833; see also E. Dole to mother, 22 May 1841.

49. C. Knapp, "Journal 1836–1846," 14 November 1839; Bingham, *A Residence of Twenty-one Years*, p. 559; A. Cooke, "Journal 1833–1871," 14 November 1839; F. Jewett, *Luther Halsey Gulick* (London: Elliot Stock,

1895), p. 23; M. Whitney to H. Whitney, 4 December 1839; M. Whitney to S. Whitney, 18 August 1834; M. Whitney to M. Whitney (daughter), 28 July 1830; S. Williston, *William Richards* (Cambridge, Mass.: privately printed, 1969 [1938]), p. 46.

50. M. Chamberlain, "Journal 1825–1849," 29 March 1840 and 8 April 1841; Castle, *Life of Samuel Northrup Castle*, pp. 108–109.

51. C. Armstrong to L. Lyons, 5 August 1844; M. Parker, "Journal (B)," December 1848.

52. D. Dole to ABCFM, 11 January 1842.

53. Judd Family, *Fragments II: Family Records of the House of Judd* (Honolulu: Paradise of the Pacific Press, 1911), p. 114; L. Chamberlain to M. Chamberlain's sister and brother-in-law, 7 September 1848.

54. M. Parker to M. Chamberlain, n.d; T. Coan to brother H. Coan, 26 June 1835; M. Whitney to sister Maria, 1 November 1836; J. Cooke to C. Montague, 28 January 1840.

55. C. Bailey to Mrs. J. Bailey, 23 October 1849.

56. C. Richards to M. Chamberlain, 31 January 1845; D. Bishop to F. Gulick, 10 November 1835; A. Cooke to C. Montague, 4 July 1844; Alexander, *Dr. Baldwin of Lahaina*, p. 169; Coan, *Sybil Moseley Bingham*, p. 27.

57. Armstrong, *Obituary Notice of Mrs. Angeline L. Castle*, p. 12; T. Coan to G. Coan, 13 June 1837.

58. L. Thurston to W. and A. Goodell, 24 October 1834; S. Lyman, "Journal 1830–1863," 19 August 1835; L. Lyons to M. Ives, 8 October 1849; C. Bailey to L. Lyons, 2 September [1841].

59. Judd, *Honolulu*, p. 92; P. Andrews to F. Gulick, 12 February 1844; F. Coan to F. Gulick, 1 November 1841.

60. M. Chamberlain to sister Jane, 27 December 1835.

CHAPTER 7

1. J. Jarves, cited in H. B. Restarick, *Hawaii, 1778–1920: From the Viewpoint of a Bishop* (Honolulu: Paradise of the Pacific Press, 1924), pp. 50–51.

2. M. Whitney, "Journal 1821–1860," 16 November 1825; M. Whitney "to the ladies in P. who were the contributors of the box of articles forwarded Feb 1832," 23 October 1833.

3. A. Cumings, *The Missionary's Daughter: A Memoir of Lucy Goodale Thurston of the Sandwich Islands* (New York: American Tract Society, 1842), p. 18.

4. T. Green, "Journal letter written to her sister in Connecticut on voyage to the Sandwich Islands, 1827–28," 6 June 1828; Thurston, *Life and Times*, p. 98.

5. M. Whitney to Mrs. Winton, 16 November 1842; Lyman, *Her Own Story*, p. 44; Judd, *Honolulu*, pp. 35 and 76; Bishop, *Reminiscences*, p. 19.

6. *Missionary Herald,* May 1826, p. 144; Doyle, *Makua Laiana,* p. 75; Wyllie, *Answers to Questions,* p. 59; see S. Lyman, "Journal 1830-1863," 10 January 1835.

7. S. Lyman, "Journal 1830-1863," 24 January 1837.

8. Judd, *Honolulu,* pp. 55-56; Lyman, "Journal 1830-1863," 30 August 1836; C. Forbes to ABCFM, 23 July 1836, ABCFM-Hawaii papers; Lyman, *Her Own Story,* p. 74.

9. ABCFM, "Answers by the Sandwich Island Missionaries to the Questions of the Circular of March 15, 1833," typescript, HMCSL, p. 53; Thurston, *Life and Times,* pp. 89-90; M. Whitney to daughter Maria, 21 February 1833.

10. M. Whitney to N. Ruggles, October 1840; F. Coan to Mrs. R. Anderson, 20 January 1837; F. Coan to Mrs. H. Hill, 30 August 1837.

11. S. Dibble, "Review of 'A Visit to the South Seas' by Rev. C. S. Stewart," n.d. [ca. 1831], ABCFM-Hawaii papers.

12. Sandwich Islands Mission, "Unpublished Minutes of the General Meetings of the Sandwich Islands Mission," 1826, typescript, p. 48.

13. *Missionary Herald,* October 1829, p. 316; S. Whitney, "Journal Kauai 2 April-1 June 1826," 30 April 1826, ABCFM-Hawaii papers.

14. C. Armstrong, "Journal 1831-1838," 29 October 1832; Judd, *Honolulu,* p. 14.

15. Bingham, *A Residence of Twenty-one Years,* p. 474; E. Clark, *A Word Relating to Marriage* (Honolulu: Mission Press, 1844).

16. Wyllie, *Answers to Questions,* p. 32. See also "An Act to Discourage Prostitution, by Regulating the Passages of Young Females Visiting Sea Ports," HMCSL.

17. M. Whitney to Mrs. G. Homer, 16 June 1829; Damon, *Father Bond of Kohala,* p. 158.

18. *Missionary Herald,* July 1832, p. 221; J. J. Jarves, *Scenes and Scenery in the Sandwich Islands* (Boston: James Munroe, 1844), p. 126.

19. M. Whitney to N. Ruggles, 30 June 1837; C. Richards to F. Gulick, April [1834?].

20. Judd, *Honolulu,* p. 8; *Missionary Herald,* July 1832, p. 221; Thurston, *Life and Times,* p. 90; M. Dibble to sister, 9 September 1833; A. Korn, (ed.), *The Victorian Visitors* (Honolulu: University of Hawaii Press, 1958); see also M. Anderson, *Scenes in the Hawaiian Islands and California* (Boston: American Tract Society, 1865), pp. 61-62.

21. S. Lyman, "Journal 1830-1863," 5 January 1835; Bishop, "Recollections of the Hawaiian Mission," in HMCS, *Jubilee Celebrations,* p. 99.

22. F. Coan to Mrs. H. Hill, 30 August 1837; Wight, *Memoirs of Elizabeth Kinau Wilder,* p. 23; M. F. Armstrong, *Richard Armstrong: America Hawaii* (Hampton, Va.: Normal School Press, 1887), p. 43.

23. Doyle, *Makua Laiana,* p. 99.

24. Hawaiian Association, *Extracts from the Records of the Hawaiian Association from 1828-1836* (Honolulu: Mission Press, 1837), pp. 13-14.

25. Frear, *Lowell and Abigail*, p. 76; Clark, *A Word Relating to Marriage*, (Silva, trans.), p. 1.

26. E. Spaulding and W. Richards, "A Brief History of Temperance for Twelve Years at the Sandwich Islands," ABCFM–Hawaii papers; *Missionary Herald*, July 1829, p. 209; Wyllie, *Answers to Questions*, p. 82.

27. M. Chamberlain, "Journal 1825–1849," 13 May 1830.

28. P. Gulick to ABCFM, 27 April 1829, ABCFM–Hawaii papers; Bingham, *A Residence of Twenty-one Years*, p. 137.

29. T. Coan to F. Coan, 24 December 1852; Lyman, "Journal 1830–1863," 12 March 1837; M. Parker to Mrs. L. Frisbie, April 1836.

30. M. Chamberlain to sister, 11 March 1830; Damon, *Father Bond of Kohala*, p. 172.

31. M. Chamberlain to sister, 11 March 1830; Emerson, *Pioneer Days in Hawaii*, pp. 58 and 139.

32. Clark, *A Word Relating to Marriage*.

33. Damon, *Father Bond of Kohala*, p. 158; L. Lyons, "Report on Waimea Station, 1837," typescript, p. 1, Mission Station Reports; Ludlow, "Clarissa Chapman Armstrong," p. 276.

34. Emerson, *Pioneer Days in Hawaii*, p. 92; J. Cooke, "Journal Aboard the *Mary Frazier* 1837," 19 March 1837; J. Cooke, "Extracts from a Journal, 1837"; Doyle, *Makua Laiana*, p. 126.

35. ABCFM, *Instructions of the Prudential Committee*, p. 101.

36. L. Brown, Report to ABCFM, 1836; L. Brown to R. Anderson, 21 February 1845, ABCFM–Hawaii papers.

37. Dibble, *History of the Sandwich Islands*, p. 267; M. Whitney, "Report of the Maternal Association at Waimea, Kauai, 13 May 1837."

38. Wyllie, *Answers to Questions*, pp. 49 and 65; L. Lyons to ABCFM, n.d. [1836].

39. Sandwich Islands Mission, *A Few Words (of Advice) for Parents* (Lahainaluna: Mission Press, 1842), p. 3; L. Thurston to P. and E. Taylor, 14 September 1852.

40. D. Baldwin, "Medical Journal 1836–1843," 1842; Judd, *Honolulu*, p. 47; Judd, *Fragments: Family Record*, pp. 56–57.

41. Sandwich Islands Mission, *A Few Words (of Advice)*, p. 8.; M. Dibble to sister, 9 September 1833; S. Lyman, "Journal 1830–1863," 29 December 1835; Emerson, *Pioneer Days in Hawaii*, p. 71.

42. L. Lyons to ABCFM, 6 September 1833, ABCFM–Hawaii papers; Judd, *Honolulu*, p. 46; Judd, *Fragments IV*, p. 12.

43. S. Lyman, "Journal 1830–1863," 17 January 1837; see also 18 February 1834 and 2 February 1835.

44. F. Coan to Miss Bates, 27 May 1837; *Mother's Magazine*, October 1837, p. 239; M. Whitney, "Report of the Maternal Association of Waimea, Kauai, 13 May 1837"; S. Lyman, "Journal 1830–1863," 2 February 1835.

45. *Mother's Magazine*, July [1833], letter from Laura Judd; L. Lyons to R. Anderson, 15 September 1835, ABCFM–Hawaii papers; R. Armstrong, "Journal on My Voyage to the Sandwich Islands," 8 November 1837; M. Smith to L. Lyons, 28 May 1840; S. Lyman, "Journal 1830–1863," 27 October 1836, 30 November 1836, and 21 January 1837; W. Richards to ABCFM, excerpts of a journal kept at Lahaina, Maui, 14 June 1826.

46. F. Coan to M. Robinson, 2 October 1838.

47. L. Andrews, E. Clark, and S. Dibble, report to ABCFM, 1836–1837, ABCFM–Hawaii papers; L. Andrews to ABCFM, 2 December 1835, ABCFM–Hawaii papers.

48. Sandwich Islands Mission, *Extracts from the Minutes of a General Meeting*, June 1832, pp. 11–12.

49. M. Ogden to M. Chamberlain, 27 June [1837?]; F. Coan to L. Lyons, August 1843.

50. F. Coan to L. Lyons, August 1834.

51. Sandwich Islands Mission, *Extracts from the Minutes of a General Meeting*, 1848, pp. 5–16, and 1849, p. 6; A. Cooke to M. Montague, 20 July 1848.

52. J. Cooke, "Extracts from a Journal, 1837," 4 July 1837; F. Coan to J. Church, 14 September 1835.

53. L. Judd to Mrs. R. Anderson, August 1841; Alexander, *Dr. Baldwin of Lahaina*, p. 171; R. Armstrong, "Journal 1840–1858," 18 July 1849.

54. S. Lyman, "Journal 1830–1863," 22 January 1838; F. Coan to T. Coan, 21 January 1849; M. Whitney to mother, 6 January 1840; M. Whitney to brother I. Partridge, 28 July 1845; Doyle, *Makua Laiana*, p. 132; Sandwich Islands Mission, General Letter of the Missionaries, 5 May 1849, ABCFM–Hawaii papers.

55. M. Chamberlain, "Journal 1825–1849," 11 May 1831.

CHAPTER 8

1. Sandwich Island missionaries, general letter to ABCFM, 5 May 1849, ABCFM–Hawaii papers.

2. C. Armstrong to R. Chapman, 27 August 1848; E. Clark to R. Anderson, 10 May 1849, ABCFM–Hawaii papers.

3. ABCFM, *General Letter to the Sandwich Islands Mission, 1851*, p. 2 (R. Anderson to missionaries, 29 April 1851); Coan, *Titus Coan*, p. 58; ABCFM, *General Letter to the Sandwich Islands Mission, 1851*, p. 2 (R. Anderson to missionaries, 14 February 1851); ibid., p. 5 (R. Anderson to J. Smith, 30 April 1851); T. Coan to F. Coan, 22 May 1851.

4. M. Chamberlain to Mrs. R. Anderson, 3 November 1849, ABCFM–Hawaii papers; M. Chamberlain to R. Anderson (ABCFM), 7 September 1850, ABCFM–Hawaii papers.

5. T. Coan to F. Coan, 23 May 1851; ABCFM, *General Letter to the Sandwich Islands Mission, 1851,* p. 2 (R. Anderson to missionaries, 3 December 1851); J. Hobbs, *Hawaii: A Pageant of the Soil,* (Stanford: Stanford University Press, 1935), p. 283.

6. Hobbs, *Hawaii,* p. 283.

7. L. Brown to R. Anderson, 16 July 1852, ABCFM–Hawaii papers; see letter of Maria Chamberlain to ABCFM, 14 November 1851, ABCFM–Hawaii papers; M. Whitney to E. Dow, 7 October 1834.

8. See Hobbs, *Hawaii,* for full details of land transactions by missionaries.

9. See HMCS, *Missionary Album,* biographical entries; C. Armstrong to L. Lyons, 15 March 1859; M. Chamberlain to Mrs. R. Anderson, 15 August 1853, ABCFM–Hawaii papers; T. Coan to F. Coan, 19 May 1856.

10. M. Chamberlain to Mrs. R. Anderson, 3 November 1849, ABCFM–Hawaii papers; R. Hitchcock to Mr. Worcester (ABCFM), 22 April 1856, ABCFM–Hawaii papers; R. Hitchcock to R. Anderson, 7 August 1861, ABCFM–Hawaii papers; R. Hitchcock to J. Smith, 28 December 1888.

11. M. Whitney to R. Anderson, 18 June 1863, ABCFM–Hawaii papers; E. Whitney to E. Dow, 20 January 1863.

12. Alexander, *Mission Life in Hawaii,* pp. 124–125; F. Coan to T. Coan, 8 November 1852; F. Coan to T. Coan, 7 May 1857; F. Coan to T. Coan, 4 April 1861; F. Coan to T. Coan, 16 August 1866; L. Lyons, "Memorials of the Reinforcement of 1837," in HMCS, *Jubilee Celebration,* p. 158; Doyle, *Makua Laiana,* p. 197.

13. S. Lyman, "Journal 1830–1863," 15 December 1853; Lyman, *Her Own Story,* pp. 155 and 175; L. Judd to L. Judd (daughter), 18 May [1855]; Korn, *The Victorian Visitors,* pp. 37, 47, and 74; F. Coan to T. Coan, 15 May 1861.

14. Thurston, *Life and Times,* pp. 168–175 and 295; T. Coan to F. Coan, 17 January 1855; L. Thurston to R. Anderson, 18 May 1866, ABCFM–Hawaii papers; L. Thurston to Hawaiian Board, 30 April 1868, ABCFM–Hawaii papers; L. Thurston to Dr. L. Gulick, 14 September 1869, ABCFM–Hawaii papers; L. Thurston, Last Will and Testament, 27 June 1876, ms., HMCSL.

15. Hawaiian Missionary Society (HMS), "Minutes of the Hawaiian Missionary Society, June 1851–June 1857," ms., Sandwich Islands Mission collection; Hawaiian Missionary Society, "Letter File 1852–1857," Sandwich Islands Mission collection; Hawaiian Missionary Society, "Minutes of the Hawaiian Missionary Society, June 1851–June 1857," ms., Sandwich Islands Mission collection.

16. C. Armstrong to L. Lyons, 26 April 1862.

17. C. Armstrong to L. Lyons, 4 April 1864; C. Armstrong to Lorenzo and Lucia Lyons, 24 January 1865; C. Armstrong to L. Lyons, 16 May 1864. Abigail Smith took over the Women's Mission Board in her later years; A. Smith to Dr. Clark, 27 March 1882; M. Castle to M. E. Castle, 29 November 1884.

18. Nellist, *Women of Hawaii*, p. 61; M. Parker to Mrs. L. Frisbie, 20 September 1856; ABCFM, *General Letter to the Sandwich Island Mission, 1851*, p. 2 (R. Anderson to missionaries, 14 February 1851); HMCS, *Fifth Annual Report, 1857* (Honolulu: Government Press, 1857), p. 9.

19. F. Gulick to J. Gulick, 21 February 1849; C. Armstrong to L. Lyons, 4 April 1864.

20. HMCS, *First Annual Report, 1853*, p. 17; F. Gulick to J. Gulick, 30 June 1866; HMCS, *Sixteenth Annual Report, 1868*, p. 8; HMCS, *Seventeenth Annual Report, 1869*, p. 9.

21. M. Hitchcock to M. Castle, 12 March 1868.

22. P. Taylor, "Memories of the Origin of the Cousins' Meeting," 27 May 1897, Children of the Mission; see also her "Shifting Views of the Life of Your Mother, from 1821–1894," Children of the Mission.

23. C. Armstrong to R. Chapman, 27 August 1848; P. Thurston to R. Anderson, 22 November 1852, ABCFM–Hawaii papers; HMCS, *Second Annual Report*, p. 15.

24. HMCS, *Third Annual Report, 1855*, p. 15; Anderson, *Scenes in the Hawaiian Isles*, p. 199; HMCS, *Twentieth Annual Report, 1872*, p. 17; HMCS, *Thirty-eighth Annual Report, 1890*, p. 33.

25. Thurston, *Life and Times*, p. 287; M. Rice and M. Smith, "Life and Work at Punahou," in HMCS, *Jubilee Celebration*, p. 190; Coan, *Titus Coan*, p. 150.

26. E. Anderson, *Words of Advice to the Women of Hawaii* (Honolulu: Mission Press, 1863), pp. 1–2; HMCS, *Forty-eighth Annual Report, 1900*, p. 59; Central Committee of the Hawaiian Mission Centennial, *The Centennial Book: One Hundred Years of Christian Civilization in Hawaii, 1820–1920* (Honolulu: Central Committee, 1920), p. 12.

27. Thurston, *Life and Times*, p. 189.

BIBLIOGRAPHY

ARCHIVAL SOURCES

The sources which were crucial for this study are located in the Hawaiian Mission Children's Society Library in Honolulu. Their manuscript archive is a rich resource for researchers wishing to understand the activities, motivations, and personal styles of the American women and men who undertook the task of evangelization among Hawaiians in the nineteenth century. The archive contains the official records of the American Board of Commissioners for Foreign Missions (ABCFM), including microfilms of those records held in the ABCFM collection in the Houghton Library, Harvard University, and in addition the personal papers of women collected together by their descendants who founded the library and museum.

The most informative records were the Missionary Letters and Missionary Journals, which contained manuscripts written by the vast majority of women and men involved in the enterprise. Some of these manuscripts were collected in the Dole papers and the Bingham Family papers, while journals and letters in the Children of the Mission collection offered insight into mission offspring at various stages of their lives. Women's experiences were aired in the minutes left by the Maternal Association of the Sandwich Islands Mission and the Maternal Association of Honolulu; antislavery activism is documented in the records of the Hawaiian Antislavery Society. Station reports, the proceedings of the Sandwich Islands Mission and the Hawaiian Evangelical Association, and the instructions sent by the home body grouped in the ABCFM–Hawaiian collection provided understanding of the discussion—among male missionaries in the field and between the ABCFM's Boston headquarters and their Hawaiian missionaries—of the progress of affairs in the islands. Of the Houghton Library records, the Letters of Candidacy, covering the women as well as the men, were particularly useful. In addition the archive of the London Missionary Society at London University provided material on the Reverend William Ellis' involvement in the mission.

The notes indicate clearly the location of archival sources. Readers interested in more detail of sources should consult my doctoral thesis, "Paths of Duty: American Missionary Wives in Early Nineteenth Century Hawaii," which is held in the Baillieu Library at the University of Melbourne and in the Hawaiian Mission Children's Society Library in Honolulu.

PUBLISHED PRIMARY SOURCES

ABCFM. *Circular to Missionaries of the ABCFM, 15 March 1833.* Boston: ABCFM, 1883.

———. *Dr. Anderson's Address to the Hawaiian Evangelical Association.* n.p., n.d. [Honolulu, 1863].

———. *General Letters to the Sandwich Islands Mission.* (Annual.) Boston: The Board, 1831–1860.

———. *Instructions of the Prudential Committee of the American Board of Commissioners for Foreign Missions to the Sandwich Islands Mission.* Lahainaluna: Mission Seminary Press, 1838.

"A Lady." *Conversations on the Sandwich Island Mission.* Boston: Sabbath School Union, 1976.

Alcott, William A. *The Young Mother.* Boston: Light and Stearns, 1836.

———. *The Young Wife, or Duties of Woman in the Marriage Relation.* New York: Arno Press, 1972 [1837].

Alexander, James. *Mission Life in Hawaii: Memoir of Rev. William P. Alexander.* Oakland: Pacific Press, 1888.

Anderson, Eliza. *Words of Advice to the Women of Hawaii.* Honolulu: Mission Press, 1863.

Anderson, Mary. *Scenes in the Hawaiian Islands.* Boston: American Tract Society, 1865.

Anderson, Rufus. *History of the Sandwich Islands Mission.* Boston: Congregational Publishing Society, 1870.

———. *Memorial Volume of the First Fifty Years of the ABCFM.* Boston: ABCFM, 1861.

Anonymous. *A Few Words of Advice for Parents (Mothers) with Children.* Lahainaluna: Mission Seminary Press, 1842.

———. *The Wife for a Missionary.* Cincinnati: Truman & Smith, 1835.

Armstrong, Clarissa. *Reminiscences of a Missionary Chair.* San Francisco: C. A. Murdock & Co., 1886.

Armstrong, M. F. *Richard Armstrong: America Hawaii.* Hampton, Va.: Normal School Press, 1887.

Armstrong, Richard. *A Sermon Preached at Honolulu, March 6, 1841, at the Funeral of Angeline L., Wife of S. N. Castle.* Honolulu: Mission Press, 1841.

Baldwin, Arthur D. *A Memoir of Henry Perrine Baldwin, 1832 to 1911.* Cleveland: privately printed, 1925.

Bartlett, Samuel. *Sketches of the Missions of the American Board.* Boston: ABCFM, 1872.

Beckwith, Martha W. (ed.). *Kepelino's Traditions of Hawaii.* Bulletin 95. Honolulu: B. P. Bishop Museum, 1932.

Beecher, Catharine. *A Treatise on Domestic Economy.* Introduction by Kathryn Kish Sklar. New York: Schocken Books, 1977 [1841].

Bingham, Hiram. *A Residence of Twenty-one Years in the Sandwich Islands.* Rutland, Vt.: Charles E. Tuttle Co., 1981 [1847].

Bingham, Sybil. *Extracts from Letters of Mrs. S. M. Bingham, Relative to Sending Her Children from the Sandwich Islands to America.* New York: privately printed, 1882.

Bishop, Sereno Edwards. *Reminiscences of Old Hawaii.* Honolulu: Hawaiian Gazette Co., 1916.

Carter, H. A. P. *Kaahumanu.* Honolulu: R. Grieve, 1899.

Choules, J., and Smith, T. *The Origin and History of Missions.* Boston: Crocker & Brewster, 1838.

Clark, E. W. *A Word Relating to Marriage.* Honolulu: Mission Press, 1844.

Coan, Lydia B. *A Brief Sketch of the Missionary Life of Sybil Moseley Bingham.* n.p., n.d. [1895].

———. *Titus Coan: A Memorial.* Introduction by Rev. S. J. Humphrey. Chicago: Fleming H. Russell, 1884.

Coan, Titus. *Life in Hawaii: An Autobiographical Sketch of Mission Life and Labors (1835–1881).* New York: Anson D. Randolph & Co., 1882.

Cumings, A. P. *The Missionary's Daughter: A Memoir of Lucy Goodale Thurston of the Sandwich Islands.* New York: American Tract Society, 1842.

Dibble, Sheldon. *A History of the Sandwich Islands.* Honolulu: Thos. G. Thrum, 1909 [1843].

Dwight, Edwin Welles (ed.). *Memoirs of Henry Obookiah, a Native of Owhyhee.* Honolulu: Woman's Board of Missions, 1968 [1818].

Ellis, William. *The American Mission in the Sandwich Islands.* Honolulu: H. M. Whitney, 1866.

———. *Memoir of Mary Ellis.* Introduction by R. Anderson. Boston: Crocker & Brewster, 1836.

———. *Polynesian Researches: Hawaii.* Rutland, Vt.: Charles E. Tuttle Co., 1974 [1842].

Emerson, Oliver P. *Pioneer Days in Hawaii.* New York: Doubleday, 1928.

Fornander, Abraham. *An Account of the Polynesian Race, Its Origins and*

Migrations and the Ancient History of the Hawaiian People to the Times of Kamehameha I. 3 vols. in 1. Rutland, Vt.: Charles E. Tuttle Co., 1969 [1878, 1880, and 1885].

Gulick, Orramel, and Gulick, Ann E. *The Pilgrims of Hawaii.* New York: Fleming H. Revell Co., 1918.

Hawaiian Association. *Extracts from the Minutes of the Hawaiian Association.* Honolulu: Mission Press, 1841–1851.

———. *Extracts from the Records of the Hawaiian Association from 1823–1836.* Honolulu: Mission Press, 1837.

———. *Minutes of the Hawaiian Association May 1837.* Honolulu: Mission Press, 1837.

Hawaiian Mission Children's Society. *Jubilee Celebration of the Arrival of the Missionary Reinforcement of 1837.* Honolulu: Daily Bulletin Steam Print, 1887.

———. *Portraits of American Protestant Missionaries in Hawaii.* Honolulu: Hawaiian Gazette Co., 1901.

Hitchcock, Edward. *The Power of Christian Benevolence Illustrated in the Life and Labors of Mary Lyon.* Northampton: Hopkins, Bridgman & Co., 1852.

Holman, Lucia Ruggles. *Journal of Lucia Ruggles Holman.* Special Publication 17. Honolulu: B. P. Bishop Museum, 1931.

Ii, John Papa. *Fragments of Hawaiian History.* Edited by D. Barrere. Honolulu: Bishop Museum Press, 1983.

Jarves, James J. *Scenes and Scenery in the Sandwich Islands.* Boston: James Munroe and Co., 1844.

Jewett, Frances Gulick. *Luther Halsey Gulick.* London: Elliot Stock, 1895.

Judd, Laura Fish. *Honolulu: Sketches of the Life, Social, Political, and Religious, in the Hawaiian Islands from 1828–1861.* Honolulu: Honolulu Star-Bulletin, 1928 [1861].

Judd Family. *Fragments: Family Record of the House of Judd.* Honolulu: privately printed, 1903.

———. *Fragments II: Family Records of the House of Judd.* Honolulu: Paradise of the Pacific Press, 1911.

———. *Fragments IV: Family Records of the House of Judd.* Honolulu: Honolulu Star-Bulletin, 1928.

———. *Fragments V: Family Records of the House of Judd.* Honolulu: Honolulu Star-Bulletin, 1930.

Kamakau, Samuel M. *Ka Poʻe Kahike: The People of Old.* Edited by D. Barrere. Honolulu: Bishop Museum Press, 1979.

———. *The Works of the People of Old.* Edited by D. Barrere. Honolulu: Bishop Museum Press, 1976.

Kinney, Henry, and Kinney, Maria. *Kinney Journals: Boston to the Sandwich Islands, 1847–1848.* Edited by Charlotte Morris Thompson. Lafayette, Calif.: privately printed, 1978.

Korn, Alforns K. (ed.). *The Victorian Visitors.* Honolulu: University of Hawaii Press, 1958.

Krout, Mary H. *Reminiscences of Mrs. Mary S. Rice.* Honolulu: Hawaiian Gazette, 1908.

Liliuokalani. *Hawaii's Story of Hawaii's Queen.* Rutland, Vt.: Charles E. Tuttle Co., 1964.

Ludlow, Helen W. "Clarissa Chapman Armstrong." In Hiram C. Haydn (ed.), *American Heroes on the Mission Fields.* New York: American Tract Society, 1884.

Lyman, Henry. *Hawaiian Yesterdays: Chapters from a Boy's Life in the Islands in the Early Days.* Chicago: A. C. McClurg & Co., 1906.

Lyman, Sarah Joiner. *Sarah Joiner Lyman of Hawaii: Her Own Story.* Hilo, Hawaii: Lyman House Memorial Museum, 1970.

Malo, David. *Hawaiian Antiquities.* Honolulu: Bishop Museum Press, 1980 [1898].

Maternal Association of the Sandwich Islands' Mission. *The Names of the Mothers, Members and Children Belonging to the Maternal Association of the Sandwich Islands' Mission.* Honolulu: Mission Press, 1835.

Mitchell, John. *The Practical Church Member, Being a Guide to the Principles and Practice of the Congregational Churches of New England.* New Haven: Nathan Whiting, 1835.

More, Hannah. *The Works of Hannah More.* 2 vols. New York: Harper and Brothers, 1951.

Paris, John Davis. *Fragments of Real Missionary Life.* Honolulu: The Friend, 1920.

Pitman, Emma. *Heroines of the Mission Field.* London: Cassell, 1880.

Rice, Mary, Chamberlain, Martha, and Coan, Lydia. *In Memoriam of Juliette Montague Cooke, 1812-1896.* Papers read before the Woman's Board. n.d. [Honolulu, 1896].

Richards, William. *Memoir of Keopuolani, Late Queen of the Sandwich Islands.* Boston: Crocker & Brewster, 1825.

Sandwich Islands Mission. *A Few Words (of Advice) for Parents.* Lahainaluna: Mission Press, 1842.

————. *Extracts from the Minutes of the General Meeting of the Sandwich Islands Mission.* Honolulu: Mission Press, 1831–1853.

————. *Minutes of a General Meeting of the Sandwich Islands Mission.* Honolulu: Mission Press, 1830–1853.

Smith, Emma L. *Journal Book, 1850-1851.* Honolulu: Honolulu Star-Bulletin, 1928.

Stewart, Charles S. *Journal of a Residence in the Sandwich Islands During the Years 1823, 1824, and 1825.* Honolulu: University of Hawaii Press, 1970. (Facsimile of 3rd edition, 1830.)

————. *A Visit to the South Seas.* New York: John P. Haven, 1831.

Strong, William E. *The Story of the American Board: An Account of the First Hundred Years of the American Board of Commissioners for Foreign Missions.* Boston: Pilgrim Press, 1910.

Taylor, Persis G. *Kapiolani.* Honolulu: Robert Grieve, 1897.

Thompson L. (ed.). *Youth's Companion.* Boston: Houghton Mifflin Co., 1954.

Thurston, Lucy Goodale. *Life and Times of Mrs. Lucy G. Thurston Gathered from Letters and Journals.* Honolulu: The Friend, 1934 [1882].

Tyerman, Daniel. *Journal of Voyages and Travels.* London: F. Westley and A. H. Davis, 1831.

Wayland, Francis. *Elements of Moral Science with Questions for Examinations.* London: Religious Tract Society, 1835.

Wheeler, Daniel. *Extracts from the Letters and Journals.* London: Harvey & Darton, 1839.

Wight, Elizabeth L. *The Memoirs of Elizabeth Kinau Wilder.* Honolulu: Paradise of the Pacific Press, 1909.

Wyllie, Robert C. *Answers to Questions Proposed by R. C. Wyllie and Addressed to All the Missionaries in the Hawaiian Islands.* Honolulu: n. p., 1848.

SECONDARY SOURCES

Alexander, Mary C. *Dr. Baldwin of Lahaina.* Stanford: Stanford University Press, 1952.

————. *William Patterson Alexander in Kentucky, the Marquesas, Hawaii.* Honolulu: privately printed, 1934.

Alexander, Mary C., and Dodge, Charlotte. *Punahou, 1841–1941.* Berkeley: University of California Press, 1941.

Andrew, John A. III. *Rebuilding the Christian Commonwealth: New England Congregationalists and Foreign Missions, 1800–1830.* Lexington: University of Kentucky Press, 1976.

Barrow, Tui Terence. *Women of Polynesia.* Wellington and Sydney: Seven Seas Publishing Co., 1967.

Bass, Dorothy. " 'Their Prodigious Influence': Women, Religion and Reform in Antebellum America." In R. Ruether and E. McLaughlin (eds.), *Women of Spirit: Female Leadership in the Jewish and Christian Traditions.* New York: Simon & Schuster, 1979.

Benedetto, Robert. *The Hawaii Journals of the New England Missionaries, 1813–1894.* Honolulu: HMCS, 1982.

Berger, Peter L. *The Social Reality of Religion.* Harmondsworth: Penguin, 1973.

Berkhofer, Robert J. *Salvation and the Savage: An Analysis of Protestant Mis-*

sions and American Indian Response, 1787-1862. Lexington: University of Kentucky Press, 1965.

Bernard, Richard, and Vinovskis, Maris. "The Female School Teacher in Ante-bellum Massachusetts." *Journal of Social History* 10 (3) (March 1977): 332-345.

Bidwell, Percy W. *Rural New England at the Beginning of the Nineteenth Century.* Clifton, N.J.: Augustus M. Kelley, 1972 [1916].

Billington, Ray. *The Protestant Crusade, 1800-1860.* New York: Rinehart and Co., 1952.

Bloch, Ruth. "American Feminine Ideals in Transition: The Rise of the Moral Mother, 1785-1815." *Feminist Studies* 4 (2) (June 1978): 101-127.

Bogdan, Jane. "Care or Cure? Childbirth Practices in Nineteenth Century America." *Feminist Studies* 4 (2) (June 1978): 92-100.

Bradley, Harold W. *The American Frontier in Hawaii: The Pioneers, 1789-1843.* Gloucester, Mass.: Peter Smith, 1968 [1942].

Brumberg, Joan Jacobs. "The Case of Ann Hasseltine Judson: Mission Hagiography and Female Popular Culture, 1815-1850." In R. Keller, L. Queens, and H. Thomas (eds.), *Women in New Worlds: Historical Perspectives on the Wesleyan Tradition.* Vol. 2. Nashville: Parthenon Press, 1982.

————. *Mission for Life: The Story of the Family of Adoniram Judson.* New York: Free Press, 1980.

Burstyn, Joan. "Catharine Beecher and the Education of American Women." *New England Quarterly* 47 (3) (1974): 386-403.

Carroll, Berenice (ed.). *Liberating Women's History: Theoretical and Critical Essays.* Urbana: University of Illinois Press, 1974.

Castle, William R. *Life of Samuel Northrup Castle.* Honolulu: Castle Foundation, 1960.

————. *Reminiscences of William Richards Castle 1849-1935.* n.p.: privately printed, 1960.

Central Committee of the Hawaiian Mission Centennial. *The Centennial Book: One Hundred Years of Christian Civilization in Hawaii, 1820-1920.* Honolulu: Central Committee of the Hawaiian Mission Centennial, 1920.

Chaney, Charles L. *The Birth of Missions in America.* Pasadena: Carey Library, 1976.

Chinen, Jon. *The Great Mahele: Hawaii's Land Division of 1848.* Honolulu: University of Hawaii Press, 1958.

Cott, Nancy. *The Bonds of Womanhood: "Woman's Sphere" in New England, 1780-1835.* New Haven: Yale University Press, 1977.

————. "Young Women in the Second Great Awakening." *Feminist Studies* 3 (1975): 15-29.

Cross, Whitney. *The Burned-over District: The Social and Intellectual His-*

tory of Enthusiastic Religion in Western New York. Ithaca: Cornell University Press, 1950.

Damon, Ethel M. *David Belden Lyman: Sarah Joiner Lyman.* n.p., n.d [Honolulu, 1932].

———. *Father Bond of Kohala.* Honolulu: The Friend, 1927.

———. *Koamalu.* Honolulu: privately printed, 1931.

——— (ed.). *Letters from the Life of Abner and Lucy Wilcox 1836–1869.* Honolulu: privately printed, 1950.

———. *Sanford Ballard Dole and His Hawaii.* Palo Alto: Pacific Books, 1957.

Davis, Natalie Zemon. " 'Women's History' in Transition: The European Case." *Feminist Studies* 3 (3/4) (1976): 83–103.

Daws, Gavan. "Honolulu in the Nineteenth Century: Notes on the Emergence of Urban Society in Hawaii." *Journal of Pacific History* 26 (1967): 77–96.

———. *Shoal of Time: A History of the Hawaiian Islands.* Honolulu: University of Hawaii Press, 1968.

Dening, Greg. "Ethnohistory in Polynesia: The Value of Ethnohistorical Evidence." *Journal of Pacific History* 1 (1966): 23–42.

———. *Islands and Beaches: Discourse on a Silent Land: Marquesas, 1774–1880.* Melbourne, Melbourne University Press, 1980.

Dodge, Charlotte P., and Silverman, Arthur. *Hawaiian Mission Children's Society, 1852–1970.* Honolulu: HMCS, 1969.

Douglas, Ann. *The Feminization of American Culture.* New York: Knopf, 1977.

Doyle, Emma Lyons. *Makua Laiana: The Story of Lorenzo Lyons.* Honolulu: Advertiser Publishing Co., 1953.

Du Bois, Ellen C. *Feminism and Suffrage: The Emergence of an Independent Women's Movement in America, 1848–1869.* Ithaca: Cornell University Press, 1978.

Du Bois, Ellen C., and others. "Politics and Culture in Women's History: A Symposium." *Feminist Studies* 6 (1) (Spring 1980): 26–64.

Dublin, Thomas. *Women at Work: The Transformation of Work and Community in Lowell, Massachusetts, 1826–1869.* New York: Columbia University Press, 1979.

Dye, Nancy S. "History of Childbirth in America." *Signs* 6 (1) (Autumn 1980): 97–108.

Etienne, Mona, and Leacock, Eleanor (eds.). *Women and Colonization: Anthropological Perspectives.* New York: Praeger, 1980.

Frear, Mary D. *Lowell and Abigail: A Realistic Idyll.* New Haven: privately published, 1934.

French, Thomas. *The Missionary Whaleship.* n.p.: Vantage Press, n.d. [ca. 1961].

Furnas, J. C. *Anatomy of Paradise: Hawaii and the Islands of the South Seas.* New York: William Sloane Associates, 1947.

Geertz, Clifford. *The Interpretation of Cultures.* New York: Basic Books, 1973.

Gething, Judith R. "Christianity and Coverture: Impact on the Legal Status of Women in Hawaii, 1820–1920." *Hawaiian Journal of History* 2 (1977): 188–220.

Goldman, Irving. *Ancient Polynesian Society.* Chicago: University of Chicago Press, 1970.

Greven, Philip. *The Protestant Temperament: Patterns of Child-rearing, Religious Experience, and the Self in Early America.* New York: Knopf, 1977.

Grimshaw, Patricia. " 'Christian Women, Pious Wife, Faithful Mother, Devoted Missionary': Conflicts in Roles of American Missionary Women in Nineteenth Century Hawaii." *Feminist Studies* 9 (3) (Fall 1983): 489–522.

———. "New England Missionary Wives, Hawaiian Women, and 'The Cult of True Womanhood.' " *Hawaiian Journal of History* 19 (1985): 71–100.

Gunson, Niel. "The Deviations of a Missionary Family." In J. W. Davidson and D. Scarr (eds.), *Pacific Island Portraits.* Canberra: ANU Press, 1973.

———. *Messengers of Grace: Evangelical Missionaries in the South Seas, 1791–1860.* Melbourne: Oxford University Press, 1978.

Halford, Francis J. *Nine Doctors and God.* Honolulu: University of Hawaii Press, 1954.

Handy, E. S. C. *Polynesian Religion.* Bulletin 34. Honolulu: Bishop Museum, 1927.

———. *Ancient Hawaiian Civilization.* Honolulu: Kamehameha Schools, 1933.

Handy, E. S. C., and Pukui, Mary. *The Polynesian Family System in Ka'u, Hawaii.* Rutland, Vt.: Charles E. Tuttle Co., 1972.

Hanson, F. Allen. "Female Pollution in Polynesia." *Journal of Polynesian Society* 91 (3) (September 1982): 335–382.

Hawaiian Mission Children's Society. *Missionary Album.* Honolulu: HMCS, 1969.

Hersh, Blanche, G. *The Slavery of Sex: Feminist-Abolitionists in America.* Urbana: University of Illinois Press, 1978.

Hewitt, Nancy A. *Women's Activism and Social Change: Rochester, New York, 1822–1872.* Ithaca: Cornell University Press, 1984.

Hobbs, Jean. *Hawaii: A Pageant of the Soil.* Stanford: Stanford University Press, 1935.

Hogeland, R. "Co-education of the Sexes at Oberlin College: A Study in

Social Ideas in Mid-Nineteenth Century America." *Journal of Social History* 6 (2) (1962): 160–177.

Howard, Alan, and others. "Traditional and Modern Adoption Patterns in Hawaii." In V. Carroll (ed.), *Adoption in Eastern Oceania*. Honolulu: University of Hawaii Press, 1970.

Hunter, Jane. *The Gospel of Gentility: American Women Missionaries in Turn-of-the-Century China*. New Haven: Yale University Press, 1984.

James, Janet Wilson (ed.). *Women in American Religion*. Philadelphia: University of Pennsylvania Press, 1980.

Judd, I. V., and Gerrit, P. *Dr. Judd: Hawaii's Friend*. Honolulu: University of Hawaii Press, 1960.

Kaufman, P. *Women Teachers on the Frontier*. New Haven: Yale University Press, 1984.

Kelly-Gadol, Joan. "The Social Relations of the Sexes: Methodological Implications of Women's History." *Signs* 1 (1976): 809–823.

Kent, Noel J. *Hawaii: Islands Under the Influence*. New York: Monthly Review Press, 1983.

Kerber, Linda K. "Daughters of Columbia: Educating Women for the Republic, 1787–1805." In Stanley Elkins and Eric McKitrick (eds.), *The Hofstandter Aegis: A Memorial*. New York: Knopf, 1974.

———. "The Republican Mother: Women and the Enlightenment—An American Perspective." *American Quarterly* 28 (Summer 1976): 187–205.

Kirkpatrick, Doris. *The City and the River: The Story of Fitchburg, Massachusetts*. Fitchburg: Fitchburg Historical Society, 1971.

Kuykendall, Ralph. *The Hawaiian Kingdom, 1778–1854*. Vol. 1. Honolulu: University of Hawaii Press, 1938.

Langmore, Diana. "A Neglected Force: White Women Missionaries in Papua, 1874–1914." *Journal of Pacific History* 17 (1982): 138–157.

Lasch, Christopher, and Taylor, William. " 'Two Kindred Spirits': Sorority and Family in New England, 1839–1845." *New England Quarterly* 36 (1963): 23–41.

Lerner, Gerda. *The Grimké Sisters from South Carolina: Rebels Against Slavery*. Boston: Houghton Mifflin Co., 1967.

———. "The Lady and the Mill Girl: Changes in the Status of Women in the Age of Jackson, 1800–1840." *Midcontinent American Studies Journal* 10 (Spring 1969): 5–14.

———. *The Majority Finds Its Past: Placing Women in History*. New York: Oxford University Press, 1979.

MacCormack, Carol, and Strathern, Marilyn (eds.). *Nature, Culture and Gender*. Cambridge: Cambridge University Press, 1980.

McLoughlin, William G. *Cherokees and Missionaries, 1789–1839*. New Haven: Yale University Press, 1984.

————. *Revivals, Awakenings, and Reform: An Essay on Religion and Social Change in America, 1607-1977*. Chicago: University of Chicago Press, 1978.

Maurer, Oscar. *Three Early Christian Leaders of Hawaii*. Honolulu: Hawaiian Evangelical Association, 1945.

Melder, Keith. *Beginnings of Sisterhood: The American Woman's Rights Movement, 1800-1850*. New York: Schocken Books, 1977.

Menton, Linda K. " 'Everything That Is Lovely and of Good Report': The Hawaiian Chiefs' Children's School, 1839-1856." Ph.D. thesis, University of Hawaii, 1982.

Miller, Char. *Fathers and Sons: The Bingham Family and the American Mission*. Philadelphia: Temple University Press, 1982.

Morgan, Theodore. *Hawaii: A Century of Economic Change, 1778-1876*. Cambridge: Harvard University Press, 1948.

Nellist, George F. *Women of Hawaii*. Honolulu: Paradise of the Pacific Press, 1929.

North, Douglass C. *The Economic Growth of the United States, 1790-1960*. New York: Norton, 1966.

Norton, Mary Beth. *Liberty's Daughters: The Revolutionary Experience of American Women, 1750-1800*. Boston: Little, Brown, 1980.

Ortner, Sherry. "Gender and Sexuality in Hierarchical Societies: The Case of Polynesia and Some Comparative Implications." In S. Ortner and H. Whitehead (eds.), *Sexual Meanings: The Cultural Construction of Gender and Sexuality*. Cambridge: Cambridge University Press, 1981.

Peterson, Barbara Bennett. *Notable Women of Hawaii*. Honolulu: University of Hawaii Press, 1984.

Phillips, Clifton J. *Protestant America and the Pagan World: The First Half Century of the American Board of Commissioners for Foreign Missions, 1810-1860*. Cambridge: Harvard University Press, 1969.

Potter, J. "The Growth of Population in America, 1700-1860." In D. V. Glass and D. Eversley (eds.), *Population in History*. London: Edward Arnold, 1965.

Pukui, Mary Kawena. "Hawaiian Beliefs and Customs During Birth, Infancy and Childhood." *Bishop Museum Occasional Papers* 16 (17). Honolulu: Bishop Museum, 1942.

Ralston, Caroline. "Hawaii, 1778-1854: Some Aspects of *Maka'ainana* Response to Rapid Cultural Change." *Journal of Pacific History* 19 (1-2) (1984): 21-40.

Restarick, Henry B. *Hawaii, 1778-1920: From the Viewpoint of a Bishop*. Honolulu: Paradise of the Pacific Press, 1924.

Richards, Mary A. *Amos Starr Cooke and Juliette Montague Cooke: Their Autobiographies Gleaned from Their Journals and Letters*. Honolulu: privately printed, 1941.

———. *The Hawaiian Chief's Children's School.* Rutland, Vt.: Charles E. Tuttle Co., 1970.

Rosaldo, Michelle. "The Use and Abuse of Anthropology: Reflections on Feminism and Cross-Cultural Understanding." *Signs* 5 (3) (Spring 1980): 389–417.

Rosaldo, Michelle, and Lamphere, Louise (eds.). *Women, Culture and Society.* Stanford: Stanford University Press, 1974.

Rothman, Ellen. *Hands and Hearts: A History of Courtship in America.* New York: Basic Books, 1984.

———. "Sex and Self-Control: Middle-Class Courtship in America, 1770–1870." *Journal of Social History* (Spring 1982): 409–426.

Ryan, Mary. *Cradle of the Middle Class: The Family in Oneida County, New York, 1790–1865.* Cambridge: Cambridge University Press, 1981.

———. *The Empire of the Mother: American Writing About Domesticity, 1830–1860.* New York: Harrington Park Press, 1985.

———. "The Power of Women's Networks: A Case Study of Female Moral Reform in Antebellum America." *Feminist Studies* 5 (1) (Spring 1979): 66–86.

Sahlins, Marshall. *Historical Metaphors and Mythical Realities: Structure in the Early History of the Sandwich Islands Kingdom.* Ann Arbor: University of Michigan Press, 1981.

———. *Social Stratification in Polynesia.* Seattle: University of Washington Press, 1958.

Schmitt, Robert C. *Demographic Statistics of Hawaii: 1778–1965,* Honolulu: University of Hawaii Press, 1968.

———. *The Missionary Censuses of Hawaii.* Pacific Anthropological Records no. 20. Honolulu: B. P. Bishop Museum, 1973.

Silverman, Jane. "To Marry Again." *Hawaiian Journal of History* 17 (1983): 64–75.

Sinclair, Marjorie. *Nahi'ena'ena: Sacred Daughter of Hawai'i.* Honolulu: University of Hawaii Press, 1976.

———. "The Sacred Wife of Kamehameha I, Keopuolani." *Hawaiian Journal of History* 5 (1971): 3–23.

Sklar, Kathryn Kish. *Catherine Beecher: A Study in American Domesticity.* New Haven: Yale University Press, 1973.

Slater, Peter G. *Children in the New England Mind: In Death and in Life.* Hamden, Conn.: Archon Books, 1977.

Smith, Bradford. *Yankees in Paradise: The New England Impact on Hawaii.* Philadelphia: J. B. Lippincott Co., 1956.

Smith, Daniel Scott. "The Demographic History of Colonial New England." In Michael Gordon (ed.), *The American Family in Social-Historical Perspective.* New York: St. Martin's Press, 1973.

Smith, Page. *Daughters of the Promised Land: Women in American History.* Boston: Little, Brown, 1970.

Smith-Rosenberg, Carroll. "Beauty, the Beast and the Militant Woman: A Case Study of Sex Roles and Social Stress in Jacksonian America." *American Quarterly* 23 (October 1971): 562–584.

———. "The Female World of Love and Ritual: Relations Between Women in Nineteenth Century America." *Signs* 1 (Autumn 1975): 1–29.

———. "The New Woman and the New History." *Feminist Studies* 3 (1/2) (1975): 185–198.

Vinovskis, Maris A. *Fertility in Massachusetts from the Revolution to the Civil War.* New York: Academic Press, 1981.

Vinovskis, M., and Bernard, R. "Beyond Catharine Beecher: Female Education in the Antebellum Period." *Signs* 3 (4) (Summer 1978): 856–869.

Wagner, Sandra E. "Mission and Motivation: The Theology of the Early American Mission in Hawaii." *Hawaiian Journal of History* 19 (1985): 62–70.

Welter, Barbara. "Anti-Intellectualism and the American Woman: 1800–1860." In *Dimity Convictions.* Athens: Ohio University Press, 1976.

———. " 'She Hath Done What She Could': Protestant Missionary Careers in Nineteenth Century America." In J. James (ed.), *Women in American Religion.* Philadelphia: University of Pennsylvania Press, 1980.

———. "The Cult of True Womanhood, 1820–1860." *American Quarterly* 18 (1966): 151–174.

———. "The Feminization of American Religion: 1800–1860." In M. Harman and L. Banner (eds.), *Clio's Consciousness Raised: New Perspectives on the History of Women.* New York: Harper & Row, 1974.

Williston, Samuel. *William Richards.* Cambridge, Mass.: privately printed, 1969 [1938].

Wishy, Bernard. *The Child and the Republic: The Dawn of Modern American Child Nurture.* Philadelphia: University of Philadelphia Press, 1968.

Young, Chester R. "American Missionary Influence on the Union of Church and State in Hawaii During the Regency of Kaahumanu." *Journal of Church and State* 9 (Spring 1967): 165–179.

PERIODICALS

Missionary Herald. 1821–1840.
Mother's Magazine. Edited by Mrs. A. G. Whittelsey. 1836–1845.
The Panoplist and Missionary Magazine. 1816–1820.
Youth's Companion. 1827–1849.

INDEX

dren, 98; on reform of Hawaiian
society, 170–171, 175–176, 177–178;
and Roman Catholicism, 114, 122;
salaries of, 104; and use of Hawaiian
labor, 36–37, 44–46, 104–105, 111–
112; on women's status, 77–80, 124–
127. *See also* American Board of
Commissioners for Foreign Missions
(ABCFM); Missionary wives
Missionary children: ABCFM attitude
toward, 7, 36, 43; careers of, 188–190;
deaths of, 140, 148–149; first arrivals
in Hawaii of, 25, 35, 37, 46–47; and
formation of Hawaiian Mission Children's Society, 190–192; language
acquisition of, 131–132; marriages of,
190; religious condition of, 131–132,
147–149; and return to United States,
133–135, 188–189. *See also* Missionary
wives
Missionary Herald, xx, 3, 9, 34, 49, 122,
186
Missionary wives: ABCFM attitude
toward, 6–7, 18–19, 25; arrival in
Hawaii of, 26–27; attitudes toward
Hawaiians of, 57–62, 63, 104–106,
111–113, 133, 145, 168–169, 171–
173, 178, 190; backgrounds of, 1–4,
12–22; childbearing by, 36, 80, 82,
89–92, 94–98, 140; childrearing by, 7,
36, 43, 102, 131–135, 137–140, 141–
149, 188–190; courtships and enlistment of, 1–5, 8–9, 12–22; deaths of,
121–122, 183–184; domestic labor of,
34–35, 43, 102–113; education of, 16–
18, 19–20; fertility control of, 90–91;
health of, 92–94, 106, 112–113, 150–
152; historians on, xix–xx; influence of
religious revivals on, 3, 20–22; and
links with United States kin, 54–56,
108; marital relations of, 70–73, 80–
84, 87–88; in Marquesas mission, 122–
124; and relations with mission
women, 65–70; and relations with
non-mission Europeans, 62–65; religious views of, 75–77, 79; and

response to geographical isolation, 51–
54, 68–69; and Sandwich Islands'
Maternal Association, 115–119; status
of, 77–80, 113–114, 124–127; teach-
ing and evangelization by, 35, 37, 44,
114, 119, 120–121, 124–127, 156–
161, 171–173; travel in islands of, 53–
54, 68–69; widowhood and old age of,
183–187. *See also* American Board of
Commissioners for Foreign Missions
(ABCFM); Missionaries; Missionary
children
Molokai, 51, 66, 85, 101, 189
Moral Reformer, The, 106
More, Hannah, 76
Moseley, Sybil. *See* Bingham, Sybil
Moseley
Mother's Magazine, 121, 128, 129–130
Mount Holyoke Seminary, 18, 19, 149,
188
Munn, Bethuel, 10–11
Munn, Louisa Clark, 11, 93

Nahienaena, 40
Naihe, 41, 162
Naihekukui, 34
Newell, Ursula. *See* Emerson, Ursula
Newell
New England, xi, 1–2, 7, 9, 11, 12, 14–
15, 19, 52, 63, 79, 101, 108, 112, 115,
136, 155, 187, 191
New England, 12
New York (state), xi, 3–4, 7, 9, 14, 20
Norridgewock Young Ladies Academy,
19

Oahu, 31, 48, 51, 65, 168, 190
Oberlin College, 19, 124, 149, 188
Ogden, Maria, 66, 67, 81, 121, 167, 175,
183, 187

Panoplist and Missionary Magazine, xiii
Paris, Ella, 189
Paris, John, 183
Paris, Mary Aletta, 189
Paris, Mary Grant, 93

ABOUT THE AUTHOR

Patricia Grimshaw, a New Zealander, teaches women's studies and American history at the University of Melbourne in Australia, where she has lived for the past twenty years. Her research interests focus on women's history and family history in the Pacific. She is the author of *Women's Suffrage in New Zealand* and has co-edited several books.

Production Notes

This book was designed by Roger Eggers.
Composition and paging were done on the
Quadex Composing System and typesetting
on the Compugraphic 8400 by the design
and production staff of University of
Hawaii Press.

The text typeface is Garamond No. 49
and the display typeface is ITC Garamond.

Offset presswork and binding were done by
Vail-Ballou Press, Inc. Text paper is
Glatfelter Offset Vellum, basis 50.